The Many Faces of Crisis

STUDIES IN EUROPEAN INTEGRATION, STATE AND SOCIETY

Edited by Magdalena Góra, Zdisław Mach and Katarzyna Zielińska

VOLUME 6

PETER LANG

Marek A. Cichocki/ Tomasz Grzegorz Grosse

The Many Faces of Crisis

An Analysis of Crisis Management from an Economic and Political Perspective

PETER LANG

Bibliographic Information published by the Deutsche Nationalbibliothek
The Deutsche Nationalbibliothek lists this publication in the Deutsche Nationalbibliografie; detailed bibliographic data is available online at http://dnb.d-nb.de.

Library of Congress Cataloging-in-Publication Data
A CIP catalog record for this book has been applied for at the Library of Congress.

The texts in this publication are synthesis of the research conducted by the Natolin European Centre as a part of a project financed by the National Science Centre (Poland). The decision number: DEC-2013/11/B/HS5/04170.

NATIONAL SCIENCE CENTRE POLAND

Editor for English version: Peter Sakowicz

ISSN 2193-2352
ISBN 978-3-631-79125-7 (Print)
E-ISBN 978-3-631-79198-1 (E-PDF)
E-ISBN 978-3-631-79199-8 (EPUB)
E-ISBN 978-3-631-79200-1 (MOBI)
DOI 10.3726/b15718

Peter Lang – Berlin · Bern · Bruxelles · New York · Oxford · Warszawa · Wien

This publication has been peer reviewed.

www.peterlang.com

Contents

Marek A. Cichocki

Introduction. The apparent dimension of the crisis as a research challenge

Presence of the crisis has become an apparent phenomenon in the contemporary world, particularly in Europe. This is a new situation compared to previous decades, when after WW2 the Western world was developing at varying degrees but under the general assumption that political and economic processes maintained their continuity, controllability and rationality. Certainly this development process experienced some shocks, e.g. the famous oil crisis of the 1970s, but still it proceeded within the framework of a defined process, within expanding and foreseeable institutional and legal structures, in an environment increasingly diversified but at the same time increasingly interdependent, and mutually linked. As a result of the collapse of the Soviet Union in the early 1990s and the relatively peaceful transformation of the post-communist part of the European continent, an optimistic conviction started to prevail about the solidification of a relatively predictable road of further development on a global scale, from the most advanced core of the Western world to its peripheries, and then on to more and more areas of the world. The emergence of global terrorism and the manifestation of its outcomes in the early 21st century greatly question further developmental prospects in various regions of the world. However, there are still no premises in place which might lead one to believe that the developmental form of the expanded Western world itself will be peaceful and devoid of any serious crises as was assumed. The second decade of the 21st century introduces a fundamental change in this respect. The crisis, which is mainly financial, affecting not only the functioning of the institutions of advanced capitalism themselves and of the globalized financial market being the bloodstream of the contemporary world economy, but also undermining the sense of their underlying values, beliefs, certainties and rules of political and social order, hits hard on the very core of the West. From this moment on all fundamental questions seem to be reopened; both in public debate and in the accompanying academic debate one of the significant issues becomes the question of the crisis as a phenomenon, the identification of its causes, the character of its course, decisive factors, and last but not least the question of what means are available today to well-developed modern western societies to counteract crises and predict their emergence as far as possible.

The increasingly obvious nature of the manifestations of the crisis in its various dimensions: financial, social, geopolitical, migration-related or institutional, entails a challenge related to capabilities which contain a crisis. On the one hand this is a practical problem of management, related to the issue of political leadership and its ability to create an effective anti-crisis strategy. However, on the other hand we are dealing with a challenge of a theoretical nature, i.e. the necessity of such a conceptualization of the issue of a crisis that would capture its various dimensions – not only economic or political (which seem the most obvious), but also social and cultural. Questions of the inevitability of the emergence of crises and methods for the reduction of their destructive outcomes have always been a niggling issue in political and economic thought. An in-depth reflection related to crisis as a phenomenon is also encountered in the Western world in the period of late, developed western capitalism, i.e. in the late 20th century, when opinions prevailed about the irreversibility and predictability of development. A large body of literature on the said topic is an outcome of this reflection. In Poland, after the period of breakthrough that took place in 1989, besides a few notable exceptions, the problem of crisis did not become the subject of any serious thought. It seems that the issue of transformation, its inevitability and certain assumptions being taken for granted, removed the issue of crisis from sight. Only in recent years has this perspective changed in Poland, opening up the need to deal with the problem in a systematic manner.

This book is the result of an attempt to address the issue of a crisis and methods of crisis management from the perspective of economic and political science theories. Such a joint approach follows from the conviction that in the case of contemporary crises we are dealing with e.g. in Europe, the aspects of economy and politics which are impossible to separate. This is the main premise of the project financed from the National Science Centre funds and carried out by the authors of this volume of papers. It enabled the search for a shared theoretical and methodological thought in those two fields of knowledge with a view to investigating the phenomenon of crisis and attempting to explain it. Consequently this book aims to show relationships between the aforementioned during the performance of anti-crisis actions, i.e. through crisis management and the deployment of any attempted necessary reforms. The dynamics of the mutual relationship between economics and politics, which becomes manifested during a crisis, becomes particularly visible in relation to specific challenges faced by policy-makers. This is mainly the issue of growth that put the task, before politics, of the recovery of economic growth and political stability, which were undermined by the crisis. As a matter of fact this challenge should not be treated too statically, as a return to the lost *status* perspectives both in the period preceding the emergence of a crisis, i.e. the accumulation of various disadvantageous factors, and also *quo;* it shall refer to the fundamental question of how in the situation where the economic and political stability was impaired we can restore conditions for further safe and responsible development, for which economic growth and political stability themselves are important but inadequate factors. The second core challenge in the economic and political dynamics of a crisis is the problem of structural balance, which may be both the cause of the crisis and the fundamental determinant for an anti-crisis strategy. Structural imbalances can be related to divergent economic determinants (e.g. structural differences of a macroeconomic nature), political determinants (geopolitical differences) or organizational determinants (governance structures). Another challenge is related to the skills and institutions allowing for effective crisis management. This concerns first and foremost the problem of political leadership, the ability to create and apply political anti-crisis strategies, as well as the ability to coordinate actions and flexibility towards changing the dynamic determinants of a crisis. The last challenge constituting a point of reference of the dynamics of the economic-political relationship in a crisis is the challenge of political legitimacy. The fundamental question in this context is whether the deficit of the said legitimacy may effectively block the undertaking of anti-crisis actions and how it can positively influence those actions and under what conditions.

This publication presents the effects of research carried out under the project called *Crisis management challenges in economic and political perspective.* Each chapter of this publication is the final report of the research in the respective areas addressed by each member of the research team. In the chapter titled "Eurozone crisis", Tomasz Grzegorz Grosse analyses the character of the anti-crisis measures in the Eurozone undertaken by EU institutions and member states after 2009. In his part he focuses mainly on the issue of developmental conditions in a crisis, on the causes underlying the internal, systemic imbalance of the Eurozone, on the political component of crisis management (leadership and the political arena) and finally on the issue of the democratic legitimacy of the process of anti-crisis actions. In the chapter titled "Asian crisis" Piotr Koryś analyses the crisis in Southeast Asian countries in late 1990s, attempting to describe its causes, course and consequences for a changed arrangement of economic and political power between the states of the entire region. This analysis also allows readers to see interesting parallels between the Asian crisis and the current one in the Eurozone, highlighting the similarities of certain phenomena and fundamental differences. In the chapter titled "Regulatory impact assessment and the creation of the economic policy in Poland", Łukasz Hardt focuses mainly on the quality and risks related to decisions made by the government. He also reflects on the current state-of-play of research on the quality of governance in the state, its traditional and modern forms, and tries to identify the major problems of governance quality in relation to the case of Poland with particular focus on the role of the regulatory impact assessment system. In the chapter titled "Public finance crisis and state fiscal competence", Jan Fałkowski addresses one of the fundamental problems of the ability of contemporary states to pursue public policies from the viewpoint of a state's fiscal policy. This problem became glaringly visible in the context of the financial crisis in Europe of recent years, which confronted some states with the threat of total bankruptcy and the necessity to revise existing fiscal policies. However, as Fałkowski demonstrates, this leads governments to embark on a dangerous game with democratic constituencies and social needs, which grow during a crisis and fundamentally influence the ability to perform rational reforms of state policies and the related necessary changes of fiscal policy. In the last chapter titled "From crisis to strategy" Marek Cichocki addresses the relationship between the crisis and the nature of strategies undertaken by policy-makers. From the viewpoint of democratic public opinion expecting the government to launch swift and effective actions in the face of crisis, this relationship seems obvious. However, the problem itself of building the strategy and ability for strategic planning action as the fundamental governance elements remains unsolved on the part of such political actors as states and governments. The joint conclusions of the project related to crisis management problems were put together by Tomasz Grzegorz Grosse in the final conclusions.

This book in no way exhausts the entirety of the issue related to crisis and crisis management. Many problems were only signalled by the authors in the hope that they will become the subject-matter of in-depth research in the future. As has been pointed out before, in Poland there is a clearly visible need to develop research and reflections of the problem of crisis both in social and political science, as well as economics. In the case of our project and the ensuing publications, it was not our top priority to exhaust the topic, as this would have been unrealistic; we wanted first and foremost to combine the political science and economic perspectives with the research on crisis phenomenon and crisis management. This task yielded quite an interesting research plan with multiple practical conclusions, either from the viewpoint of a public administration's actions or the pursuance of policies by the state. We hope this book will help readers to become familiar with the research results, attract their interest to the covered issues, and in some cases provoke them to embark on their own research.

Tomasz Grzegorz Grosse

The Eurozone crisis

Abstract: The chapter presents an analysis of the Eurozone crisis, reflecting on political and economic challenges, structural problems, especially in the context of the geopolitical system of Europe, as well as crisis management and integration process together with legitimisation questions. The study proves why the defence of the Eurozone was attempted, aiming in particular at the opposition to strong secession tendencies. Furthermore, according to the author, it is difficult to explain why the crisis has not led to an "institutional breakthrough" towards a democratic federation and triggered sharp rivalry for power, as well as over crisis costs distribution between member states instead. The answer to this question should be attached to the problem of political legitimisation. Although the crisis did not cause any formal changes of the treaties in Europe, there have been several informal adjustments within the system. The author defines the described systemic modifications as a model of "asymmetric confederation", whose main features include not only the uneven distribution of political power between the core and peripheries, but also the asymmetric levels of political legitimisation.

Keywords: Eurozone crisis, developmental crisis, structural crisis, crisis management, political legitimacy, geopolitics, asymmetric confederation

Introduction

Any crisis reveals a given system's dysfunctions and limitations. This may ensue from institutional gaps or internal discrepancies inherent in the system. A crisis is most frequently defined as a sudden and acute disruption in the "normal" working of the system, when the aforementioned dysfunctions and discrepancies become emphasized and aggravated[1]. Nevertheless, crises go through an incubation period; going through what one may call the stage of the gradual accumulation of crisis-generating factors. A crisis not only externalizes the faults and dysfunctions of a given system, but also becomes an opportunity for internal adjustments. This relates first and foremost to the bridging of basic institutional contradictions and gaps, but at times also relates to the reconstruction of political legitimization and the ideological foundations required for the strength and stability of a given system. We are, therefore, dealing with a crisis on the one

1 B. Badie, D. Berg-Schlosser, L. Morlino (eds.) (2011): *International Encyclopedia of Political Science*, vol. 2, Sage London, pp. 489–493.

hand, and with crisis management by political authorities, or attempted reforms, on the other.

The Eurozone crisis concerned not only specific economic dysfunctions, but also the political authority system – the foundations for the functioning of a single currency. As a result, besides the outcomes of an economic crisis, we could also observe dysfunctions related to crisis management and the difficulties in overcoming problems within the existing political institutions. Consequently, we were faced with systemic crisis. An analysis of a systemic crisis should take four fundamental segments into account. They are: (1) development problems, (2) structural problems, (3) management problems, and (4) the problem of the inadequate legitimization of a given system[2].

(1) Development problems

Among various aspects of the crisis, the issue of economic growth is of paramount importance. Major symptoms of the phenomenon include weakening of the GDP growth rate, increased unemployment, shrinking economic production and trade (including international). Other symptoms include declining social welfare and widening inequalities. Several reasons underlying growth issues may include: depletion of the resources of a given economic system, as well as diminishing utility of core economic processes and institutions.

Economic growth problems translate into the lessening of the significance of a given political system or entity in international relations. This concerns, among other things, diminishing benefits (or growing costs) following on from a system's functioning for its major participants. The problem of the weakening of an international position may be related to difficulties of an economic nature as well as improper management of the economy. For example, the slowing down of economic growth rate plus the impoverishment of the society can corrupt the geopolitical potential of a given system in the international arena[3]. This is most frequently related to the regular loss of competitive advantages compared to other geopolitical actors or arrangements. This may also result from an accumulation of losses following on from the dysfunctions of one's own economic

---

2 For more details see: T. G. Grosse (2013) (ed.): *Między polityką a rynkiem. Kryzys Unii Europejskiej w analizie ekonomistów i politologów* [Between politics and the market. The crisis of the European Union in the analysis of economists and political scientists], Warsaw: Uczelnia Łazarskiego.

3 R. Gilpin (1987): *The Political Economy of International Relations*, Princeton: Princeton University Press, p. 112.

system. But what is most important, the aforementioned tendency ensues from long-term – and disadvantageous for a given system – mechanisms of economic exchange or other dysfunctional economic processes.

Growth challenge may also be analysed in a systemic context as development of a given political system. This applies particularly in the case of systems being in the process of construction, with European integration processes being a good example. In this case neo-functional concepts theoretically seem to be the best method to explain the integration process in Europe. These concepts perceive integration processes as the gradual transfer of competencies from member state to European level, i.e. the expanded scope of European law and reinforcement of the competencies of EU institutions, as well as the "spill over" of integration from economic cooperation onto the political plane[4]. Particular catalysers for the described processes are crisis situations, which in a way coerce further development of integration with a view to improving the functionality of governance and the efficiency of decision-making processes[5].

(2) Structural problems

The structural dimension in economics is strictly connected with geopolitical structures. In the case of an economic crisis, the most frequent problem is the improper structure of the economy (also with regard to production factors and costs), leading to the lowering of its international competitiveness. This is also the most frequent reason for the underlying emergence of problems with economic growth. For example, the problem of a monetary regime can be excessive internal macroeconomic disparities, including those related to the structural elements of particular economies.

Under a geopolitical approach we can list at least a few symptoms of a structural crisis. Firstly, this aspect concerns a growing imbalance between the main actors within a given geopolitical arrangement. This covers the widening disproportions between their potential and the related change in power relations[6]. Also of great significance is the issue of perceptions of one's own international role, including

---

4 E. B. Haas (1964): *Beyond the Nation State. Functionalism and International Organisation*, Stanford: Stanford University Press.

5 See: P. C. Schmitter (1970): *A Revised Theory of Regional Integration*, International Organisation, vol. 24, No. 4, pp. 836–868.

6 Ch. F. Doran (1991): *System in Crisis, New Imperatives of High Politics at Century's End*, Cambridge: Cambridge University Press, xii, xiii, 2; K. Waltz (1979): *Theory of International Politics*, Reading: Addison-Wesley, p. 69; S. Hoffmann (1968): *Gulliver's Troubles: Or the Setting of American Foreign Policy*, New York: McGraw Hill, p. 17.

that within a specified geopolitical arrangement[7]. This encompasses the ambitions of particular political leaders concerning positions within the power hierarchy dominant in a given system. In such situations the structural factor for crisis accumulation is not only by disproportions of real geopolitical potentials, but also by dissonances between the ambitions and perceptions of one's own placement within a given power system.

Under liberal theory in political sciences, the problem of excessive structural differences concerns the entire system of international cooperation (e.g. regional one[8]). The system is more stable if the benefits and costs of integration processes are distributed relatively uniformly across particular countries. This means that in the name of the principle of solidarity and with care for the stability of the entire system in mind, richer and geopolitically more powerful states assist the weaker ones. Under realist theory, importance is assumed by the differences in the potentials and structure of mutual relations (or perceptions of those relations), mainly between dominant states[9]. Here ambitions are at their peak and rivalry for leadership is at its greatest. In the case of states with weaker international positions, the geopolitical ambitions of their elites are lower. They are most frequently on the same bandwagon as the policies of major world powers or are dependent on them in political and economic terms. It is worthwhile adding that the growing asymmetry between the benefits and costs within a given economic regime can also be included among the structural factors. Such asymmetry is responsible for the systematic accumulation of gains and losses of particular states; this influences the structure of their geopolitical potential within a given arrangement and their mutual power relations.

(3) Management problems

Problems of management in a crisis are present in relation both to the political system and economic regime. With regard to economy this entails, among other things, the loss of politicians' impact on economic processes. This is related to a trend aimed at the separation of economy from electoral policy (e.g. through the introduction of apolitical agency institutions) or the takeover of power

7 Ch. F. Doran (1991), pp. 21, 31, 33, 37.

8 See: W. Mattli, A. Stone Sweet (2012): Regional Integration and the Evolution of the European Polity: On the Fiftieth Anniversary of the Journal of Common Market Studies, *Journal of Common Market Studies*, vol. 50, no. S1, pp. 1–17.

9 Ch. F. Doran (1991), p. 31.

over regulatory processes by economic interests (something termed *regulatory capture*[10]). Other sings of management problems include weakening of the autonomy of public authorities in relation to the pressure exerted by economic entities. A good example of such pressure is because of the disciplining impact of financial markets on the fiscal policies of public authorities.

The aforementioned phenomena entail the weakening of power 'over oneself'. This can also be defined as the loss of sovereignty or autonomy in internal policy. This is related, among other things, to the impact of financial markets, external powers or difficulties with internal governance within a specific political system. Symptoms of the latter include problems with making the right political decisions and their subsequent efficient implementation. This may ensue from excessive rivalry between main political actors, as well as from conflicting interests between them. Another cause may be related to the absence of institutions that might enable the resolution of such contradictions and also of those that would take care of the well-being of the entire political arrangement protecting it from vested interests. This would cover the issue of the distribution of costs and benefits within a specific political system. Excessive disproportions of this nature are destabilizing for the entire system in the long run, even though they may bring about short-term benefits to the dominant entity or privileged social groups.

Extreme symptoms of a given system's dysfunction are such limitations to crisis management that preclude them from being overcome within a given political system. For example, they hamper the use of more effective anti-crisis instruments or allow only for partial or short-term solutions, which fail to resolve any systemic problems fully, or can even increase costs of the crisis or provoke side effects leading to even more dysfunctions. This is of huge geopolitical importance because it translates into the position of a given entity (political system) in the international arena. Its internal problems are usually an incentive for external powers to interfere to the detriment of the said entity.

Crisis management entails additional difficulties, which follow directly from a difficult economic or political situation. Given such circumstances, the policymakers are subjected to pressures of time or other external crisis-generating

---

10 A. Baker (2010): Restraining Regulatory Capture? Anglo-America, Crisis Politics and Trajectories of Change in Global Financial Governance, *International Affairs*, vol. 86, no. 3, pp. 647–663; J. Bhagwati (1998): The Capital Myth: The Difference between Trade in Widgets and Dollars, *Foreign Affairs*, May–June, pp. 7–16; G. Duménil, D. Lévy (2011): *The Crisis of Neoliberalism*, Cambridge – London: Harvard University Press, p. 25.

factors. This is conducive for the narrowing of their decision-making perspective, i.e. for focusing on ad-hoc, rather than strategic actions. The intensification of crisis-related difficulties combined with intra-systemic limitations give rise to the situation of disequilibrium, as political science calls it[11]. It increases the uncertainty of the main actors, among other things due to a lack of access to information and difficulty with situation assessment. This is conducive for erroneous calculations, emotional responses to current events and irrational decision-making. A situation of systemic crisis, therefore, may easily transform into a serious internal or international conflict.

A crisis usually requires extraordinary modes of action, although it may be resolved quite simply with the use of already available instruments as before. This type of conservatism, however, can hamper the overcoming of problems. A crisis situation may also lead to long-term consequences of a systemic nature, for example by permanently increasing the power hierarchy (which is initially treated only as a method to improve the effectiveness of measures counteracting the hardship) or by turning extraordinary measures into lasting management methods in a specified political system. In the case of uniting Europe, this may concern not only systemic issues or dominant integration advancement methods, but also routine management and socialization methods, which literature sometimes places under the blanket umbrella term of Europeanization[12].

(4) Legitimization problems

Crises of lesser weight are manifested through weakened legitimization, i.e. through social approval for a specific government. On the other hand a systemic crisis is accompanied by more fundamental legitimization issues, i.e. ones related to social approval for a socio-economic order or political system. This is most

---

11 J. D. Steinbruner (1974): *The Cybernetic Theory of Decision: New Dimensions of Political Analysis*, Princeton: Princeton University Press; B. Bueno de Mosquita (1978): *Systemic Polarization and the Occurrence and Duration of War, Journal of Conflict Resolution*, vol. 22, no. 2, pp. 241–267; R. N. Lebow (1981): *Between War and Peace*, Baltimore: The Johns Hopkins University Press; I. L. Janis, L. Mann (1997): Decision Making: A Psychological Analysis of Conflict, Choice and Commitment, *New York: The Free Press*; Ch. F. Doran (1991), pp. 22, 26–29, 41.

12 See: Ch. Bretherton, M. L. Mannin (2013) (eds.): *The Europeanization of European Politics*, New York: Palgrave Macmillan; R. Coman, T. Kostera, L. Tomini (2014) (eds.): *Europeanization and European Integration: from Incremental to Structural Change*, Houndmills-Basingstoke, New York: Palgrave Macmillan; T. G. Grosse (2012): *W objęciach Europeizacji* [In the embrace of Europeanization], Warsaw: ISP PAN.

frequently related not only to current dissatisfaction with a crisis situation, but also to earlier systemic problems or gaps present in the said area. For example, if the system of power was not adequately based on democratic institutions, then the crisis situation is likely to aggravate the chronic problem of a democratic deficit.

A phenomenon accompanying legitimization problems is the fact that economic or political ideas being the ideological basis for a specific system become exhausted. Given such a situation, the aforementioned ideas become empty truisms, which cease to justify the need to advance a given political system. Therefore, the weakening of social identification with such a system may be a sign of a crisis. This is most frequently related to the widening gap between unfulfilled social expectations and the real state of affairs. As an example, if utilitarian issues, i.e. ones related to the improvement of citizens' living conditions and well- being, are the basis of social support for a specific order, then a long-term economic crisis becomes a particularly difficult challenge for such a system's legitimization. Thus, a legitimization crisis additionally contributes to the weakening of the political system, consequently lowering its geopolitical potential in external relations.

* * *

All four aforementioned dimensions were visible during the Eurozone crisis. First of all there were difficulties in restoring economic growth and the crisis-generated weakening of geopolitical potential. Furthermore, the crisis revealed the problems of excessive economic disparities in the Eurozone and the structural differences between core states and the periphery, as well as growing disequilibrium within the core of integrating Europe, i.e. between France and Germany. This became a source of excessive rivalry between those states, hampering crisis management. And finally, there was the issue of political legitimization deficit. All dimensions of the crisis will be described at greater length in a further part of the chapter. They are rooted in the weaknesses of the geopolitical system supporting the monetary regime, and consequently in an ailment of the political system emerging in the integration of Europe.

Two aspects of development

Europe has been afflicted by problems in at least two ways: economically and politically. In the case of the economic aspects of the Eurozone's dysfunctions, the weakening of the economic growth rate and rising unemployment, proved to be particularly painful, while applied methods to overcome the crises largely contributed to the aggravation of those problems, at least in the mid-term perspective. This is due to the fact that the adopted anti-crisis tactics deepened the recession in many states of the monetary union. It must also be kept in mind that the specifics of the functioning of subsequent monetary regimes in Europe has consisted of the systemic limitation of the growth and employment potential, accompanied by the neglect for actions aimed to stimulate economic innovation and competitiveness[13].

Back in the 1960s economists pointed out to boundary conditions necessary for the permanence of the monetary union. According to Mundell's theory of optimum currency areas[14] the indispensable elements include high labour resources mobility to offset economic tensions in underdeveloped parts of the monetary union (so-called asymmetrical shocks). Fiscal instruments comprise another adjustment mechanism; for example, investment programmes (stimulating economic growth in weaker regions of the monetary union) or so-called automatic stabilizers in a business cycle, i.e. social programmes launched during a recession and rises in unemployment[15]. To be effective, they have to be performed in a centralized manner across the entire monetary union. This requires a fiscal federation (i.e. a fiscal union and a strong central budget). An additional systemic element should be the control of capital markets and capital flows within the monetary union as well as in external relations[16]. Without such control, excessive financial investments are possible in some regions of the monetary union. They result not only in so-called speculative bubbles, but first and foremost in the further widening of macroeconomic gaps. In consequence they aggravate the basic problem threatening the permanence of the monetary union.

---

13 B. Eichengreen (2007): *The European Economy Since 1945. Coordinated Capitalism and Beyond*, Princeton - Oxford: Princeton University Press, pp. 252–277; J. Cohen (2009): *Toward a Leaderless Currency System*, in: E. Helleiner, J. Kirshner (eds.): *The Future of the Dollar*, Ithaca and London: Cornell University Press, pp. 142–165.

14 R. Mundell (1961): A Theory of Optimum Currency Areas, *American Economic Review*, vol. 51, pp. 657–665.

15 P. Kenen (1969): The Theory of Optimum Currency Areas: An Eclectic View, in: R. Mundell, A. Swoboda (eds.): *Monetary Problems of the World Economy*, Chicago: University of Chicago Press, pp. 41–60.

16 P. Krugman (1993): Lessons of Massachusetts for EMU, in: Torres F., Giavazzi F. (eds.): *Adjustment and Growth in the European Monetary Union*, Cambridge: Cambridge University Press, pp. 241–269; D. Folkerts-Landau, P. Garber (1992): The ECB: A Bank or a Monetary Policy Rule, in: M. Canzoneri, V. Grilli, P. Masson (eds.): *Establishing a Central Bank: Issues in Europe and Lessons from the US*, Cambridge: Cambridge University Press, pp. 86–110.

The direct reason underlying the crisis was the financial slump caused be an external factor i.e. the collapse of the US banking system (in 2008); nevertheless, it became just a catalyst for a deep crisis in Europe, which had been maturing for a long time before and resulted from dysfunctions within the Economic and Monetary Union (EMU) itself. Excessive macroeconomic diversification between particular member states led to the accumulation of imbalances within the Eurozone, particularly regarding the economic competitiveness between the economically weakest states, located mainly in southern Europe, and the richest, located in the very centre of the continent. This phenomenon was manifested in an imbalance of current accounts between those states, including export surpluses in some, and trade deficits in others. According to scholars' forecasts, this generated an asymmetry of costs and benefits ensuing from monetary regime functioning, which resulted in growing private and public debt in the least competitive countries[17]. As already mentioned, the basic method for overcoming such problems should be investment transfers from rich states of the monetary union into the weakest ones with a view to restoring the competitiveness of the latter, i.e. stimulating economic development, employment and improving the trade balance[18]. In the conditions of the crisis, the dominant political majority in the Eurozone considered macroeconomic disparities to be an internal problem of the weakest economies, i.e. one requiring no EMU intervention, or even less so a response from those economies of the monetary union that have the greatest export surpluses. The only response to this fundamental problem of the EMU was the introduction of the monitoring of the macroeconomic situation by EU institutions, on the basis of which suggestions will be presented for structural reforms to be implemented by particular countries.

The adopted anti-crisis tactics not only failed to provide an answer to the greatest problem of the Eurozone, but also transferred adjustment costs mainly onto weaker states and ones immersed in crisis[19]. Moreover, in mid-term the said tactics deepened the problems of economic growth and employment

17 See: M. Wolf (2014): *The Shifts and the Shocks. What We've Learned – and Have Still to Learn – from the Financial Crisis*, London: Allen Lane, pp. 59–64.

18 R. Germain, H. Schwartz (2014): The Political Economy of Failure : The Euro as an International Currency, *Review of International Political Economy*, vol. 21, no. 5, pp. 1095–1122 [1106]; S. Collignon (2014): Political Lessons from the Economics of the Euro-crisis, in: M. J. Rodrigues, E. Xiarchogiannopoulou (eds.): *The Eurozone Crisis and the Transformation of EU Governance*, Burlington: Ashgate, pp. 85–106 [95–96].

19 P. A. Hall (2014): Varieties of Capitalism and the Euro Crisis, *West European Politics*, vol. 37, no. 6, pp. 1223–1243 [1231]; S. Collignon (2014), p. 99.

in those states. This is attributable to the fact that the solution proposed by European policymakers was the so-called internal devaluation, which was aimed at reducing production costs in the weakest states of the euro area. But such actions triggered deflation pressure and slowed down the economic growth rate. It consequently led to a rise in unemployment and was accompanied by a very slow rate of restoring the competitiveness of domestic exports (resulting in among other things, enforced reductions of local wages and social benefits). This caused the crisis to drag on, social and political costs to escalate, as well as a rise in Euroscepticism and support for extreme and populist parties. The applied method of crisis resolution, therefore, deepened the economic growth problems, as it was underpinned by the superiority of the vested interests of the richest states over the stability and rationality of the functioning of the entire arrangement. Since the very establishment of the European Communities, scholars have pointed out to the said phenomenon as one of the greatest threats to integration advancement[20]. The crisis also led to a weakening of the potential of the European Union in the international arena, and hampered the raising of financing for the pursuance of active foreign policy.

The political system in place in Europe suffers from chronic economic growth problems, and the applied method of the Eurozone crisis resolution is just an example of the said phenomenon. This problem was noticed by the first commentators of regional cooperation in Europe, who attached particular significance to the functionality of the integration process[21]. Simultaneously they argued that an absence of mutual benefits together with excessive external costs following from integration are likely to hamper any advancement of such cooperation. Dysfunctionality of the monetary regime ensues from design faults in the Eurozone, including in particular, the absence of relevant institutions enabling fiscal transfers (investment and social) in a crisis. The aforementioned shortcomings hamper economic development in Europe. Additionally, the crisis generated more debts (despite the fact that debt reduction was allegedly the priority of anti-crisis measures), which will certainly encumber further growth.

Growth problems can also be analysed from another perspective. The main method for the stimulation of development in the EU was first and foremost by subsequent rounds of Community enlargements, and the facility for core states to grow richer on the basis of expansion of the single market into states with

20 See: E. B. Haas (1961): International Integration: The European and the Universal Process, *International Organization*, vol. 15, no. 3, pp. 366–392.

21 *Ibidem.*

relatively weaker economies. This type of expansion is sometimes described in literature as internal colonialism or the exploitation of semi-peripheries by the core in a given political system[22]. This is related to a growing imbalance of costs and benefits between entities of the most competitive and weakest economies, with the weaker powers of political influence located in the peripheries. A particular example of the application of this mechanism proved to be the monetary union, which – as I have already mentioned – in the long-term accumulated imbalances on current accounts between the said two groups of states. Such a development method within the monetary union (across the entire European Union) not only proved asymmetrical for some particular countries, but also resulted in long-term consequences for the potential of the entire united Europe. This is attributable to the neglect for measures which would have supported economic innovation and competitiveness[23]. Moreover, actions counteracting excessive economic and social inequalities within the EU were highly inadequate.

Besides the economic aspects, the growth category can be examined in a political dimension. The development of a given political system can be understood, among other things, as the gradual strengthening of power within a rising political core. In the case of the European Union, political development so understood translates into the increased powers of EU institutions, expansion of European law and the depletion of sovereign competencies of member states. This draws on neo-functional assumptions guiding integration in Europe, as part of which subsequent crises enforce advances of integration, including in particular expansion of the powers of supranational (Community) institutions in relation to member states. Moreover, advances of integration should lead to a gradual reduction of the powers of intergovernmental institutions and intergovernmental decision-making processes for the benefit of Community method[24] or federal.

---

22 For more details see: T. G. Grosse (2012): *W objęciach Europeizacji* [In the embrace of Europeanization], pp. 225–240. See a classic book on internal colonialism: M. Hechter (1998): *Internal Colonialism: The Celtic Fringe in British National Development*, New Brunswick: Transaction Publishers; 2nd edition.

23 For more details see: T. G. Grosse (2015): *Kryzys innowacyjności w Europie* [Crisis of innovation in Europe], Przegląd Europejski, no. 1 (35), 2015, pp. 11–32.

24 The Community method is characterized by (i) the central role of the Commission in formulating proposals; (ii) qualified majority voting (QMV) in the Council as a rule; (iii) involvement of the European Parliament with varying intensity depending on the decision-making procedure; and (iv) the role of the Court in ensuring judicial accountability. G. De Baere (2008): *Constitutional Principles of EU External Relations*, Oxford-New York: Oxford University Press, p. 73.

During the Eurozone crisis, there was indeed an expansion of European law and of the powers of European institutions in relation to member states; this concerned in particular the supervisory competences of the EU over the fiscal policies pursued in EMU countries. I define this process as the reinforcement of "negative fiscal federalism" in Europe. I say this because it consisted of ever stronger limitations by European law and institutions of the fiscal policies pursued by EU members, particularly by EMU states. Simultaneously, against neo-functional assumptions the crisis did not lead to increased powers of Community institutions, such as the Commission or Parliament in relation to intergovernmental institutions. Anti-crisis policy was dictated by the biggest and richest EMU states, particularly in accordance with German and French preferences, and not by the technocratic institutions of the EU or the European Parliament. The latter fulfilled a rather legitimizing role for prior informal decisions made by leading states and a few of their most influential politicians[25]. The crisis also became an opportunity for the reconfiguration of power in Europe, and more precisely for its restoration by some member states over supranational institutions[26]. This concerned both a reduction of the political autonomy of the Commission, Parliament and other European institutions (e.g. the European Central Bank [ECB]), and among other things by subjecting them to stronger control by intergovernmental institutions and the informal influences of the most powerful member states. This process also concerned the reconfiguration of power within intergovernmental institutions themselves, as well as by subjecting them to a stronger political influence from the richest EMU states, and also by a strengthening of the power of selected Eurozone states over the remaining part of the EU. The latter process is called "political segmentation" into the Eurozone and its external integration circle (i.e. other EU members)[27]. A symptom of the growing importance of the biggest euro area states was the transfer of the crisis costs onto the weakest EMU members, while the process of segmentation in Europe was related to the institutional strengthening of the Eurozone, particularly of the intergovernmental institutions of the zone, as well as to the increased informal influence of those institutions in the decision-making process across the

25 See: F. Schimmelfennig (2015): Liberal Intergovernmentalism and the Euro Area Crisis, *Journal of European Public Policy*, vol. 22, no. 2, pp. 177–195 [191]; M. Ryner (2015): Europe's Ordoliberal Iron Cage: Critical Political Economy, the Euro Area Crisis and Its Management, *Journal of European Public Policy*, vol. 22, no. 2, pp. 275–294.

26 F. Schimmelfennig (2015), p. 191.

27 For more details see: T. G. Grosse (2015): Can "Differentiated Integration" Lead to a Federation in Europe? *Yearbook of Polish European Studies*, vol. 18.

EU. One can hardly refer to the described process as integration advancement. One should rather speak of a change of the integration model towards an "asymmetrical confederation", i.e. a political system where the dominant position is assumed by the most powerful states, which on one hand influence smaller and peripheral states, and control the functioning of major supranational institutions in Europe on the other[28].

The political and economic system in Europe is still incomplete and unstable in the long run. The fundamental problem of the Eurozone was the fact that the centralization of monetary policy was pursued during the decentralization of fiscal policy without introducing "positive fiscal federalism", i.e. joint fiscal instruments within the monetary union that would allow for the distribution of investment and social funds into trouble-stricken parts of the EMU. These institutional gaps are defined as "functional dissonances" associated with the EMU, because they hamper the resolution of problems of the monetary union, consequently disturbing its effective functioning in a long-term perspective[29]. The centralization of fiscal policy at the level of the monetary union would require the introduction of a political union of democratic nature, and consequently the supplementation of an electoral democracy with political communities functioning at national level with electoral institutions and the building of a political community within the EMU (or across the entire EU)[30]. The crisis did not become an opportunity to bridge those institutional gaps or the aforementioned *functional dissonances*. Instead, power was reconfigured towards the strengthening of the political force of the strongest states in relation to the weaker, peripheral states as well as those immersed in misfortune. This type of power asymmetry – less and less toned down by Community institutions (which were subjected to a loss of autonomy and also became exposed to the power of the biggest states) – led to multiple political tensions in Europe, which negatively influence the stability of the integration process.

---

28 For more details see: T. G. Grosse (2015): *Changing the Integration Model: On the Fiasco of the Neo-functional Vision of the Crisis.*

29 A. Niemann, D. Ioannou (2015): European Economic Integration in Times of Crisis: A Case of Neofunctionalism? *Journal of European Public Policy*, vol. 22, no. 2, pp. 196–218 [201].

30 N. Jabko (2015): *The Elusive Economic Government and the Forgotten Fiscal Union*, in: M. Matthijs, M. Blyth (eds.): *The Future of the Euro*, Oxford – New York: Oxford University Press, pp. 70–89.

The geopolitical arrangement and stability of the monetary regime

The single currency system in Europe can be treated as a specific example of an international regime[31] applicable in monetary relations. According to scholars any monetary regime is rooted in a geopolitical arrangement[32]. If a given geopolitical arrangement is weak, than the monetary system is prone to crises. This follows from the fact that a monetary regime is based on political power and draws on a specific geographic area. In this sense it has a direct relationship with a specific geopolitical arrangement (understood as a system of political power within a given territory).

Dysfunctions of a geopolitical arrangement supporting the monetary regime may be caused by many factors. One of them is the weakness of a regional hegemon, who e.g. imposes its own currency or dominates politically within the regional currency system. Here one may refer to the conclusions of the famous book by Charles Kindleberger[33] asserting that a benevolent hegemon is indispensable for the stability of a given monetary regime. This term also denotes a type of dominant power which assumes responsibility for the functioning of the entire regime, so that it is not guided exclusively by its own interests. For that reason, its leadership position is accepted by other entities and legitimized within the international community. In the case of the Eurozone there is no such regional hegemon. The position of Germany is dominant in the economic area but much less so in the area of politics. This state can be defined as a leading European power, but not as a hegemon, particularly one assuming full responsibility for the stability of the single currency, in accordance with the rationality of the functioning of such an arrangement and not solely with regard to its own interests.

In crisis, Germany was guided first and foremost by its own preferences and economic ideas of ordoliberalism, with one example being the imposition of

31 D. J. Puchala, R. F. Hopkins (1982): International Regimes: Lessons from Inductive Analysis, *International Organization*, vol. XXXVI, no. 2, pp. 245–276.

32 E. Helleiner, J. Kirshner (2009): Summing Up and Looking Ahead: The Future of the Future of the Dollar, in: E. Helleiner, J. Kirshner (eds.): *The Future of the Dollar*, Ithaca and London: Cornell University Press, pp. 216–227; D. P. Calleo (2009): Twenty-First Century Geopolitics and the Erosion of the Dollar Order, in: E. Helleiner, J. Kirshner (eds.): *The Future of the Dollar*, Ithaca and London: Cornell University Press, pp. 164–190.

33 C. P. Kindleberger (1973): *The World in Depression: 1929–1939*, London: Allen Lane, The Penguin Press.

austerity measures and the transfer of adjustment costs onto the more severely trouble-stricken states. It also tried to minimize its responsibility for financing the crisis costs, and consistently refused any proposal for increased fiscal redistribution between rich and poor euro area states. Consequently the attitude of Germany failed to win full approval from other EMU members, so it did not win the adequate legitimization required to fulfil the hegemonic function[34]. A large portion of its proposals were challenged, and if they were eventually implemented, this mainly followed from conditions set by Berlin on financial aid. The uniquely powerful position of Germany in crisis was based on this state's financial potential, required to save the Eurozone. Not all of the Berlin proposals were put into practice and sometimes German politicians had to make concessions during negotiations. Almost each time, however, the concessions were made on their terms. This was the case of the stormy negotiations on the third bailout package for Greece (in 2015). The price paid by the Greek government for financial aid and the avoidance of Grexit was its commitment to make drastic fiscal savings, increase taxes and introduce a reform of welfare and pension schemes, and to guarantee repayment of debts to creditors through the establishment of a 50-billion EURO privatisation fund.

The institutional shape of the EMU was conducive for the accumulation of economic imbalances between the core states (Germany in particular), and other states[35]. The monetary regime, therefore, increased the benefits of Germany and enhanced its economic and geopolitical potentials compared to other members of the monetary union. This is why some define the monetary union in Europe as a German system[36], where Berlin defines the main rules and political directions and derives geoeconomic benefits. This is how the design of the system, similarly to earlier monetary regimes in Europe[37], has contributed to the widening of structural gaps in the geopolitical area.

---

34 S. Bulmer (2014): Germany and the Eurozone Crisis: Between Hegemony and Domestic Politics, *West European Politics*, vol. 37, no. 6, pp. 1244–1263 [1250].

35 This was demonstrated by a Harvard University professor, B. Friedman, in his speech at the Brussels Economic Forum, *Sources of Economic Growth*, Brussels, 31–05–2012.

36 A. Moravcsik (2012): Europe After the Crisis. How to Sustain a Common Currency, *Foreign Affairs*, vol. 91, no. 3, pp. 54–68; J. Story, J. Walter (1997): *Political Economy of Financial Integration in Europe. The Battle of the System*, Cambridge Massachusetts: The MIT Press, pp. 74, 85, 89, 93, 99.

37 For more details see: T. G. Grosse (2012): *Trzy cykle kumulacji doświadczeń reżimu monetarnego w Europie* [Three cycles of experiences accumulation of monetary regime in Europe], Warsaw: Myśl Ekonomiczna i Polityczna, no. 3 (38) 2012, pp. 32–54.

The German policy in times of crisis is mainly a result of internal factors, first and foremost of the reluctance among German voters to allow for the redistribution of their taxes into poorer Eurozone states[38]. Nevertheless, it is also a continuation of post-war policies, when leaders of the country focused on economic reconstruction and also tried to restore prestige to their state and geopolitical potential on the basis of economic development. This was an attempt to transpose geopolitical rivalry from military to economic, while the development of an internal market in Europe, followed by the establishment of a single currency, was intended to be the basic framework for commercial and investment expansion[39]. This was a geoeconomic strategy, or at least a strategy leading to express geoeconomic outcomes: Germany became the main economic power in Europe, with the greatest financial potential, as well as being the only one with the greatest discretionary power in European policy in the situation of the Eurozone crisis. The only limitation for this model of geoeconomic expansion proved to be the fact that it did not win full approval of other states, which was manifested during the crisis in the political disputes with France and its allies from southern Europe.

The specific geopolitical situation in Europe, which consisted of the relatively equal geopolitical potentials between the three biggest states[40] (together with the absence of a clear European hegemon, notwithstanding the external impact of the USA) – was reflected in the integration process. This is so because it led to the open (or incomplete) contracting of international agreements[41], as it was impossible to negotiate final and holistic contracts. An example of this phenomenon was the single currency system, which from the very start displayed serious institutional deficiencies and inconsistencies. A consequence of the discussed situation is the necessity to constantly correct and supplement the aforementioned system. So far this has pushed the integration process forward, but at the same time given rise to political tensions and rivalry between the main actors. The crisis has proved that the aforementioned method sometimes results in significant costs and dysfunctions in the incomplete system.

---

38 S. Bulmer (2014), pp. 1245–1249.

39 See: S. F. Szabo (2015): *Germany, Russia and the Rise of Geo-Economics*, London: Bloomsbury Academic.

40 Here I have in mind countries with the greatest economic, demographic and military potential: Germany, France and the United Kingdom.

41 See: A. Cooley, H. Spruyt (2009): *Contracting States: Sovereign Transfers in International Relations*, Princeton: Princeton University Press, p. 161.

Another element of the EMU's weakness in the geopolitical dimension is the fact that it lacks a proper systemic basis. Scholars point out to the absence of the transfer of political sovereignty from nation-states to the monetary union[42]. The lack of such transfer is the fundamental reason underlying the weakness of the decision-making process. The single currency is based on a quite fragile agreement between sovereign states, which can easily change and is frequently subject to tough political bargaining. The lack of adequate transfer of sovereignty also contributes to problems of political legitimization for power at the Union level. Other scholars argue[43] that the monetary union in Europe is based neither on a political (democratic) federation nor on a system resembling an EU nation-state. This is rather a confederation of sovereign states with a superstructure in the form of supranational institutions, which do not have adequate political mandate. Therefore, the monetary union lacks an institution of *positive fiscal federalism* (e.g. joint taxes and a budget guaranteeing the single currency).

Scholars[44] have pointed out that unless the aforementioned institutions are introduced, the monetary union for Europe makes economic sense only within a narrow group of core states. This concerns countries with structurally similar economies to, i.e. Germany, France, the Benelux countries and Denmark. From the very start, therefore, the EMU faced the dilemma pointed out by economists: it would either arise in a narrow group of core states or should be augmented by relevant institutions. European politicians, however, made a different choice. In the name of geopolitical considerations related to European integration, they established the EMU with a broad structure – incorporating South European states into it. Simultaneously they did not agree on a proper institutional architecture that would provide guarantees for the Union's stability in a long term perspective. This is how negligence on the part of policy-makers and the weaknesses of the political arrangement became the direct cause behind the accumulation of economic dysfunctions and costs in the monetary regime.

In the period of the Eurozone crisis, a discussion has surfaced on a similar topic within the group of the biggest policy-makers. Some of them have

---

42 B. J. Cohen (2009), pp. 142–165.

43 See: D. Calleo (2002): *Rethinking Europe's Future.* Princeton–Oxford: Princeton University Press; D. P. Calleo (2009), p. 188. B. Eichengreen (2011): *Exorbitant Privilege: The Rise and Fall of the Dollar and the Future of the International Monetary System*, Oxford: Oxford University Press, pp. 121–150.

44 T. Bayoumi, B. Eichengreen (1993): Shocking Aspects of European Monetary Unification, in: Torres F., Giavazzi F. (eds.): *Adjustment and Growth In the European Monetary Union*, Cambridge: Cambridge University Press, pp. 193–229.

decided that the best way to cut the crisis short would be for Greece to leave the Eurozone in view of the fact that this country structurally differs so much from the rest and the introduction of fiscal reforms encounters serious resistance in local policies. Such a position was presented, among other things, in 2015 by the German finance minister[45]. His proposal was rejected in the name of geopolitical interests, and particularly in view of the threat that Grexit might destabilize the south-eastern part of Europe and open it to Russian influences. This is why the Americans were against the Eurozone's decomposition; at the European forum the cohesion of the euro area was most actively defended by the French, and by the head of the European Council – Donald Tusk[46]. Geopolitical factors influenced the final position of Chancellor Merkel, contradicting the proposals of her finance minister.

The problem of geopolitical arrangement in Europe is additionally compounded by strong political and economic rivalry between the strongest powers. The period of crisis became a catalyst for a struggle for power and over the distribution of costs related to the rescuing of the monetary regime. It became an opportunity for political and systemic adjustments in the EU, i.e. changes related to the geopolitical system being the support base for the Eurozone. It turns out that the changes and disputes about the distribution of financing in Europe were of paramount importance for political elites. The issue of crisis resolution was just a pretext or background for such a geoeconomic gameplay.

As already mentioned, structural adjustments, and only to a limited extent, concerned the bridging of any macroeconomic gaps, and even then, were mainly related to the geopolitical arena. Paris aimed to diminish the imbalance of potentials and relational power between a more and more powerful Germany and a weakening France. For example, an increased financial distribution in the Eurozone could deplete the capital resources of Germany. This in turn could change the monetary union's functioning in a way which would permanently enforce high spending by the said state. Paris also aimed at a gradual reduction of benefits for the German economy under this system; also through the limitation of the German economy's competitive advantages compared to other Eurozone

45 *German Finance Minister Wants Greece Out Of Euro*, Forbes, July 11, 2015, http://www.forbes.com [last accessed on: 29.07.2015].

46 Greece Talks: 'Sorry, but There Is No Way You Are Leaving this Room', *Financial Times*, July 13, http://www.ft.com [last accessed on: 29.07.2015]. The article's title is a quote from a statement by Donald Tusk at the European Council summit when he prevented leaving of negotiations by the prime minister of Greece and chancellor of Germany without prior negotiation of a compromise saving the eurozone's cohesion.

economies. Berlin consistently opposed a transfer union (something I call a *positive fiscal federalism*), i.e. non-repayable investment transfers aimed to improve the competitiveness of the economies of southern Europe; it rejected proposals to reduce the debts of some states and communities in the Eurozone, as well as to introduce social transfers from EMU level with the aim of counteracting mass unemployment and restoring demand in the most crisis-stricken states. But Berlin backed down under pressure from the scale of difficulties (as well as the pressure from Paris), and agreed to provide financial support in the form of loans stabilising the banking system and budgets of particular countries, at the same time imposing very stringent conditions on those countries, relating among other things to fiscal reforms[47].

After the change of power in the Élysée Palace in mid-2012, there was a stronger mobilisation of Paris and other Eurozone capitals to pressurise Berlin. An example of the distribution channels conflict between the aforementioned countries was the issue of the establishment of a banking union (agreed at the euro area summit in June 2012[48]). A coalition of states under French leadership was aimed at creating a powerful instrument for the refinancing of troubled banks, established as part of the aforementioned project. Moreover, it wanted to enable such banks the direct use of aid from the European Stability Mechanism (ESM) (i.e. a fund dedicated to rescuing crisis-stricken eurozone states). At the same time representatives of Germany, the Netherlands and Finland, i.e. states enjoying the highest financial ratings and largely providing support under the ESM – tried to block the facility[49]. Berlin also wanted to hamper the establishment of a bank refinancing fund (so-called single resolution mechanism) and European deposit insurance system[50] or at least delay the creation of such banking union instruments[51].

---

47 See: A. Crespy, V. Schmidt (2014): The clash of Titans: France, Germany and the discursive double game of EMU reform, *Journal of European Public Policy*, vol. 21, no. 8, pp. 1085–1101 [1086].

48 *Euro Area Summit Statement,* Brussels, 29 June 2012. See: S. McPhilemy (2014): Integrating rules, disintegrating markets: the end of national discretion in European banking? *Journal of European Public Policy*, vol. 21, no. 10, pp. 1473–1490.

49 *The other moral hazard*, The Economist, 29th September 2012.

50 No More Bail-outs: Germany Blocks Juncker's Eurozone Reform Drive, *The Telegraph*, Thursday 17 September 2015.

51 This is evidenced by 2013 European Council Conclusions. See: *Conclusions*, European Council, EUCO 156/12, Brussels 18/19 October 2012, p. 7.

French policy was aimed at introducing growth-stimulating instruments in the Eurozone. One of the outcomes of those efforts was the action package adopted in June 2012 under the name of Compact for Growth and Jobs[52]. It concerned, among other things, the recapitalization of the European Investment Bank and an increase in the volume of loans granted by this institution, the release of so-called project bonds aimed at financing projects in key transport, energy and broadband infrastructure, as well as the reallocation of unutilized funds from the EU cohesion policy. Another example of the Paris policies was the proposal to establish a separate budget for the Eurozone area (or so-called "fiscal capacity" of the said zone). In this case, Berlin's actions were limited to the minimization of the scale of this instrument, among other things through a proposal to base its financing on a new tax on financial transactions. This source of revenues was not only too scarce but also highly uncertain, because at that time not all EMU states approved of its introduction[53]. The discussion about the *fiscal capacity* of the Eurozone virtually came to a stop in 2013. Nevertheless, concessions made by Germany on this issue were aimed at blocking a much more dangerous proposal for Berlin to issue Eurobonds.

Another action of French diplomacy was the reinforcement of *political segmentation* in the EU in accordance with the "two-speed Europe" mechanism. Those processes were to be based on the Eurozone and its institutional strengthening. This concerned, among other things, the elevated status of the Euro group and its support through the expansion of the administrative apparatus. Besides the aforementioned budget for the Eurozone area, other proposals were also discussed, such as the appointment of a separate chamber for the monetary union within the European Parliament and a division within the European Commission into commissioners representing the Eurozone and the rest of the EU[54]. Also the idea of appointing a banking union and stepping up banking supervision concerned mainly with the Eurozone. According to the press release from the European Commission, this was to constitute a milestone for the deepening of political integration within the monetary union[55].

---

52 See: *Conclusions,* European Council, EUCO 76/12, 28–29 June 2012, Brussels, Annex, pp. 11–12.

53 *Eleven EU Countries Agree on Transaction Tax*, Der Spiegel, 09.10.2012.

54 Final report by the Reflection Group on the Future of the EU by the Foreign Affairs Ministers of Austria, Belgium, Denmark, France, Spain, the Netherlands, Luxembourg, Germany, Poland, Portugal and Italy, 17 September 2012, www.msz.gov.pl, downloaded on: 29.09.2012.

55 Commission Proposes New ECB Powers for Banking Supervision as a Part of a Banking Union, *European Commission*, Press Release, Brussels, 12 September 2012, p. 2.

Germany was reluctant to reinforce European integration solely within the Eurozone, because this would have excessively strengthened the position of Paris and its allies in Europe. Germany, therefore, also stressed the necessity to open new solutions concerning the Eurozone to those states that would want to adopt the European single currency in the future or that declare voluntary participation in negotiated agreements. This concerned Poland among other states, which at that time was a close ally of Germany. Berlin also agreed for the stepping up of economic governance – in accordance with the French suggestion to establish an economic government for the Eurozone – but only to use those instruments for the strengthening of fiscal discipline and also to cover the procedure for EU states remaining outside of the Eurozone area[56].

Another sign of the French tactics was the aim to increase the politicization of the decisions related to economic governance in the EMU. This was related, among other things, to the proposal to step up the status of the Eurogroup and increase its competencies with regard to the coordination of economic policies between member states. It is worthwhile pointing out that the aforementioned actions had already been proposed by France, i.e. in the period when the shape of the monetary union was negotiated on the turn of the 1980s and 1990s[57]. At that time they aimed to limit the influence of Germany on how the monetary regime would function, including in particular German rules related to fiscal policy and its anti-inflationary approach to monetary policy. So the goal was to make economic rules within the system more flexible, but first and foremost to weaken the influence of Berlin on the directions of economic policies. According to the terminology applied in literature[58], these actions can be defined as attempts to diminish the structural power of Germany within the monetary regime.

Crisis management crisis

The weakness of the political centre is the main problem of the geopolitical system underlying the functioning of the single currency. This weakness resulted mainly in the slow decision-making process, the inadequacy of those decisions to the emerging problems (which fundamentally restricted the effectiveness of actions), as well as the lack of proper political legitimization for those

56 A. Crespy, V. Schmidt (2014), p. 1093.

57 J. Story, J. Walter (1997), p. 87.

58 See: D. M. Andrews (2006): Monetary Power and Monetary Statecraft, in: D. M. Andrews (ed.): *International Monetary Power*, Ithaca – London: Cornell University Press, pp. 7–28.

decisions[59]. There were some visible attempts to find solutions to the aforementioned weaknesses, but they failed to bring about the expected outcomes. Sometimes attempts were made to resolve one ailment of the system at the cost of aggravating other problems. The real problem was that the political system functioning in the EU was unable to resolve effectively all the dysfunctions of the decision-making process at the same time. This necessitates a fundamental systemic change, not merely a correction of the existing political governance.

Political economists have repeatedly pointed out to difficulties related to the undertaking of long-term actions in democracies[60]. This is connected with the narrowing of the time perspective of actions undertaken by politicians due to short timeframes of subsequent elections. Also during the Eurozone crisis, the impact of electoral effect on the behaviour of political elites was clearly visible. This was related mainly to the avoidance of such decisions that would give rise to social controversies. In the case of the richest states, this entailed reluctance for excessive involvement in financial measures connected to rescuing the Eurozone area states threatened with bankruptcy. There was also a visible conservative attitude among political elites and the avoidance of making too risky or breakthrough decisions, which might have jeopardized their chances in elections. The preference, therefore, was for the use and improvement of already existing solutions rather than for the introduction of new instruments[61]. At the same time the pressing problems of the Eurozone required bold decisions made within a strategic perspective.

There was also a visible influence of financial markets on the actions of politicians. The tackling of the crisis was reduced mainly to the reassurance of financial investors. In the critical situation, markets gained a much greater influence over the actions of politicians than local voters. This testified not only to

---

59 S. McPhilemy (2014); J. Caporaso, Min-hyung Kim, W. N. Durrett, R. B. Wesley (2015): Still a Regulatory State? The European Union and the Financial Crisis, *Journal of European Policy*, vol. 22, no. 7, pp. 889–907.

60 See: W. D. Nordhaus (1975): The Political Business Cycle, *Review of Economic Studies*, vol. 42, pp. 169–182; E. Dal Bo, M. Rossi (2011): Term Length and Political Performance, *Review of Economic Studies*, vol. 78, pp. 1237–1263; J. Ferejohn (1986): Incumbent Performance and Electoral Control, *Public Choice*, vol. 50, pp. 5–25; A. Glazer, M. Robbins (1985): How Elections Matter: A Study of U.S. Senators, *Public Choice*, vol. 46, pp. 163–172.

61 A. Verdun (2015): A Historical Institutionalist Explanation of the EU's Responses to the Euro Area Financial Crisis, *Journal of European Public Policy*, vol. 22, no. 2, pp. 219–237.

the perspective in which the crisis was perceived by the elites (instability of the financial sector took centre stage), but may also indicate deeper problems of European democracy[62]. This proves that the decision-making perspective was superficial and ad hoc. The response to signs of the crisis (among other things – the destabilization of financial markets) was much more important for politicians than the resolution of its fundamental causes. It is worthwhile adding that what really helped to reassure markets in 2012 was not the institutional reform boldly undertaken in the EMU, but the actions of the ECB related to quantitative easing and the announcement of the facility to buy out unlimited numbers of the bonds of the monetary union states[63].

Another example of the weakness of the political centre was the propensity to undertake partial reforms, instead of systemic ones. In many cases this only concerned the improvement of existing economic governance mechanisms in the EU. As an example, prior regulatory instruments were strengthened with regard to fiscal discipline towards member states (i.e. *negative fiscal federalism* was deepened), but political agreement was lacking to introduce new redistribution instruments (i.e. mechanisms of *positive fiscal federalism*)[64] and to rebuild the "supporting political infrastructure so that political actors could negotiate distributional conflicts"[65]. Moreover, the strategic problem of inequality with regard to economic competitiveness in the Eurozone was ignored; focus of attention was placed on the issue of excessive debt and the disturbances in the banking system instead. This resulted from the aforementioned lack of courage to undertake deeper reforms and from the conservatism of political elites. Another cause underlying the situation was a deficit of political leadership in a time of crisis. But to the greatest extent, governance dysfunctions resulted from the divergent interests and geoeconomic rivalry of the main actors.

A characteristic feature of governance in the EMU is the trend towards "asymmetric rationality". I understand this term as superiority of the interests of some member states over rationality of the functioning of the entire system. Those were the interests of dominant states that determined the institutional shape and anti-crisis policy in the eurozone[66]. Moreover, the rationality of the main political actors than stability (and rationality) of the entire system mattered much more

62 For more details see: T. G. Grosse (2012): Changes in Western Democracy: A Systemic Crisis, or a Chance to Overcome It? *Politeja*, nr (3) 21, pp. 133–154.
63 ECB 'Ready to Do Whatever It Takes', *Financial Times*, July 26, 2012.
64 See: J. Caporaso, Min-hyung Kim, W. N. Durrett, R. B. Wesley (2015).
65 R. Germain, H. Schwartz (2014), p. 1105.
66 S. Bulmer (2014), pp. 1245–1249; P. A. Hall (2014), p. 1233.

in the applied method of governance. This resulted in a trend towards the maximization of economic benefits by the dominant member states in the mid-term perspective and in the accumulation of troubles in the long-term. After some time, unresolved problems ceased to be simply local, but began to threaten the stability of the entire regime. We can conclude, therefore, that there was a crisis management of the crisis in the Eurozone in the period of 2010–2015. The management crisis was the cause of several economic difficulties both in Europe and globally. European authorities were unable to clean up the banking system or create a proper banking union. Although the ECB managed to calm the financial markets in 2012, it did not solve the structural problems of the EMU, but only postponed them till later. The elite of the Eurozone area focused their efforts on pro-cyclical fiscal austerity rather than on growth and employment. The monstrous financial costs of rescuing this system were not utilised optimally[67]. The financing exceeded almost twice the total volume of German war reparations after WWI and the American aid under the Marshall Plan after WWII[68]. The crisis contributed not only to a loss of credibility in the currency itself, but also in the political system of the EU[69].

The basic mechanism for the improvement of governance in Europe was the strengthening of the power of the strongest member states. This was performed through the improvement of intergovernmental governance, a stronger hierarchy between dominant and weaker states, stepped up control over Community institutions, and through segmentation into various integration circles.

A consequence of the division into a "two-speed Europe" was the change of the geopolitical arrangement in Europe. The political core around Berlin and Paris was strengthened. This core had a much stronger influence than before over other Eurozone states and EU countries. Additionally the role of Paris and Berlin was enhanced by the fact that the United Kingdom increasingly distanced itself from European integration. The latter included, among other things, declarations that the UK would withdraw from yet another area of European policies, or even

---

67 See: P. B. Whyman (2015): Keynes and the International Clearing Union: A Possible Model for Eurozone Reform?, *Journal of Common Market Studies*, vol. 53, no. 2, pp. 399–415; J. Caporaso, Min-hyung Kim, W. N. Durrett, R. B. Wesley (2015).

68 Both operations – converted into USD value of 2010 – exceeded USD 500 billion The financing allocated to rescuing of the Eurozone is estimated by the International Monetary Fund at over USD 1 trillion. See: D. Marsh (2011): Faltering Ambitions and Unrequited Hopes: The Battle for the Euro Intensifies, *Journal of Common Market Studies*, vol. 49, Annual Review, pp. 45–55.

69 For more details see: R. Germain, H. Schwartz (2014).

leave the EU[70]. An important symptom of the UK's distancing from continental policy was its refusal to participate in the European Fiscal Compact[71]. This was provoked by leading Eurozone states, which decided to develop the treaty outside of the Community framework due to the impossibility to arrive at a compromise with some EU member states. This led in fact to the exclusion from the proceedings of the states opposing the German and French proposals (agreed at the informal meeting of the leaders of both countries in Deauville, in October 2010). The enhanced cooperation mechanisms, therefore, provided for under Community law, were deliberately discounted; under these mechanisms, the consent of all EU members is required to enhance the cooperation of a group of states[72]. Moreover, the role of non-EMU states diminished in those intergovernmental negotiations. At the same time the influence of Berlin and Paris on the shaping of the said treaty increased significantly[73]. The decision-making influence of the German-French tandem was additionally enhanced by an increased and more frequent practice of the application of the majority voting system in the EU; and as part of the post-Lisbon system for the calculation of a qualified majority, the Eurozone area states can outvote non-EMU states. A similar majority principle was adopted during the crisis even for the ratification of new treaties. In the case of the aforementioned Fiscal Compact, it could enter into force once ratified by 12 EMU states, although from that moment on its rules were binding on all remaining signatories[74].

Segmentation of the Union in accordance with the "two-speed Europe" mechanism introduces division into different integration circles. This is conducive for the strengthening of the power hierarchy between core and peripheral states (i.e. those not only located on the outskirts of the EU but first and foremost having little influence on decisions made in the Union). This is stressed in an analysis by

---

70 See: *Britain Losing Allegiance to the EU*, Der Spiegel, 15.10.2012. At the time of the writing of this chapter the UK made a dash for the referendum on further membership in the EU, but it was not yet resolved.

71 The Treaty on Stability, Coordination and Governance in the Economic and Monetary Union, an intergovernmental treaty signed on 2 March 2012 in Brussels by 25 member states of the EU (except the Czech Republic and the United Kingdom).

72 See art. 20 Treaty on the European Union and art. 326–334 of the Treaty on the functioning of the European Union.

73 G. Tsebelis, H. Hahm (2014): Suspending Vetoes: How the Euro Countries Achieved Unanimity in the Fiscal Compact, *Journal of European Public Policy*, vol. 21, no. 10, pp. 1388–1411.

74 G. Tsebelis, H. Hahm (2014), p. 1396.

George Soros[75]. In his opinion, the introduction of new financial aid instruments for the Eurozone conditioned by stringent political criteria establishes a permanent power hierarchy between the richest states (lenders) and poorer (borrowers). It covers both subordination at the geopolitical level as well as economic dependence, of which the long-term outcome will include asymmetric benefits and costs following from the participation in European integration between the two groups of countries.

An example of the hierarchic impact of core states on the weaker ones and those located outside the Eurozone was the declaration on the establishment of a banking union. The aforementioned union was open to non- euro area states, but under asymmetric rules. The latter had to accept most obligations and new regulations, but with very little influence over decision making procedure[76]. Moreover, one can expect that any supervision performed by the ECB will be preferential for the economic situation and interests of financial institutions coming from the monetary union. This concerns in particular the macro-prudential measures performed with regard to capital groups functioning within both the euro area insider and outsider states.

It is worthwhile pointing out that earlier systemic adjustments in Europe were made through the strengthening of the Community model of integration. One of the mechanisms was the increased delegation of powers to European institutions or the fostering of so-called "positive integration" (through the introduction of joint or harmonized regulations at the EU level). During the common currency crisis, the situation was clearly different. Adjustments related to governance were made, among other things, through the strengthening of technocratic institutions, but with stronger subordination to the political will of the biggest EMU states. Moreover, informal and formalized intergovernmental mechanism also became stronger[77]. This came about for two fundamental reasons. First, from the reluctance of a large part of the states to resolve governance problems through the strengthening of the Community method, previously being the leading supranational cooperation mechanism. Second, anti-crisis decisions

---

75 G. Soros (2012): *The Tragedy of the European Union and How to Resolve It*, New York Review of Books, September 10, 2012.

76 See: *Commission proposes a package for banking supervision In the Eurozone – frequently asked questions*, European Commission, Brussels – Strasbourg, 12 September 2012, *p.* 7.

77 U. Puetter (2012): Europe's Deliberative Intergovernmentalism: The Role of the Council and European Council in EU economic governance, *Journal of European Public Policy*, vol. 19, no. 2, pp. 161–178; for more details see: Ch. J. Bickerton, D. Hodson, U. Puetter (2015): *The New Intergovernmentalism*, Oxford – New York: Oxford University Press.

related to the coordination of economic policies went beyond Community institutions competencies in many areas. In consequence, intergovernmental coordination became the more obvious choice.

A symptom of the growing role of hierarchic governance in the EMU was the top-down imposition of conditions governing financial aid granted in the crisis, formally via European institutions, but in fact dictated by creditors, including in particular the richest member states[78]. These terms were not infrequently imposed against the will of local societies. A good example was a rejection in the Greek referendum (in 2015) of the conditions governing aid proposed by international institutions, followed by coercing the Greek government to accept more austere terms than those subjected to the referendum voting.

This established completely new standards for the Europeanization mechanism. They have increasingly consisted of the imposition by dominant states of political solutions on subordinated countries, and entrusted their implementation to European institutions – formally independent, but in fact being a political disguise to enable the implementation of the will of the strongest actors. The Europeanization processes were intensively promoted by pro-European political narrations. In times of crisis the aforementioned narrations stigmatized weak and crisis-stricken states as ones "living beyond their means" and "at the expense of others", casting them in the roles of "sinners" notoriously violating EU law regulations. At the same time thrifty countries, abiding by fiscal discipline, were indicated as imitable examples. The aforementioned interpretations aimed to justify tough terms of financial aid and the necessity for the biggest EMU debtors to make sacrifices, while at the same time justifying the limited dimension of European solidarity towards the worst crisis-stricken countries[79].

Compared to the earlier applied "soft" governance methods, such as the open method of coordination, enforcement of the adopted solutions became stronger in the crisis. This took place through strictly international agreements (including treaties concluded outside the EU), but also through entrusting the implementation of those agreements into the competence of European institutions. For example, the European Commission was responsible for the implementation of the so-called European Semester for the evaluation of budget policies and fiscal

---

78 Central role in the determination of detailed aid terms was played by Eurogroup (i.e. the Eurozone finance ministers) and representatives of the so-called troika (the European Commission, ECB and the International Monetary Fund).

79 For more details see: M. Matthijs, K. McNamara (2015): The Euro Crisis' Theory Effect: Northern Saints, Southern Sinners, and the Demise of the Eurobond, *Journal of European Integration*, vol. 37, no. 2, pp. 229–245.

reforms in member states. Nevertheless, scholars have pointed out that contract management in Europe changed during the crisis[80]. Enforcement of agreements between member states had previously been based on the delegation of relevant powers to supranational technocratic institutions, whose credibility was based on an unbiased and apolitical approach to the equal treatment of all states and proceeding in accordance with European law and procedures. Contract enforcement in the crisis was based to a greater extent on the political and financial power of some states over others and on the growing politicization of delegation institutions, which aimed at their informal subordination to the will of the strongest states. The Commission and other agency institutions consequently became instruments for the enforcement of asymmetric intergovernmental agreements rather than autonomic guarantors of a state's equality and respect for law. Studies indicate[81], that e.g. the politicization of the Commission resulted in increased arbitrariness and discretion of the application of fiscal regulations towards particular states, which not only increased the number of derogations from the application of EU law, but also made such derogations conditioned by behind-the-scenes political bargaining taking place at intergovernmental levels.

An intergovernmental approach entails stronger politicization of decisions made at the European level, and in particular it increases the informal influence of dominant states over the functioning of all European institutions. Consequently such technocratic institutions as the Commission or the ECB became the arena for political rivalry between the biggest players and instruments for political pressure on the weaker and peripheral states. The process of segmentation into various integration circles in Europe also serves the purpose of reinforcing the hierarchy between member states. The aforementioned trends do improve the effectiveness of the decision-making process, but also create permanent tensions between dominant states and those subjected to stepped-up political pressure.

Legitimization of the geopolitical arrangement

Geopolitical arrangement is mainly legitimized with regard to the issue of security. Benefits from economic development also have great importance for its social acceptance. Moreover, legitimization criteria are strongly related to values

---

80 For more details see: R. Bellamy, A. Weale (2015): Political Legitimacy and European Monetary Union: Contracts, Constitutionalism and the Normative Logic of Two-Level Games, *Journal of European Public Policy*, vol. 22, no. 2, pp. 257–274.

81 D. Hodson (2014): Eurozone Governance: Recovery, Reticence and Reform, *Journal of Common Market Studies*, vol. 52, Annual Review, pp. 186–201.

prevalent in a given political culture and follow on from historical traditions. In the case of post-war geopolitical order which took shape in Western Europe, the issue of security and peace-keeping were of fundamental importance. European integration processes ensured the attainment of both objectives, which contributed to a high level of approval both by political elites and particular societies. Nevertheless, the criterion of peace in Europe weakened over time since the end of WWII, and the issue of security declined in importance since the fall of the Cold War order and the diminishing threat from Russia[82]. The challenge of prosperity growth for citizens of Europe has prevailed. An additional criterion – at least for some social groups – was the fair distribution of costs and benefits following from integration processes[83]. The crisis greatly undermined the faith of Europeans that the monetary regime leads to better prosperity and more jobs, diminishes inequalities and ensures solidary distribution of the costs of European integration.

Troubles of legitimization of integration processes in Europe should also be considered in the context of a local political culture. Among other things it is based on democratic values. Consequently it combines political legitimization with voters' control over public authorities. The problem was becoming more and more urgent as more competencies were transferred from the level of national democracies onto the EU level. As part of the two-tier political system in place in Europe (i.e. simultaneously at the national and European levels)[84], power was shifted – step by step – from control of the voters in nation-states into European institutions and transnational elites, which did not have proper democratic authorisation[85].

Selection of integration methods by political elites was of central significance here. It was based on the tactical avoidance of politicization, particularly related to electoral policies[86]. Therefore, at the European level, we have democracy present more in the realm of declarations and pro-European marketing, than in the

82 This is likely to change and the security challenge will grow in Europe, bearing in mind the aggravation of the Russian-Ukrainian conflict and the problem of excessive immigration in 2015.

83 See: L. Tsoukalis (2003): *What Kind of Europe?*, Oxford – New York: Oxford University Press, 43–65.

84 See: T. G. Grosse (2012): *Dwupoziomowy system polityczny w Europie* [The two-tier political system in Europe], Przegląd Europejski, no. 2 (25), 2012, pp. 7–26.

85 See: G. Majone (1996): *Regulating Europe*, London: Routledge, p. 287.

86 See: P. De Wilde, M. Zürn (2012): Can the Politicization of European Integration be Reversed?, *Journal of Common Market Studies*, Vol. 50, no. S1, pp. 137–153.

form of specific democratic institutions, based on all-European direct elections[87]. Elections for the European Parliament are some kind of exception. Nevertheless, they are more national than European elections. They indeed take place with a breakdown into particular countries, with voters voting for national parties, and with local affairs being the main subject of debates. According to Giandomenico Majone, Parliament is unable to effectively offset the democracy deficit in the EU because it does not represent a European *demos*, and consequently cannot refer to European interests. Moreover, it has no power over European taxes either, or to appoint an EU government, nor to initiate legislation (which means it greatly departs from major parliamentarian standards in Europe)[88]. Instead of developing fully democratic institutions in the EU, European policy-makers sometimes try to evade voter's verdicts in member states. They fear that national democracy may hurt integration advancement. A good example is the avoidance of referenda as a method of authorizing political decisions concerning the future of the EU. This is no surprise as the European project has been put at risk many times by those few referenda held on European affairs in recent years. As an example, lost referenda in the Netherlands and France in 2005 frustrated the European constitution project[89].

A symptom of depoliticisation tactics was the delegation of power to technocratic institutions, as well as basing the integration process on a regulatory system. This is how the power of officials and judges was supposed to tone down the influence of politicians, including in particular adverse trends related to the vested interests of national electoral policies[90]. The aforementioned integration mechanism constitutes a fundamental part of the so-called Community method, which for many years was a dominant way of the EU's development. According to some opinions[91] – in view of the scale of the transfer of competencies to EU institutions – keeping distance in relation to electoral policy is impossible in the

---

87 For more details see: P. Mair, J. Thomassen (2010): Political Representation and Government in the European Union, *Journal of European Public Policy*, vol. 17, no. 1, pp. 20–35.

88 G. Majone (2014): From Regulatory State to a Democratic Default, *Journal of Common Market Studies*, vol. 52, no. 6, pp. 1216–1223 [1217].

89 See: T. G. Grosse (2014): *Kryzys demokracji w Europie* [Crisis of democracy in Europe], Przegląd Europejski, no. 3, pp. 24–52.

90 See: Neyer J. (2010): Justice, Not Democracy: Legitimacy in the European Union, *Journal of Common Market Studies*, Vol. 48, No. 4, pp. 903–921.

91 P. De Wilde, M. Zürn (2012), p. 150.

long-term perspective. This is another of the reasons underlying the loss of trust in the Community method among some of European policy-makers.

An additional phenomenon is the growing asymmetry of the political influence on the course of European affairs between the biggest and the peripheral states. The aforementioned trend became reinforced as majority voting was disseminated in EU bodies. It became additionally augmented in the time of crisis, among other things, through the conditional provision of financial support from European instruments[92]. This was how the diversified decision-making process translated into an uneven scope of sovereignty (subjectivity) of particular states, and consequently into the stronger or weaker influence of national voters on European affairs. Some governments had a greater chance to respect the will of their voters than others. A good illustration of this can be seen by an event of 2011, when a commission of the German Bundestag drew up an opinion on the draft budget of Ireland (i.e. the budget of a state covered with an aid programme), before it was presented for democratic authorisation in the Irish Parliament[93]. While the Bundestag fully controlled the funds of its taxpayers (in this case it supervised how the German loan would be utilised), the democratic institutions in states covered by assistance programmes resembled administrative units implementing European guidelines[94]. The aforementioned phenomenon of the "differentiation of the quality of democracy" between member states is also defined as a declining degree of political pluralism in Europe, or even recognised as something threatening the stable functioning of the Union[95].

Both in states of central political importance and in those of less significance, on the periphery and immersed in troubles – local societies rebelled against the external commands and costs of the crisis. Nevertheless, the core states had more institutionalized democratic systems, i.e. those that remained in better condition. Social protests, therefore, were channelled via democratic institutions, among

---

92 Democratic legitimization deficit of aid programmes in the Eurozone is pointed out – among other things – by: A. Hinarejos (2015): *The Euro Area Crisis in Constitutional Perspective*, Oxford – New York: Oxford University Press, pp. 161–166. K. Tuori, K. Tuori (2014): *The Eurozone Crisis. A Constitutional Analysis*, Cambridge: Cambridge University Press, chapter 7.

93 This example is provided by: G. Majone (2014), p. 1221.

94 See: D. Chalmers (2012): The European Redistributive State and a European Law of Struggle, *European Law Journal*, vol. 18, no. 5, pp. 667–693 [693].

95 See: E. Haas, P. Schmitter (1964): Economics and Differential Patterns of Political Integration: Projections about Unity in Latin America, *International Organization*, vol. 18, no. 4, pp. 705–737.

other things through the activities of parliamentary opposition or constitutional court. Moreover, those states to a greater degree were able to influence European instruments and use them to improve the economic situation or minimization of crisis costs. At the same time weaker and peripheral states as a rule were not only harder hit by the crisis but also subjected to stronger external pressures. This resulted in a wave of street protests, more frequent changes of governments and a growing support for extreme and populistic parties.

In summary, one can argue that the integration progress so far was based on the supranational agreements of elites around the Community model. Such agreements were in fact concluded above the heads of citizens and accompanied by attempts to restrict the influence of electoral democracy on European affairs. European societies were fed with European ideals and the intensive promotion of integration as an unambiguously beneficial project, in political, economic and social dimensions. Instead of democratic legitimization procedures, the authorisation of the integration processes was based on utilitarian issues – related to the tangible benefits and improvement of the quality of life of a majority of citizens. Utilitarian legitimization was based on economic development and the improvement of social conditions.

In the situation of a protracting economic crisis, which has been present in some states since 2008 – it became increasingly difficult to avoid the impact of national democracy on the integration processes. Support for integration ideas faltered while the popularity of euro-sceptical views rose[96]. In crisis-stricken countries voters opposed more savings imposed by the European institutions and representatives of the states being the biggest creditors of European loans. They demanded more just cost distribution within the EU. At the same time citizens of the richest countries rebelled against the excessive distribution of funds coming from their taxes to rescue the situation in other states of the monetary union, consequently negating the solidarity rule in place as part of the existing integration formula.

This is how the crisis led to a situation that can be termed as a "legitimization paradox". Theoretically the crisis should be the motivation to overcome economic difficulties and political barriers, i.e. to pave the way towards the establishment

96 See: R. Gomez (2015): The Economy Strikes Back: Support for the EU during the Great Recession, *Journal of Common Market Studies*, vol. 53, no. 3, pp. 577–592; J. D. Medrano (2012): The Limits of European Integration, *Journal of European Integration*, vol. 34, no. 2, pp. 191–204; T. G. Grosse (2015): A Potential for Revolution in Europe? in: B. J. Góralczyk (ed.): *European Union on The Global Scene: United or Irrelevant*? Warsaw: Centre for Europe, University of Warsaw, pp. 203–223.

of a fully democratic federation in Europe, which could effectively resolve the arising problems. Instead, it stimulated democracy at national levels, resulting – at least in some member states – under intensive pressure of regaining control by national electoral institutions over local fiscal policy and increased supervision over European policies. This hampered the centralization of fiscal policy, including in particular the introduction of the mechanisms of *positive fiscal federalism* in the EMU, and at the same time strengthened particularistic trends in EU policies. Consequently, the stimulation of national communities in the name of the reconstruction of democratic legitimization hampered the introduction of the most optimal economic and political reforms in the EU, and at the same time blocked the possibility to reduce the democratic deficit at EU level.

It is highly characteristic how this deficit was intended to be reduced in the time of the crisis. First, bearing in mind that democratic institutions at national level included the basis for the legitimization of European actions, an attempt was made to strengthen the participation of national parliaments in decision-making processes[97]. This mainly concerned the use of instruments planned under the Lisbon Treaty[98]. The second method was comprised by a proposal to strengthen the role of Eurodeputies coming from the Eurozone or to establish a separate chamber of the European Parliament for the Eurozone area, which might have deepened the division into a "two-speed Europe"[99]. Both legitimization improvement mechanisms remained at the preliminary stage of the discussion and moreover, they did not fully resolve the problem of democratic deficit in Europe. Even more so because utilitarian issues remain the main legitimization point of reference for European integration.

Conclusions: Towards a change of integration model in Europe

In this chapter I have performed a simultaneous analysis of the Eurozone crisis at four levels, consequently reflecting on (1) economic and political development

---

97 *Conclusions*, European Council, EUCO 156/12…, p. 10.

98 See: Protocol 1 TFEU. *Treaty on the Functioning of the European Union (TFEU)*, Official Journal of the European Union 2008 C 115, reflecting the changes introduced by the Protocol on amendments to the Treaty of Lisbon (Official Journal of the European Union 2009 C 290. For more details see: T. Winzen (2012): National Parliamentary Control of European Union Affairs: A Cross-national and Longitudinal Comparison, *West European Politics*, 35:3, pp. 657–672; I. Cooper (2012): A 'Virtual Third Chamber' for the European Union? National Parliaments after the Treaty of Lisbon, *West European Politics*, 35:3, pp. 441–465.

99 See: *Final report by the Reflection Group* …, p. 2.

challenges, (2) structural problems, particularly in the context of the geopolitical system functioning in Europe, (3) regarding crisis management methods, and (4) integration processes together with legitimization issues. All these threads combine and mutually complement the analysis.

The performed analysis proves why the defence of the Eurozone was attempted, including in particular the opposition to strong secession tendencies. To a greater extent, geopolitical factors were responsible for such development. They were related on one hand to the willingness to maintain Euro-Atlantic influences over the entire EMU territory, and with support for the integration process, for which the European currency was a flagship project on the other. Additionally this was accompanied by the aim to rebuild political influences in the EU (among other things attempted by France) on the basis of the deepening of integration in the Eurozone area and political division into the "two-speed Europe". Another– albeit less significant – factor was the interdependence of economic interests in the Eurozone, which were conducive for aid programmes for the most crisis-stricken states and new actions initiated by the ECB.

It is, however, more difficult to explain why the crisis has not led to an "institutional breakthrough" towards a democratic federation[100], and triggered sharp rivalry for power, as well as over crisis costs distribution between member states instead. The answer to this question should be looked for in the sphere of political legitimization. The crisis activated national democracy, and also brought about electoral politicization from the national level to EU policy. This triggered re-nationalization trends, resulting – among other things – in the strengthening of the role of intergovernmental institutions, and in the increased influence of member states on the functioning of the remaining European institutions. Another effect was the narrowing down of the perspective of policy-makers mainly in defence of particularistic national interests, while interests of the entire Eurozone became of secondary importance to them (or were treated in an instrumental way). This perception hampered the most optimal resolution of the eurozone's dysfunctions, and in particular blocked the possibility to carry out thorough reforms towards a political federation and *positive fiscal federalism*.

The crisis did not cause any formal changes in the political system in Europe. Nevertheless, there have been several informal adjustments within the system, which have significantly modified its modus operandi. Consequently, European integration processes are decreasingly based on the Community model. The

---

100 For more details: T. G. Grosse (2015): *Overcoming Crisis in the Economic and Monetary Union,* Przegląd Europejski, 1 (39), pp. 28-51.

aforementioned model was based on the relative equilibrium between various European institutions and the gradually increasing autonomy of Community institutions (such as the European Commission or the European Parliament) from intergovernmental levels. The balance of power was also kept separate between the most powerful and weaker member states under the Community model. This equilibrium was warranted by Community institutions and the cohesion of the EU regulatory system. The basic principle of the discussed model was of solidarity towards weaker integration participants.

During the time of the crisis the Community model became eroded, while at the same time a new integration model was rising, one where growing political influences were held by the strongest member states. Such elements as the asymmetry of power between intergovernmental and other European institutions became more prominent, as well as the hierarchy between the most powerful and weaker, peripheral states. An additional process was the growing *political segmentation* in the EU in accordance with the "two-speed Europe" mechanism.

The crisis-induced changes partly aimed towards the centralization of power in Europe, can be seen by the transfer of certain fiscal competencies from the national to European level. However, this process was not accompanied by the proper reinforcement of political institutions in the EU, which was detrimental for democracy in Europe. At the same time the described systemic trend can hardly be termed a strengthening of the "technocratic federation". There was indeed growth in technocratic (including the Commission and the ECB) enforcement competencies but under stronger intergovernmental supervision, and more precisely in accordance with the will of the strongest member states. This turned Europeanization into an instrument of asymmetric power of the core states over the politically weaker peripherals.

For this reason, I propose to define the described systemic tendencies as an "asymmetric confederation", whose main features include not only the uneven distribution of political power between the core and peripheries, but also the asymmetric level of political legitimization – being greater in the more powerful member states and reduced in the weaker and more peripheral member states. This may lead to the materialization of a forecast by Urlich Beck that unless the Union reforms itself during the crisis towards a full (i.e. democratic) federation, it will aim towards a neo-colonial system[101].

During those few years of crisis, Europe failed to fully overcome its economic problems, and in particular to eliminate any macroeconomic diversification and

101 U. Beck, *German Europe*, Polity Press, Cambridge 2013, p. 44.

institutional shortcomings in the monetary union. The economic recovery, therefore, in the Eurozone area in 2015 may prove unsustainable. And as yet, there are still no guarantees that the EU will succeed in maintaining cohesion in the Eurozone or prevent disintegration or secession processes. Methods applied to overcome political problems have remained largely the same as before. They are aimed at keeping the political groups in power which support integration, approve of the realities in which Europeanization functions, and which have originated from the political mainstream. Radical and Eurosceptical groups have been the basic threat for the political system. Given such a situation, equally risky for the stabilization of the political situation in the two-tier European system also proved to be democracy at national level, including in particular the possibility that power will be taken over by populist political groups. Such development has been blocked by the solidary actions of mainstream elites both in member states and at the European level.

References

Andrews D. M. (2006): Monetary Power and Monetary Statecraft, in: D. M. Andrews (ed.): *International Monetary Power*, Ithaca–London: Cornell University Press, pp. 7–28.

Badie B., Berg-Schlosser D., Morlino L. (eds.) (2011): *International Encyclopedia of Political Science*, vol. 2, London: Sage, pp. 489–493.

Baker A. (2010): Restraining Regulatory Capture? Anglo-America, Crisis Politics and Trajectories of Change in Global Financial Governance, *International Affairs*, vol. 86, no. 3, pp. 647–663.

Barker A. et al. (2015): Greece Talks: 'Sorry, but There Is No Way You Are Leaving This Room', *Financial Times*, July 13, http://www.ft.com [last accessed on: 29.07.2015].

Bayoumi T., B. Eichengreen (1993): Shocking Aspects of European Monetary Unification, in: F. Torres, F. Giavazzi (eds.): *Adjustment and Growth in the European Monetary Union*, Cambridge: Cambridge University Press, pp. 193–229.

Beck U. (2013): *German Europe*, Cambridge: Polity Press.

Bellamy R., A. Weale (2015): Political Legitimacy and European Monetary Union: Contracts, Constitutionalism and the Normative Logic of Two-Level Games, *Journal of European Public Policy*, vol. 22, no. 2, pp. 257–274.

Bhagwati J. (1998): The Capital Myth: The Difference between Trade in Widgets and Dollars, *Foreign Affairs*, vol. 77, no. 3, May–June, pp. 7–16..

Bretherton Ch., Mannin M. L. (eds.) (2013): *The Europeanization of European Politics*, New York: Palgrave Macmillan.

Britain Losing Allegiance to the EU, *Der Spiegel*, 15.10.2012.

Bueno de Mosquita B. (1978): Systemic Polarization and the Occurrence and Duration of War, *Journal of Conflict Resolution*, vol. 22, no. 2, pp. 241–267.

Bulmer S. (2014): Germany and the Eurozone Crisis: Between Hegemony and Domestic Politics, *West European Politics*, vol. 37, no. 6, pp. 1244–1263.

Calleo D. P. (2002): *Rethinking Europe's Future*. Princeton–Oxford: Princeton University Press.

Calleo D. P. (2009): Twenty-First Century Geopolitics and the Erosion of the Dollar Order, in: E. Helleiner, J. Kirshner (eds.): *The Future of the Dollar*, Ithaca–London: Cornell University Press, pp. 164–190.

Caporaso J., M. H. Kim, W. N. Durrett, R. B. Wesley (2015): Still a Regulatory State? The European Union and the Financial Crisis, *Journal of European Policy*, vol. 22, no. 7, pp. 889–907.

Chalmers D. (2012): The European Redistributive State and a European Law of Struggle, *European Law Journal*, vol. 18, no. 5, pp. 667–693.

Cichocki M. (2015): *Unia w Unii? Strefa euro w przebudowie* [Union in the Union? The Euro Area under Reconstruction], Nowa Europa, Warsaw: CEN.

Cohen J. (2009): Toward a Leaderless Currency System, in: E. Helleiner, J. Kirshner (eds.): *The Future of the Dollar*, Ithaca–London: Cornell University Press, pp. 142–165.

Collignon S. (2014): Political Lessons from the Economics of the Euro-crisis, in: M. J. Rodrigues, E. Xiarchogiannopoulou (eds.): *The Eurozone Crisis and the Transformation of EU Governance*, Burlington: Ashgate, pp. 85–106.

Coman R., Kostera T., Tomini L. (eds.) (2014): *Europeanization and European Integration: From Incremental to Structural Change*, Houndmills-Basingstoke–New York: Palgrave Macmillan.

Commission Proposes a Package for Banking Supervision in the Eurozone – Frequently Asked Questions, European Commission, Brussels–Strasbourg, 12 September 2012.

Commission Proposes New ECB Powers for Banking Supervision as a Part of a Banking Union, European Commission, Press Release, Brussels, 12 September 2012.

Conclusions, European Council, EUCO 156/12, Brussels, 18/19 October 2012.

Conclusions, European Council, EUCO 76/12, Brussels, 28–29 June 2012.

Cooley A., H. Spruyt (2009): *Contracting States: Sovereign Transfers in International Relations*, Princeton: Princeton University Press.

Cooper I. (2012): A 'Virtual Third Chamber' for the European Union? National Parliaments after the Treaty of Lisbon, *West European Politics*, vol. 35, no. 3, pp. 441–465.

Coppola F. (2015): German Finance Minister Wants Greece Out Of Euro, *Forbes*, July 11, 2015, http://www.forbes.com [access: 29.07.2015].

Crespy A., V. Schmidt (2014): The Clash of Titans: France, Germany and the Discursive Double Game of EMU Reform, *Journal of European Public Policy*, vol. 21, no. 8, pp. 1085–1101.

Dal Bo E., M. Rossi (2011): Term Length and Political Performance, *Review of Economic Studies*, vol. 78, pp. 1237–1263.

De Baere G. (2008): *Constitutional Principles of EU External Relations*, Oxford–New York: Oxford University Press.

De Wilde P., M. Zürn (2012): Can the Politicization of European Integration Be Reversed?, *Journal of Common Market Studies*, Vol. 50, no. S1, pp. 137–153.

Doran Ch. F. (1991): *System in Crisis, New Imperatives of High Politics at Century's End*, Cambridge: Cambridge University Press.

Duménil G., D. Lévy (2011): *The Crisis of Neoliberalism*, Cambridge–London: Harvard University Press.

Eichengreen B. (2007): *The European Economy since 1945. Coordinated Capitalism and Beyond*, Princeton–Oxford: Princeton University Press.

Eichengreen B. (2011): *Exorbitant Privilege: The Rise and Fall of the Dollar and the Future of the International Monetary System*, Oxford: Oxford University Press.

Eleven EU Countries Agree on Transaction Tax, Der Spiegel, 09.10.2012.

Euro Area Summit Statement, 29 June 2012, Brussels.

Euro Exit by Southern Nations Could Cost 17 Trillion Euros, Der Spiegel, 17.10.2012.

Ferejohn J. (1986): Incumbent Performance and Electoral Control, *Public Choice*, vol. 50, pp. 5–25.

Final Report by the Reflection Group on the Future of the EU. If the Foreign Affairs Ministers of Austria, Belgium, Denmark, France, Spain, the Netherlands, Luxembourg, Germany, Poland, Portugal and Italy, 17 September 2012, www.msz.gov.pl, downloaded on: 29.09.2012.

Folkerts-Landau D., P. Garber (1992): The ECB: A Bank or a Monetary Policy Rule, in: M. Canzoneri, V. Grilli, P. Masson (eds.): *Establishing a Central Bank: Issues in Europe and Lessons from the US*, Cambridge: Cambridge University Press, pp. 86–110.

Germain R., H. Schwartz (2014): The Political Economy of Failure: The Euro as an International Currency, *Review of International Political Economy*, vol. 21, no. 5, pp. 1095–1122.

Gilpin R. (1987): *The Political Economy of International Relations*, Princeton: Princeton University Press.

Glazer A., M. Robbins (1985): How Elections Matter: A Study of U.S. Senators, *Public Choice*, vol. 46, pp. 163–172.

Gomez R. (2015): The Economy Strikes Back: Support for the EU during the Great Recession, *Journal of Common Market Studies*, vol. 53, no. 3, pp. 577–592.

Grosse T. G. (2012): Changes in Western Democracy: A Systemic Crisis, or a Chance to Overcome It?, *Politeja*, vol. 3, no. 21, pp. 133–154.

Grosse T. G. (2012): Dwupoziomowy system polityczny w Europie [The Two-Tier Political System in Europe], *Przegląd Europejski*, vol. 2, no. 25, 2012, pp. 7–26.

Grosse T. G. (2012): Trzy cykle kumulacji doświadczeń reżimu monetarnego w Europie [Three Cycles of Experiences Accumulation of Monetary Regime in Europe], Warsaw: Myśl Ekonomiczna i Polityczna, vol. 3 , no. 38, 2012, pp. 32–54.

Grosse T. G. (2012): *W objęciach europeizacji* [In the embrace of Europeanization], Warsaw: ISP PAN.

Grosse T. G. (ed.) (2013): *Między polityką a rynkiem. Kryzys Unii Europejskiej w analizie ekonomistów i politologów* [Between Politics and the Market. The Crisis of the European Union in the Analysis of Economists and Political Scientists], Warsaw: Uczelnia Łazarskiego.

Grosse T. G. (2014): Kryzys demokracji w Europie [Crisis of democracy in Europe], *Przegląd Europejski*, vol. 3, pp. 24–52.

Grosse T. G. (2015): A Potential for Revolution in Europe? in: B. J. Góralczyk (ed.): *European Union on the Global Scene: United or Irrelevant*? Warsaw: Centre for Europe, University of Warsaw, pp. 203–223.

Grosse T. G. (2015): Can "Differentiated Integration" Lead to a Federation in Europe? *Yearbook of Polish European Studies*, vol. 18, pp. 15-38..

Grosse T. G. (2015): Changing the Integration Model: On the Fiasco of the Neo-Functional Vision of the Crisis, in: J. Nadolska, T. Wallas, K. Wojtaszczyk (eds.): *Z kim, którędy I dokąd? Dylematy integracyjne Polski i Unii Europejskiej*, Warsaw: ASPRA.

Grosse T. G. (2015): Kryzys innowacyjności w Europie [Crisis of innovation in Europe], *Przegląd Europejski*, vol. 1, no. 35, 2015, pp. 11–32.

Grosse T. G. (2015): Overcoming Crisis in the Economic and Monetary Union, *Przegląd Europejski*, vol. 1, no. 39, pp. 28–51.

Haas E., P. Schmitter (1964): Economics and Differential Patterns of Political Integration: Projections about Unity in Latin America, *International Organization*, vol. 18, no. 4, pp. 705–737.

Haas E.B. (1961): International Integration: The European and the Universal Process, *International Organization*, vol. 15, no. 3, pp. 366–392.

Haas E.B. (1964): *Beyond the Nation State. Functionalism and International Organisation*, Stanford: Stanford University Press.

Hall P. A. (2014): Varieties of Capitalism and the Euro Crisis, *West European Politics*, vol. 37, no. 6, pp. 1223–1243.

Hechter M. (1998): *Internal Colonialism: The Celtic Fringe in British National Development*, New Brunswick: Transaction Publishers; 2nd edition.

Helleiner E., J. Kirshner (2009): Summing Up and Looking Ahead: The Future of the Future of the Dollar, in: E. Helleiner, J. Kirshner (eds.): *The Future of the Dollar*, Ithaca and London: Cornell University Press, pp. 216–227.

Hinarejos A. (2015): *The Euro Area Crisis in Constitutional Perspective*, Oxford–New York: Oxford University Press.

Hodson D. (2014): Eurozone Governance: Recovery, Reticence and Reform, *Journal of Common Market Studies*, vol. 52, Annual Review, pp. 186–201.

Hoffmann S. (1968): *Gulliver's Troubles: Or the Setting of American Foreign Policy*, New York: McGraw Hill.

Jabko N. (2015): *The Elusive Economic Government and the Forgotten Fiscal Union*, in: M. Matthijs, M. Blyth (eds.): *The Future of the Euro*, Oxford–New York: Oxford University Press, pp. 70–89.

Janis I. L., L. Mann (1997): *Decision Making: A Psychological Analysis of Conflict, Choice and Commitment*, New York: The Free Press.

Kenen P. (1969): The Theory of Optimum Currency Areas: An Eclectic View, in: R. Mundell, A. Swoboda (eds.): *Monetary Problems of the World Economy*, Chicago: University of Chicago Press, pp. 41–60.

Khan M. (2015): No More Bail-Outs: Germany Blocks Juncker's Eurozone Reform Drive, *The Telegraph*, Thursday 17 September 2015.

Kindleberger C. P. (1973): *The World in depression: 1929–1939*, London: Allen Lane, The Penguin Press.

Krugman P. (1993): Lessons of Massachusetts for EMU, in: F. Torres, F. Giavazzi (eds.): *Adjustment and Growth in the European Monetary Union*, Cambridge: Cambridge University Press, pp. 241–269.

Lebow R. N. (1981): *Between War and Peace*, Baltimore: The Johns Hopkins University Press.

Mair P., J. Thomassen (2010): Political Representation and Government in the European Union, *Journal of European Public Policy*, vol. 17, no. 1, pp. 20–35.

Majone G. (1996): *Regulating Europe*, Routledge: London.

Majone G. (2014): From Regulatory State to a Democratic Default, *Journal of Common Market Studies*, vol. 52, no. 6, pp. 1216–1223.

Marsh D. (2011): Faltering Ambitions and Unrequited Hopes: The Battle for the Euro Intensifies, *Journal of Common Market Studies*, vol. 49, Annual Review, pp. 45–55.

Matthijs M., K. McNamara (2015): The Euro Crisis' Theory Effect: Northern Saints, Southern Sinners, and the Demise of the Eurobond, *Journal of European Integration*, vol. 37, no. 2, pp. 229–245.

Mattli W., A. Stone Sweet (2012): Regional Integration and the Evolution of the European Polity: On the Fiftieth Anniversary of the Journal of Common Market Studies, *Journal of Common Market Studies*, vol. 50, no. S1, pp. 1–17.

McPhilemy S. (2014): Integrating Rules, Disintegrating Markets: The End of National Discretion in European banking? *Journal of European Public Policy*, vol. 21, no. 10, pp. 1473–1490.

Medrano J. D. (2012): The Limits of European Integration, *Journal of European Integration*, vol. 34, no. 2, pp. 191–204.

Moravcsik A. (2012): Europe after the Crisis. How to Sustain a Common Currency, *Foreign Affairs*, vol. 91, no. 3, pp. 54–68.

Mundell R. (1961): A Theory of Optimum Currency Areas, *American Economic Review*, vol. 51, pp. 657–665.

Neyer J. (2010): Justice, Not Democracy: Legitimacy in the European Union, *Journal of Common Market Studies*, Vol. 48, No. 4, pp. 903–921.

Niemann A., D. Ioannou (2015): European Economic Integration in Times of Crisis: A Case of Neofunctionalism? *Journal of European Public Policy*, vol. 22, no. 2, pp. 196–218.

Nordhaus W. D. (1975): The Political Business Cycle, *Review of Economic Studies*, vol. 42, pp. 169–182.

Puchala D. J., R. F. Hopkins (1982): International Regimes: Lessons from Inductive Analysis, *International Organization*, vol. XXXVI, no. 2, pp. 245–276.

Puetter U. (2012): Europe's Deliberative Intergovernmentalism: The Role of the Council and European Council In EU Economic Governance, *Journal of European Public Policy*, vol. 19, no. 2, pp. 161–178.

Puetter U. (2015): *The New Intergovernmentalism*, Oxford – New York: Oxford University Press.

Ryner M. (2015): Europe's Ordoliberal Iron Cage: Critical Political Economy, the Euro Area Crisis and Its Management, *Journal of European Public Policy*, vol. 22, no. 2, pp. 275–294.

Schimmelfennig F. (2001): The Community Trap: Liberal Norms, Rhetorical Action, and the Eastern Enlargement of the European Union, *International Organization*, vol. 55, no. 1, pp. 47–80.

Schimmelfennig F. (2015): Liberal Intergovernmentalism and the Euro Area Crisis, *Journal of European Public Policy*, vol. 22, no. 2, pp. 177–195.

Schmitter P. C. (1970): A Revised Theory of Regional Integration, *International Organisation*, vol. 24, no. 4, pp. 836–868.

Soros G. (2012): The Tragedy of the European Union and How to Resolve It, *New York Review of Books*, September 10, 2012.

Statement by the Euro Area Heads of State or Government, European Council, Brussels, 9 December 2011.

Steinbruner J. D. (1974): *The Cybernetic Theory of Decision: New Dimensions of Political Analysis*, Princeton: Princeton University Press.

Story J., J. Walter (1997): *Political Economy of Financial Integration in Europe. The Battle of the System*, Cambridge Massachusetts: The MIT Press.

Szabo S. F. (2015): *Germany, Russia and the Rise of Geo-Economics*, London: Bloomsbury Academic.

The Other Moral Hazard, *The Economist*, 29th September 2012.

Treaty on the Functioning of the European Union (TFEU), Official Journal of the European Union 2008 C 115, reflecting the changes introduced by the *Protocol on amendments to the Treaty of Lisbon* (Official Journal of the European Union 2009 C 290).

Tsebelis G., H. Hahm (2014): Suspending Vetoes: How the Euro Countries Achieved Unanimity in the Fiscal Compact, *Journal of European Public Policy*, vol. 21, no. 10, pp. 1388–1411.

Tsoukalis L. (2003): *What Kind of Europe?*, Oxford–New York: Oxford University Press.

Tuori K., K. Tuori (2014): *The Eurozone Crisis. A Constitutional Analysis*, Cambridge: Cambridge University Press.

Verdun A. (2015): A Historical Institutionalist Explanation of the EU's Responses to the Euro Area Financial Crisis, *Journal of European Public Policy*, vol. 22, no. 2, pp. 219–237.

Waltz K. (1979): *Theory of International Politics*, Reading: Addison-Wesley.

Whyman P. B. (2015): Keynes and the International Clearing Union: A Possible Model for Eurozone Reform? *Journal of Common Market Studies*, vol. 53, no. 2, pp. 399–415.

Winzen T. (2012): National Parliamentary Control of European Union Affairs: A Cross-National and Longitudinal Comparison, *West European Politics*, 35:3, pp. 657–672.

Wolf M. (2014): *The Shifts and the Shocks. What We've Learned – and Have Still to Learn – from the Financial Crisis*, London: Allen Lane.

Piotr Koryś

The Asian crisis

Abstract: The author of this chapter analyses the crisis of 1997, that changed the economic, social and political face of the Southeast Asia, aiming at describing its causes, course and consequences for an economic and political power arrangements between the states of the entire region. Although, when we see the success of China within the recent 20 years, it might seem that the crisis did not influence the region's development. However, in reality the crisis undermined the foundations of the "Asian economic miracle" and the Asian model of the developmental state, including in particular the political and economic consensus within societies of the region. Therefore, according to the author effective anti-crisis policies were of central importance for further successful development of the states and their convergence. The failure of such policies in the case of countries being at medium and lower development levels was mainly a barrier to catching-up with the highly developed countries. The chapter allows to find interesting parallels between the Asian crisis and the current one of the Eurozone, highlighting the similarities of certain phenomena and fundamental differences.

Keywords: financial crisis, developmental state, new industrialized economies, ASEAN, crisis management

Introduction

1997 was a year marked by the crisis that changed the economic, social and political face of the fastest-developing world region at that time – i.e. Southeast Asia. The timeline of the Asian crisis as a dynamic process of economic collapse, taking place first and foremost in the countries of Eastern Asia and Southeastern Asia, is defined quite precisely. In June 1997, after a series of speculative attacks squarely aimed at the local currency and in view of inadequate foreign currency reserves, the government of Thailand opted for devaluation and transition onto a floating exchange rate. The actual effects of the said decision included a dramatic fall of the Baht against the US Dollar. Later the crisis was termed "Asian flu", which refers both to Asia as the source of a potential flu pandemic, as well as the dynamics of the devaluation process, which affected the entire southeastern part of the continent, with more and more countries "becoming infected" with the financial crisis from day to day. Yeltsin's Russia proved to be last victim of the "Asian flu". The external shock delivered by the Asian crisis became the proverbial "final nail in the coffin" for the Russian economy – technologically lagging

Tab. 1: Basic indicators of the Asian financial crisis (see also Chart 1). Source: Stooq.pl.

	30.06.1997	30.09.1998	30.06.1999
Stock Exchange Indexes			
Indonesia	724,56	276,15	662,02
Korea	745,4	310,32	883
Malaysia	1077,3	373,52	811,1
Philippines	2809,21	1259,64	2485,61
Singapore	1988	939,65	2167,7
Thailand	527,28	253,82	521,77
Exchange rates, price of 1 USD in local currencies.			
Indonesia	2430	10590	6854
Korea	886	1388	1157
Malaysia	2,52	3,8	3,8
Philippines	26,35	43,6	37,9
Singapore	1,43	1,69	1,7
Thailand	27,59	43,94	40,94

and dependent on the business cycle in raw material markets. In August 1998, under the circumstances of extremely high inflation and the necessity to devaluate the Ruble, Russia declared insolvency and requested international aid. But Russian history is not part of the following story.

However, the above set timeframe fails to take note of several important components of the entire Asian crisis process (See: Tab. 1 and Chart 1). It certainly started much earlier, along with growing discrepancies within the Japanese economy, followed by the period of economic successes of the countries of Southeast Asia (termed the Asian economic miracle). The crisis can be analysed as a crisis of the periphery countries of the Japanese economic zone (the Yen zone), with highly diverse levels of development, economic structures and wealth. From this viewpoint, one can look back for the beginnings of the crisis into the 1980s. On the other hand, in economic terms, one can place the end of the crisis at the moment of the return to the former growth path or at least when the pre-crisis GDP and GDP per capita levels returned. In this way, we see that the full recovery of some countries from "Asian flu" took over a decade.

The Asian crisis can also be perceived as the structural crisis of a certain developmental model designed for the purpose of catching up with the economies of the core countries (the West) based on the following pillars: imitating the success

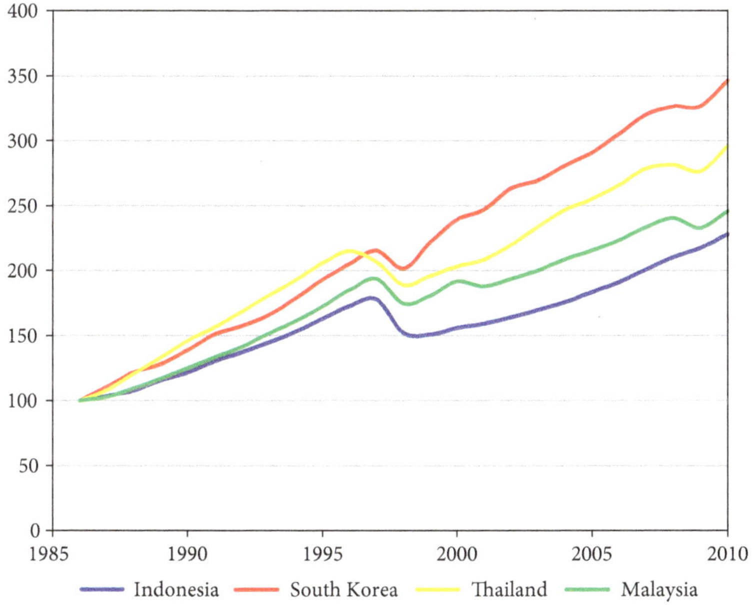

Chart 1: Crisis-exit paths. GDP dynamics in the pre- and post-crisis period for selected countries of the region (1985=100). Source: Angus Maddison historical statistics. http://www.ggdc.net/maddison/Historical_Statistics/horizontal-file_02-2010.xls.

of Japan (and NIE countries[1]) in export-oriented industrialization policies, development based on labour-intensive industrialization in the conditions of almost unlimited access to cheap – in relation to quality – labour force together with undemocratic forms of government[2]. At the same time, in contrast to East Asian countries, which had industrialised earlier, the catching up process took place in circumstances of relatively ineffective social, political and economic entities, described by Gunnar Myrdal as *soft-state*[3].

1 New industrialized economies (South Korea., Taiwan, Singapore, Hong Kong).

2 K. Akamatsu (1962): *A Historical Pattern of Economic Growth in Developing Countries*, *Journal of Developing Economies*, 1(1), pp. 3–25; T. Ozawa (2005): *Institutions, Industrial Upgrading, and Economic Performance in Japan. The 'Flying Geese' Paradigm of Catch-up Growth*, Cheltenham: Edward Elgar.

3 G. Myrdal (1968): *Asian Drama. An Inquiry into the Poverty of Nations*, New York: Pantheon.

This paper attempts to reconstruct the crisis process in the aforementioned wider aspects, offering a better perspective of both the challenges of the structural tensions that led to the manifestation of the crisis in its acute form, and the challenges of growth and governance in crisis. Moreover, the author attempts to analyse the consequences of the crisis in the perspective of future development, attaching particular importance to the processes of de-convergence of economic development, transformation of the political situation within states and the regions, as well as social outcomes of the crisis.

As in the majority of similar cases, the first symptoms of the crisis were ignored for a long time, and the state of the effective insolvency of some countries of the region, was also ignored by investors for a similar period of time. These were only several exogenous factors (speculative attacks aimed at the region's currencies, the moment Hong-Kong was relinquished by the UK to the PRC) that changed the attitudes of investors. Growing internal and international contradictions resulted in a situation where the decline of the Baht became the catalyst for an acute crisis with a regional reach.

The problem of the short- and long-term effects of the crisis has not been clearly assessed so far. Some authors point out to the success and restoration of the economic potential of the economies of ASEAN countries; others – growing in number – indicate the long-term effect of the crisis in the said economies. The only aspect not giving rise to any doubts is the success of the anti-crisis policies in NIE countries, particularly in South Korea[4].

1 The Asian economic miracle

Although the category of the Asian economic miracle describes the development and success of ASEAN countries lasting from the mid-1980s to the Asian crisis, the sources for the developmental model that founded this success should be looked for earlier in Japan and among the 4 Asian tigers (NIE countries). Starting from the mid-20th century, a specific – different from the European one – industrialization model and the ensuing developmental policy model took shape there.

"“Catching up” occurred, not just as a result of the Gerschenkronian pooling of resources or the injection of capital, or the state promotion of technical education and nationalism. These efforts certainly mattered, but they were not sufficient enough to make any Asian industrializing country adequately competitive to raise capital or secure the necessary resources, against those countries which

4 J.-S. Shin, H.-J. Chang (2003): *Restructuring Korea Inc.*, London: Routledge.

were part of the Atlantic economy during the second half of the nineteenth and the early twentieth centuries. In particular, they do not in themselves explain the international competitiveness of labour-intensive industries, represented by cotton textiles, which became the mainstay of Asia's industrialization[5]".

Based on his earlier research into proto-industrialization and the industrious revolution[6], Sugihara indicates that due to socio-economic determinants, including in particular access to production factors, in Japan and then across entire Asia, the industrialization process proceeded for a long time under a model that in Europe had characterized only a short period of proto-industrialization. It was based on the use of cheap – in relation to educational background (human capital) and productivity – labour force, and not on capital investments.

The dissemination of this model in Asia after WW2 contributed to dynamic growth of the importance of the region in the global economy (see: Chart 2) and contributed to the transformation of the eastern and south-eastern parts of the continent in the 1980s into the world's factory, and to the swift economic growth of the region.

The decade of 1980–1990 was also the last decade of Japan's fast economic growth. At the end of the said decade, the economic crisis that affected Japan led to the burst of the stock and property market speculative bubbles[7]. Post-1989 Japan until today has not been able to regain its economic dynamics; contributing factors have included both external pressure on the Yen's appreciation (which led to such appreciation and the partial departure of Japan from the exchange rate's strict control pursuant to the Plaza Accord), and disadvantageous demographic trends, as well as growing external competition from other Asian states imitating the Japanese economic policy of export promotion. At the same time the Accord became a catalyst for an inflow of investments, and consequently for further economic growth of the countries of Southeast Asia for several reasons[8].

---

5 K. Sugihara (2004): *Labor-intensive Industrialization in Global History*, Background paper for Osaka GEHN conference, [Last accessed on-line on: 28.12.2015] http://www.lse.ac.uk/economicHistory/Research/GEHN/GEHNPDF/SugiharaGEHN5.pdf

6 See: discussion on the term in: J. De Vries (2008): *The Industrious Revolution: Consumer Behavior and the Household Economy, 1650 to the Present*, New York: Cambridge University Press.

7 E. Chancellor (2000): *Devil Take the Hindmost: a History of Financial Speculation*, New York: Plume Books.

8 K. Ishida (1998): Japan's Foreign Direct Investment in East Asia: Its Influence on Recipient Countries and Japan's Trade Structure, in: E. G. Adams, S. Ichimura (eds.), *East Asian Development. Will the East Asian Miracle survive?* London: Praeger, pp. 156–169. T. Ozawa (2005).

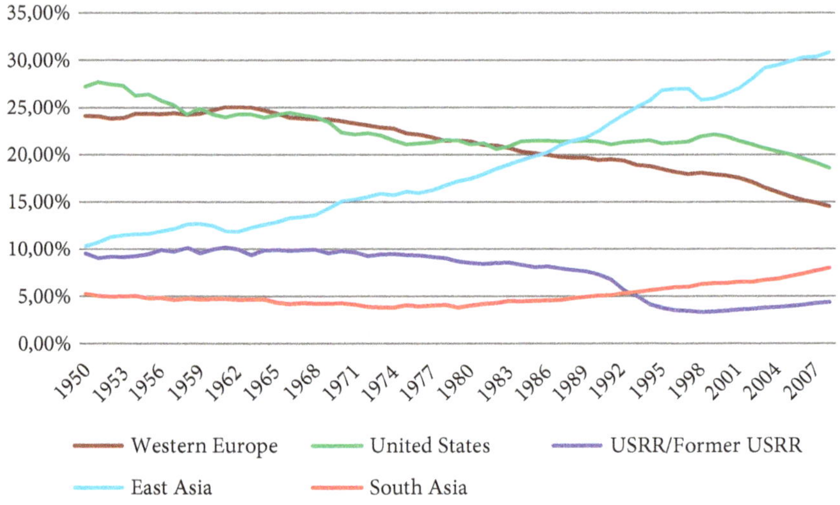

Chart 2: Regional structure of GDP worldwide. Source: Angus Maddison historical statistics. http://www.ggdc.net/maddison/Historical_Statistics/horizontal-file_02-2010.xls. Western Europe: Austria, Belgium, Denmark, Finland, France, Germany, Italy, The Netherlands, Norway, Sweden, Switzerland and The UK; South Asia: India, Bangladesh, Sri Lanka and Pakistan; East Asia: China, Japan, South Korea, Taiwan, Thailand, Malaysia, Philippines, Singapore, Hong Kong.

First, in the 1980s Japanese companies adjusted to growing external labour costs through productivity growth, automation and more intensive outward FDIs (see: Chart 3). Throughout the entire decade those investments – depending on the degree of complexity of the exported technologies/enterprises – were located either in the new industrialized economies of South-Eastern Asian countries or in the less developed ASEAN countries. Japanese foreign direct investments contributed to the industrialization of Asian countries and provided a relevant factor driving the development of their economies. Similarly there was an observable significant, albeit less relevant, inflow of capital from other economically developed regions[9].

Second, owing to the pegging of certain regional currencies (including the Thai Baht) to the US Dollar, depreciation of the US Dollar against the Yen

9 W. Thorbecke, N. Salike (2011): *Understanding Foreign Direct Investment in East Asia*, ADBI Working Paper, No. 290/2011.

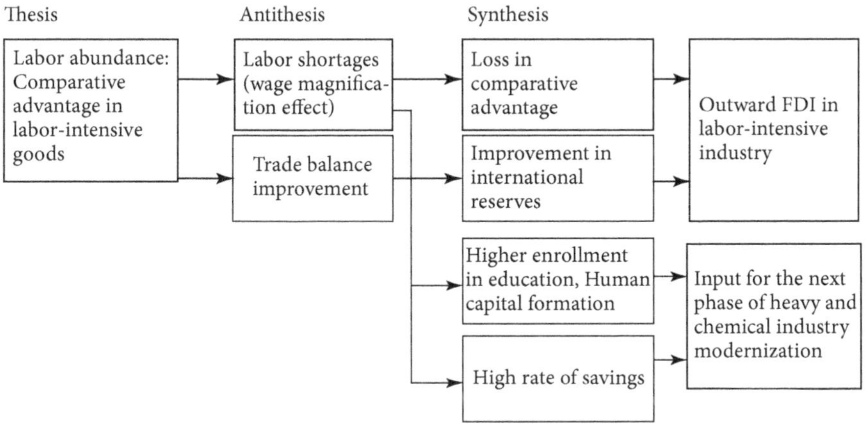

Chart 3: The mechanism governing the development of Japan and Japanese FDIs in South-East Asia (the price-knowledge/industry-flow). Source: Ozawa (2005).

automatically enhanced the competitiveness of the economies of those countries (their currencies were also depreciated against the Yen). This competitive growth determined the directions of Japan's outward FDIs. It is worthwhile stressing that the economies of the analysed countries came into the area of economic influences of Japan (in a nutshell – the Yen area), and therefore from the time of the Plaza Accord (and the partial liberalization of the Yen's exchange rate) pegging to the US Dollar could yield positive economic outcomes only if the Yen appreciated. The periods of weakening of the Japanese currency had a detrimental impact on the FDI-dependent economies of the region.

And third, the period between 1986 and 1995 was a time of political stabilization in the region. In the Philippines the Marcos regime was overthrown and the democratization process took place early in the decade. Similarly, the democratization process took place in such countries as South Korea, Taiwan and Malaysia. Conflicts in the region became non-existent (although the war between Vietnam and Cambodia lasted until 1989, by the late 1980s the conflict weakened). Nevertheless, democratization did contribute to a rise and change of corruptive practices, making economic investments less predictable (and more risky), and such processes – related to South America – had been described several dozen years earlier by Huntington[10].

10 S. P. Huntington (1968): *Political Order in Changing Societies*, New Heaven: Yale Univ. Press.

During this period many countries of the region imitated the Japanese (and already applied by South Korea and Taiwan) export promotion policy, which was made possible owing to an inflow of FDIs (chiefly from Japan). This translated into the dynamic growth of the export of goods and services and of GDP. Export in Thailand, which was one of the biggest beneficiaries of the process, grew by 15 % annually on average within the entire decade preceding the crisis, while annual economic growth exceeded 9 % in the said period. In the decade preceding the crisis, successes of the economies of Southeastern Asia, until recently troubled by conflicts and lasting economic problems, were called the Asian economic miracle[11].

Dynamic growth was largely dependent on such exogenous factors as inflows of FDIs, growing external demand for products made in the countries of the region and the loss of competitiveness by Japan (which in turn – owing to the aforementioned coupling of the region's currencies to the US Dollar rather than the Yen – was subject to fluctuations). At the same time internal dynamics of economic transformations assumed a disadvantageous character in many countries of the region. Very high GDP growth dynamics was accompanied by excessive expansion in the construction sector, sustaining current account deficit, a dramatic rise of indebtedness in private sector and (to a lesser degree) in the public sector[12].

Industrialization resulted in accelerated urbanization and an improvement in the quality of, but also in growing aspirations, which contributed to the formation of a speculative bubble in the property market (although certainly equally important was the new fashion among Westerners to spend holidays in Thailand). Starting from the early 1990s, there was a slow appreciation of the currencies of Asian countries in relation to the Yen and the Renminbi, mainly

---

11 R. Alavi (1996): *Industrialization in Malaysia. Import Substitution and Infant Industry Performance*, London: Routledge.

12 K. Wong (2001): Housing Market Bubbles and Currency Crisis. The Case of Thailand, *Japanese Economic Review*, vol. 52, No. 4, pp. 382–404; S. Saxena, K. Wong (2002): *Economic Growth, Over-investment and Financial Crisis*, Mimeo, [Last accessed on-line on: 28.12.2015] https://faculty.washington.edu/karyiu/papers/invest-crisis.pdf; A. Raquiza (2012): *State Structure, Policy Formation, and Economic Development in Southeast Asia the Political Economy of Thailand and the Philippines*. London: Routledge; S. Siriprachai (1997): Inconsistencies and Inequalities in Thai Industrialisation, in: J. D. Schmidt, J. Hersh, N. Fold (eds.) *Social Changes in Southeast Asia*, London: Longman, pp. 183–205.

following on from the appreciation of the US Dollar. Pressure on the region's currency grew even stronger due to the inflow of capital in the form of FDIs and capital investments. This process compromised the competitiveness of the economies, but it simultaneously reduced the servicing costs of the indebtedness (both private and public) denominated in foreign currencies; this reduced credit costs but at the same time lowered genuine willingness of the authorities to counteract this process.

Additionally, economic co-operation with Japan contributed to the synchronization of economic cycles in the analysed countries along with their growing interdependence. This in turn from year to year increased the likelihood that a local recession may transform into a crisis of regional nature[13].

Moreover, many Asian countries had poor quality institutions in place, which in a way complemented the low level of political stability described earlier. ASEAN countries, including in particular the Philippines, Indonesia and Thailand, were at the very top of countries with high corruption levels. It was a widespread strategy of the public administration to seek political gain, both with foreign and domestic investors, entrepreneurs, and with citizens. Despite democratization transformations, political regimes were still far removed from democracy, and in some cases they continued to be oppressive dictatorships or military junta rules (Indonesia, Thailand). The economic boom obscured the ineffectiveness of public institutions and the inefficiency of political systems, but later contributed to a deepening of the crisis and hampered its effective management.

A certain approximation of the quality of the institutions in the analysed countries on the eve of the crisis can be made on the basis of the TI Corruption Perceptions Index[14]. In 1996 countries with low corruption levels in the region included: Japan (17[15]), Singapore (7) and Hong-Kong (8). Average corruption levels were found in Malaysia (26), South Korea (27) and in Taiwan (29), while Thailand (37), the Philippines (44) and Indonesia (45) were countries with high corruption levels. A year later (results were announced in July 1997, research was carried out in the pre-crisis period) positions of the majority of countries of the regions were slightly worse (52 countries were studied): Singapore (9), Hong-Kong (18), Japan (21), Taiwan (31), Malaysia

13 S. Kim, J. H. Yoon, C. Viney (2001): Dynamic Interdependence and Volatility Transmission of Asian Stock Markets: Evidence from the Asian Crisis, *International Review of Financial Analysis*, vol. 10, No. 1, pp. 87–96.

14 Cf. Transparency International webpage: http://www.transparency.org/research/cpi.

15 Position in the ranking among 54 studied countries.

(32), South Korea (34), Thailand (39), the Philippines (40) and Indonesia (46). On each occasion China fared very poorly in the ranking, but its corruption specifics were different owing to the political system in place. Although TI indices give rise to some reservations, CPI results can be treated as an approximation of the quality of institutions. They indicate that more resilient to crisis institutions were found in better developed countries (Japan, Singapore, Taiwan, South Korea, Malaysia and Hong-Kong), while the less resilient were found in the quickly industrializing poorer countries (the majority of ASEAN countries).

Owing to the aforementioned factors, starting from the early 1990s, from year to year the situation of the majority of crisis-stricken countries deteriorated, although this was not immediately visible in the relevant indicators. As shown above, appreciation of the currencies of a majority of the countries against the Yen proceeded. There was a visible slowdown of the net capital inflow dynamics (a decreasing rate of the total FDIs' growth value), and some countries even experienced a reversal of the trend. To a large extent, the beneficiaries of the change were China and Hong-Kong, the latter being in a way a gateway to investments in China. China became an attractive destination for the location of FDIs both because of an almost unlimited supply of cheap labour, and of the political and economic stability (particularly after the Tiananmen massacre, the authorities put a lot of effort into convincing prospective investors of security and the feasibility of investments in China) guaranteed by the undemocratic regime. Consequently, against such a background, the institutional, economic and political weaknesses of other countries in the region became increasingly manifested. Among other things, along with the decline of capital inflow dynamics (or its outflow), pressure emerged to depreciate the currencies of the region.

2 Crisis – the history

As mentioned above, devaluation of the Baht forced by speculative attacks and structural weakness of the Thai economy became the catalyst for the crisis in the region. Loss of confidence in the Thai economy almost immediately affected the other economies of the region (see: Tab. 1, Chart 3), which resulted in speculative attacks against their currencies, the collapse of their exchange rates, the outflow of investment and capital, and insolvency of some countries. Consequently, there was dramatic unemployment growth, a decline of industrial production and the collapse of the construction sector (e.g. in Thailand approximately 600 thousand foreign employees in the construction industry and financial services sectors had to leave the country owing to loss of jobs, which concealed the unemployment growth rate)[16].

Another factor with impact on investment risk growth in the region was most likely caused by the change in the status of Hong Kong, which returned to China on the 1st of July 1997 (while only having to relinquish a small part of its autonomy). Uncertainty related to real China policies certainly contributed to an outflow of capital from the region, as well as aggravating the effect of the collapse of the Baht exchange rate in Thailand (which happened on 2nd July).

The crisis in some countries, starting from Thailand, led to an almost instantaneous loss of currency reserves, and consequently to a loss of the ability to influence the exchange rates. Attempts to prevent the effects of speculative attacks exhausted the reserves within several days. As a result, devaluation of currencies proved to be dynamic and profound, leading in mid-term to fast price rises expressed in domestic currency (both of investment goods and imported consumer goods, and – through increased energy costs – also of locally produced goods), and consequently to a rise in social dissatisfaction.

At the same time the banking crisis was in place, it was influenced by outflows of capital abroad and the deteriorating situation of borrowers. Moreover, the rise of exchange rate uncovered costs of very high exposure of individual borrowers to exchange rate risk: a large portion of consumer and housing loans were denominated in the US Dollar, while added to this, institutional securities proved too weak. This translated into a dramatic deterioration of the situation for banks with lending being put on hold. The lack of access to loans, increased costs of imports, and the destabilization of the economies of the region, including a growth slowdown in Japan, led quickly the collapse of the manufacturing sector. Equally important was the outflow of capital related to increasing investment risks. Under the conditions of export-oriented industrialization financed by external capital, this contributed to the collapse of industrial production and the profound crisis in the financial services sector. This is where the financial crisis finally uncovered the weaknesses and internal contradictions in the economies it had hit hard[17].

From the very outset, crisis management – both at national and supranational level – was hardly effective. And despite the alarm bells of earlier symptoms and

16 Z. Chalamwong (1998): The Impact of the Crisis on Migration in Thailand, *Asian and Pacific Migration Journal*, Vol. 7, Nos. 2–3, 1998, pp. 297–312.

17 M. Goldstein (1998): *The Asian Financial Crisis. Causes, Cures and Systemic Implications*, Washington: Institute for International Economics; Ch. Collins, A. Senhadji (2002): *Lending Booms, Real Estate Bubbles and the Asian Crisis*, IMF WP 02/20.

warning signals, the crisis came as a surprise for many countries. As a result, political elites could not cope with crisis management, particularly under the conditions of weakening legitimization (both of authoritarian and corrupt democratic regimes). This led to a transformation of the monetary and banking crisis, successively, into an economic and political crisis. The dynamics of the political crisis were high in such countries as Indonesia, South Korea and Thailand. The growth of social dissatisfaction resulted in the fall of the Suharto regime in Indonesia, political changes in South Korea (the success of the opposition in presidential elections), Thailand (protests in May 1997 and the liberalization of the regime and ensuing change of the constitution), and transitional troubles for those in power in other countries.

Supranational regional structures, ASEAN in particular, did not have sufficient resources (including institutional as well as official) to launch anti-crisis measures. Then soon after, Thailand, followed by other countries, had to turn for aid to the IMF. The IMF then prepared aid packages for the applicant countries, supplemented with structural adjustment packages, which were a precondition for the implementation of the granting of aid. The packages contained requirements which did not depart from the standard aid terms applied during the macroeconomic stabilization as set out in the 1990s by the IMF[18]. They consisted of reductions in government spending, a policy of the aggressive raising of interests rates, and the admission of bankruptcy of banks and financial institutions that had lost liquidity. In exchange for the implementation of those packages, the countries of the region obtained aid in the stabilization of their currencies. IMF aid, however, was rejected by Malaysia while South Korea paid back the stabilization loan in the shortest possible time.

At the same time, the course of the crisis was moderated by external factors, which largely contributed to the shortening of its acute phase. First, because the dynamics of worldwide economic growth remained relatively high in Asia in 1997 and 1998, particularly owing to the fact that China and India had avoided the most serious outcomes of the crisis. The crisis, therefore, remained a mainly regional event. Second, successes in the democratization process in the crisis-stricken countries most likely facilitated the introduction of anti-crisis policies by new governments. The new governments had a greater freedom in the pursuance of anti-crisis policies. Third, in some countries at least, the outflow of

---

18 IMF (2000): *Recovery from the Asian Crisis and the Role of the IMF*, IMF Report 00/05. [Last accessed on-line on: 28.12.2015] https://www.imf.org/external/np/exr/ib/2000/062300.htm.

immigrant labour reduced direct impact of the crisis (in particular – the collapse of the construction sector) on the local labour market. Fourth, the collapse of exchange rates, although disadvantageous for citizens, in the mid-term helped in the recovery of the manufacturing sector, restoring competitiveness of the economies[19].

Nevertheless, it has to be said that the outcomes of the crisis in the economies of Southeast Asian countries turned out to be relatively stable, even though the crisis did put an end to the period of the "Asian economic miracle". And although after 2–3 years, a return to growth did take place, economic development dynamics in the crisis-stricken economies proved to be clearly lower than in the period that had preceded it. In particular the countries associated in ASEAN lost the status of successors to the Asian tigers, and the economic growth dynamics of Thailand, Indonesia and Malaysia ceased to stand out against the background of the world and the region. This phenomenon cannot be unambiguously explained by the depletion of growth potential based on the catching up process: at a similar development level, the economies of such countries as South Korea and Japan attained a higher growth of dynamics while managing a high level of social cohesion. However, it is worthwhile pointing out that in the post-crisis period, the economic development environment became far less advantageous (which can be linked to the growth of the economic importance of China).

3 Challenges of the crisis

At least on the face of it, South-East Asian countries coped quite well with the challenges of crisis management. However, deeper analysis demonstrates that this was mainly due to exogenous factors that determined the successes of their anti-crisis policy.

As indicated above, the maintenance of economic growth dynamics at pre-crisis levels became unattainable for virtually all countries that experienced the crisis. In the decade between the end of the Asian crisis and the outbreak of the great recession in 2007, average growth dynamics were clearly lower than in the period preceding the crisis. If we assume that without the crisis it would have been possible to maintain average economic growth levels comparable to the pre-crisis period, the GDP per capita level in the crisis-stricken countries on the verge of another recession in (2008) would have been even as much as 50 % higher. Simultaneously, the relative economic growth of the region (the catching-up process) also slowed down compared to the technological leaders.

19 Z. Chalamwong (1998).

This concerned in particular, ASEAN countries, which had failed to follow the path taken by NIE countries[20].

The process of the industrialization of the region's economies also slowed down significantly. The role of the major global manufacturer was permanently held by the Chinese economy, and in the case of some economies of the ASEAN countries one may speak of stagnation or even de-industrialization as an outcome of the crisis. In particular the crisis affected the new technologies sectors covering high value added products. On the other hand, the significance of foreign tourism as an important branch of the economy increased (among other things, due to the depreciation of currencies). This contributed to a restoration of growth in such countries as Thailand and Indonesia, and to a decline in unemployment over the long term. Nevertheless, this resulted in the economies of some countries becoming more susceptible to business cycles in developed countries (which became manifested during the recession of 2008).

It turned out that lost opportunities for economic growth were not compensated for by democratic consolidation. The level of perception of corruption, being in a way an indicator of the quality of public institutions, improved only very slightly in the post-crisis period, and the following waves of dramatic change in the political arena and mass-scale social protests are testimony to the weakness and poor quality of the democratic regimes established after the crisis. The crisis also weakened the social cohesion of the region: its consequences were felt much less by the wealthy, but much more by the poorer social groups – as a consequence, these inequalities started to aggravate (which became visible even in such affluent countries as South Korea)[21].

In the management of the economic crisis a greater role than that of local ideas and solutions was played by requirements imposed by the IMF (in which case, one may even speak of structural violence). In the advantageous external environment (sustainable global growth, relatively fast recovery of demand for export products of those countries), accompanied by a conducive demographic situation (demographic premium, particularly visible in South Korea, but also in other countries of the region) and improvement of the competitive position attributable to reduced labour costs (resulting from the devaluation of currencies and deterioration of the situation in the labour market), as well as reforms performed on the basis of the said requirements led to the stabilization

20 K. S.Jomo (ed.) (2004): *After The Storm: Crisis, Recovery and Sustaining Development in East Asia*, Singapore: Singapore Univ. Press.

21 Cf. Koo H. (2014). *Inequality in South Korea*. East Asia Forum, 1.07, [Last accessed on: 28.12.2015] http://www.eastasiaforum.org/2014/07/01/inequality-in-south-korea/.

of the economic situation and the remedy of public finances in better-developed countries. Nevertheless, in the less developed countries, such as Indonesia, the social costs of those reforms were significant, while their successes were limited.

Part 5 below discusses the problem of the exhaustion of the South-East Asian development model based on two foundations: export-oriented industrialization and something that Akamatsu conceptualized as the 'flying wild geese pattern'[22]: the sequential appearance and development of industries within a given region and the subsequent relocation process of technologically less advanced and more labor-intensive industries from advanced to developing countries as the economies of the former grow. The crisis of such a developmental model in some countries translated into a long period of growth slowdown and deterioration of developmental positions (ASEAN countries), owing to the absence of new developmental concepts (Indonesia) or attempts to introduce solutions that proved economically ineffective, e.g. in Malaysia. The Malaysian authorities made an attempt at redefining their economic policies so as to defend the internal market – this entailed a return to protectionism with elements of import substitution policy and the introduction of capital flow control. Although these measures at least temporarily contributed to an improvement of the internal situation, in the mid-term perspective they significantly worsened the international competitiveness of Malaysia.

Rejection of the IMF's aid was an important factor influencing crisis management in Malaysia. Opinions about the consequences of the said decision are ambiguous: in the conducive external environment of the late 1990s, freedom to pursue economic policy, including in particular fiscal expansion, might have had a partially positive effect, but in the long term the costs (such as the outflow of foreign capital, and a decline in investors' trust) seem to have prevailed over benefits[23].

Having received a stabilization loan, a completely different strategy was chosen by South Korea, which complied with the IMF's recommendations, but swift repayment of the liabilities eliminated the impact of the loan fund on economic policies in that country in the long term. The crisis itself created conditions for the restructuring of the economic system. An even more conducive environment was formed for industrial production growth[24]. This process, which can be metaphorically described as *Restructuring Korea Inc.*[25], took place – at least to some

22 K. Akamatsu (1962).

23 K. S. Jomo (2004); Athukorala P. (2010): *Malaysian Economy in Three Crises*. WP in Trade and Development, No. 12/2010, ANU, Canberra.

24 K. S. Jomo (2004).

25 J.-S. Shin, H.-J. Chang (2003).

extent – to the detriment of the existing social model[26]. Since the onset of the crisis, there has been a visible increase of the wealth and income Gini coefficient, of the percentage of people living below the relative poverty threshold accompanied by reduced allocations to social spending[27]. All of this has taken place under the conditions of a low birth rate, together with an ageing society; consequently, the outcomes of such a policy are particularly felt by old age pensioners (those who built the prosperity of Korea). Some interpret the changes of economic policies in Korea as an adaptation of a neo-liberal economic model altered to suit Asian conditions. And also because of the actual adoption of solutions promoted by the IMF despite the fact that the country swiftly resigned from the Fund's aid[28].

In the mid-1990s Southeast Asian countries faced several challenges of a **structural character**, which led to a crisis and in turn was reinforced by that crisis through a series of feedbacks. Swift economic growth related to inflows of foreign investments, particularly in ASEAN countries, led to disadvantageous transformations in economic structures, including the labor market. Dramatic growth in the production and construction sectors of big cities caused robust developmental asymmetry. Dynamics of growth were so powerful that immigrants became an important factor in the labor market – e.g. in Thailand – despite the fact that the process of transformation of the societies of those countries into industrial urban societies was far from complete. Financial development of the new middle class which was forming in big cities (such as Bangkok or Jakarta) still lagged behind this group's new, global aspirations. This contributed to a rise in demand for consumption and housing loans – with the consequences described above. Economic growth, supported by political elites, which to some extent compensated for any shortcomings with regard to political freedoms (under a slightly similar modal to the Chinese), led to an increase in structural problems[29].

Moreover, many authors draw attention to the importance of the temptation of abuses in a model imitating the development strategies of South Korea or Taiwan. Pressure on the development of infrastructural projects subsidized by the state, nominating companies for success, as well as protection and support

26 D. Hundt (2009): *Korea's Developmental Alliance: State, Capital and the Politics of Rapid Development*, London: Routledge.

27 H. Koo (2014).

28 D. Hundt (2014): Economic Crisis in Korea and the Degraded Developmental State, *Australian Journal of International Affairs*, vol. 68, pp. 499–514.

29 K. S. Jomo (2003): *Southeast Asian Paper Tigers. From Miracle to Debacle and Beyond.* London: Routledge.

to companies threatened with bankruptcy or peculiar guarantees from the government that return on investment is in a way secured, created conditions for the attainment of high economic growth rate. But at the same time they created conditions for the making of sub-optimal economic decisions. Returns on new investments were declining, even below real capital costs. Simultaneously, under conditions of domestic capital shortages, capital was imported from abroad. Despite deteriorating investment conditions, companies continued investing in the institutional environment created by the governments of the countries of the region. They benefitted from the liberalization of capital turnovers introduced in the region in the late 1990s. On the other hand, investment banks ignored warning signs and willingly lent money to local intermediaries, supporting new lending in spite of growing economic imbalances[30].

The behaviour of political and civil servant elites and of the entire apparatus of power, seeking political capital in the period of prosperity, definitely contributed to an unequal distribution of the benefits from growth in the decade that preceded the crisis. Besides the profit-deriving middle classes, the greatest benefits were reaped by corrupt politicians and civil servants (being, by the way, part of the said class), while the greatest costs of ineffective and corrupt institutions were transferred mostly onto the lower classes. Among the latter, social advancement was still adequately acceptable for people migrating to the cities, while rural residents were probably not considered to be a political threat from the viewpoint of the authorities. In the cities themselves, apart from the affluent districts, areas of extreme poverty were dramatically expanding, revealing the weaknesses of the chosen developmental model.

One can indicate a certain parallel with the final years of the People's Republic of Poland, and – more widely – of the state socialist system in Eastern Europe (although quite certainly in socialism this process took place under the conditions of a crisis, and not of an economic boom). State authorities and administrations put a lot of effort into 'switching' from political to economic capital, even at the risk of growing structural tensions in the national economy. In Southeast Asia the crisis somehow exposed this face of the authorities, and perhaps made the society unwilling to tolerate it any longer. On the other hand it may be that corrupt institutions proved to be hardly flexible or willing enough to make reforms (particularly in the weaker and less affluent crisis-stricken countries), which translated into outbreaks of social unrest.

---

30 G. Corsetti, P. Pesenti, N. Roubini (1998): *Paper Tigers? A Model of the Asian Crisis*, NBER Working Paper 6783.

The weakness of Asian states in the management of structural challenges was also revealed through changes on the region's geopolitical map[31]. As a result of the crisis, Indonesia lost control over East Timor, and the country was shaken by internal conflicts. In Thailand the post-crisis years brought unstable democratization, subsequent waves of protests and a *coups d'ëtat*. The Internal weakness of Thailand contributed to the weakening of its position in the region. The actual beneficiary of those processes was China, whose regional and global position improved significantly. Simultaneously, as I have already pointed out, the policies promoted by Western institutions (particularly the IMF) in poorer countries failed to bring about the expected results, and were universally perceived as the cause underlying the long-term deterioration of living standards and conditions.

As a result, the USA-Japan partnership shaping up the geopolitical order in the region was undermined. The very access to the global markets that had been guaranteed by the USA, and creating the developmental conditions for states that were in a highly disadvantageous geopolitical position in the period of Cold War, such as Taiwan and South Korea, ceased to be sufficient enough to maintain the role of the said partnership in regional geopolitics. China, exceptionally dynamic compared to the ageing Japan, and definitely more powerful than any other country of the region, started to play a key role. However, the shifting of the development axis towards China, who became a political and economic leader, did not signify, at least in the short term, the definition of a new developmental model; instead, it marked a crisis of the existing one[32]. Only in recent years has China tried to change the situation – growing internal economic tension, however, is perceived as proof of the inefficiency of the Chinese model.

To sum up, the poor quality of state institutions failed to create the necessary conditions for a smooth exit from the crisis. Consequently, particularly in ASEAN countries, the crisis lasted relatively long (in the context of the conducive economic and political climate in the world), and its long-term consequences (such as a permanent decline in the growth rate) did not recede until 2007–2008, when another global crisis started to be felt. Countries that were at a higher level of economic, social and technological development when the crisis broke out, coped better. Despite corruption, their institutions proved to be quite efficient

---

31 IISD (2007): *Regional Integration, Trade and Conflict in Southeast Asia. The Singapore Institute of International Affairs*, IISD, [Last accessed on-line on: 28.12.2015] https://www.iisd.org/pdf/2007/tas_rta_se_asia.pdf.

32 K. E. Broedsgaard, B. Heurlin (eds.) (2002): *China's Place in Global Geopolitics: Domestic, Regional and International Challenges*, London: Routledge.

and the democratization level was high enough to manage the challenges of the crisis effectively.

The challenge of crisis management, both at the flashpoint and also in the long term, revealed the weaknesses of the majority of the states of the region. The crisis did not produce any benefits for Japan, and although it did provide an opportunity for the improvement of Japan's economic situation, it brought only losses to the majority of other states. Apart from South Korea, the most resilient proved to be the countries deriving profits from their special relations with China: Taiwan, Hong Kong, and Singapore. Each of them, in their own special way, was in that period a gateway to China: for capital from the West the route frequently led through investments in Taiwan or Hong Kong, and for Chinese goods the route to well-developed countries often led through Hong Kong and Singapore[33].

At the same time it is worthwhile stressing these were the countries that greatly narrowed down the developmental gap which had separated them from Japan in the preceding decade. Their level of technological advancement, institutional development, accompanied by significant independence in international economic relations contributed to a relatively efficient containment of the crisis. Institutions undergoing the democratization process (in South Korea and Taiwan), as well as being relatively well prepared for institutional shocks (as was the case of Hong Kong being handed over to China), or at least significantly modernized after decades of the policy of transparency (Singapore), were capable of reacting flexibly to crisis challenges. Such situations, however, did not take place in ASEAN countries.

ASEAN countries to a large extent cushioned the blow of the crisis through currency devaluation enforced by external factors (excluding Indonesia, the least developed of the crisis-stricken countries, which entered into a long period of deep recession). this, however, greatly impacted on society in general, but particularly of the developing middle-class which was taking shape at that time. Consumption loans became the most burdensome (and – to a lesser degree – the public debt – denominated in the US Dollar), as well as a rise in the prices of imported products. Moreover, an outflow of capital resulted in the loss of jobs, together with a deterioration in employment conditions.

Apart from NIE countries, having relatively modern and efficient public institutions capable of formulating developmental policies, all political measures

---

33 Ch. H. Lee (2002): *Financial Liberalization and Economic Crisis in Asia*, London: Routledge.

aimed at limiting the consequences of the crisis were taken much too late, if at all. In the majority of cases the very 'containment' of the crisis entailed the implementation of the IMF's requirements (but a negative image of the organization among the societies of the region was sustained for a long time due to the radicalism of the applied solutions; of which the geopolitical consequences have already been discussed), at least the basic resolution of tensions of a social and ethnic nature (in many countries anti-Chinese riots were a response to the crisis), and stabilization of the political crisis. The collapse of political systems left local businesses, which were dependent on clientelistic and crony networks, to their own devices.

The crisis weakened not only the governance capabilities at state, corporation and enterprise levels (the consequences of the connections between politics and business being cut loose in the region are also described below), but also at the level of international cooperation:

"The crisis undermined the coherency and structural integrity of ASEAN. The region's economic structures were destabilized with massive domestic imbalances crippling member states and reversing the successful trends of the 1980s. Many ASEAN countries returned to economic nationalism by reversing economic liberalization (an outward, export-oriented Newly Industrialized Economy (NIE) model) to protect their own domestic industries and markets, such as the case of Malaysia experimenting with controls over capital flows and currency rates[34]".

Also in the long-term, when the acute phase of the crisis ended, the capabilities of particular ASEAN countries to manage the crisis proved limited. Malaysia witnessed a move towards interventionist and protectionist policies. Both Malaysia and Thailand returned to competing for capital and investments in global markets based almost solely on the costs of cheap labour, which in turn prevented the process of modernization of the industrial sectors in those countries. While we may speak of the developmental success of NIE countries, where the export-oriented industrialisation model led in the post-crisis period to maintain and even strengthen the position of local brands and companies in the global market (such as Samsung, Hyundai, ACER, ASUS and many others), the ASEAN countries failed to repeat this success. This might have resulted from the long experience of NIE countries in the formulation and management of developmental policies. An administration prepared to do that, was also ready to introduce anti-crisis policies, while a higher level of legitimization was also conducive for that process.

34 IISD (2007).

It seems that the course of the crisis first uncovered how shallow the **legitimization** of the political regimes in Southeast Asia were. In particular in poorer Asian countries the crisis proved to be a political tsunami, which – leaving behind ruins of the previous system – created very limited conditions for the growth of stability in the newly shaped political systems. Consequences of the degradation of the legitimization of the regimes previously in the rule were also felt by the business community. Close relations between the regimes and private business were a specific trait of the Asian model of the *developmental state.*

The legitimization crisis entailed not only the inability to undertake anti-crisis actions and the ensuing feedback and fall of some regimes, or a very deep correction of their functioning. Simultaneously, the rules of the functioning of private business changed, and apart from Korea and other less crisis-stricken NIE countries, where robust companies managed to arise, this translated into a profound crisis in the business sector. The crisis was structural in nature and in the mid-term strengthened the effects of the crisis.

Most importantly, however, the economic crisis led to a crisis – if not the destruction – of the Asian model of the developmental state. In particular this can be observed in the wealthier countries of the region (Japan, NIE countries), where visible inequalities in growth took place in the post-crisis period. This was related to the reorientation of economic and social policies – and the slow departure from the *developmental state* model towards competitiveness in global markets. In poorer countries the process of consolidation of the institutions of such state has never been completed.

4 Winners and losers of the Asian crisis

China proved to be the greatest 'winner' of the Asian crisis. Virtually untouched by the crisis, China shortly became the recipient of a large portion of the capital that fled from Southeast Asian countries. Moreover, using industrial policy instruments characteristic for the Asian developmental state, China started to build their own companies successfully. It seems that during the following decade it coped better with the creation of conditions for sustainable growth than ASEAN countries had done before the crisis.

One can speak of the relative success with regard to NIE countries. South Korea, Taiwan, Singapore and Hong Kong swiftly returned to the economic growth path, maintaining their positions in the global economy. Following the development path of Japan, they closely approximated its developmental level. Even the limitations of state interventionism and links between the state and the private industrial sector did not have a negative impact on the developmental potential of those states. Economic and political liberalization lent a new developmental impulse, while companies established during the period of protectionist (export-oriented) industrialization policy (in particular Korean *chaebols*) became growth drivers, playing a similar role to that of the Japanese *keiretsu* in the period of 1970–80. However, this took place at the cost of growing social tensions, which were reflected both in the growing inequalities and deep demographic crises in those countries.

And finally, the least developed states of the region (Bangladesh, Vietnam) benefitted from the crisis, being countries increasingly treated as attractive locations for labour-intensive industries, While the location advantages of such countries as Thailand and Malaysia declined owing to the political and economic instability uncovered by the crisis and its growing labour costs.

Among the losers of the crisis, one should point out first of all the ASEAN states, and secondly – Japan. The ASEAN states were clearly 'knocked out' of the developmental path. The industrialization process slowed down; this is well illustrated by export statistics. Although industrial production grew, its share in exports remained stable. Moreover, industrial production growth dynamics (despite lower technological advancement and lower GDP levels) started to differ significantly from the one characteristic of NIE countries (except Hong Kong, where growth gained new foundations) and was only slightly higher than the dynamics of the highly developed states of (Japan and the USA).

On the other hand, Japan remained in a state of secular stagnation which had lasted since the early 1990s. In contrast to South Korea, the crisis did not lead to structural reforms, which would have increased (or restored) Japan's competitiveness. In combination with disadvantageous demographic trends this made post-crisis Japan enter into another 'lost decade'.

A detailed analysis of the economic growth dynamics in the post-crisis period indicates that – apart from China – Taiwan and South Korea were the states that coped best with the crisis, developing faster than the regional average, while other countries coped much worse. As a consequence, convergence took place in the group of wealthy countries (the poorer ones, Korea and Taiwan, were in the process of catching up with the wealthy city-states, i.e. Singapore, Hong Kong and Japan), while the growth rate of the poorest countries resulted in de-convergence in relation to the leaders. Nevertheless, within the groups of poor countries convergence did also take place.

The last, probably quite incidental, loser proved to be the big country whose wealth was based on raw materials, namely Russia being in the final period of Yeltsin's rule.

5 The Asian crisis. A crisis of the export-oriented industrialization model in Southeast Asia?

In the second half of the 1980s a group of Southeast Asian countries (mostly associated with ASEAN) made an attempt to imitate the economic development strategy implemented in Japan since the 1950s and then in South Korea and Taiwan (and the city-states of – Singapore and Hong Kong) since the 1960s[35]. The key component of this strategy was the industrialization policy, which allowed states to take advantage of the cheap labour force resources for competing in global markets, and to evade the problem of *infant industry*. This strategy was based on support for the development of light industry accompanied by the creation of incentives to save money, an active educational policy aimed to improve the quality of human capital and the search for developmental niches, including in particular technologically advanced industry sectors, where the impact of the problem of *infant industry* would be limited (such as the car and consumer electronics industry in Japan, the consumer electronics and household appliances industry in Korea and the microelectronic industry in Taiwan). Support for the establishment of industrial conglomerates also created conducive conditions for the development of initially non-competitive industry sectors.

The Industrialization of ASEAN countries was rapid in the 1980s and early 1990s but the Asian Crisis set a clear dividing mark in this process. In the following decade the industrialization dynamics of Malaysia (measured by the value of industrial production), Thailand and even of agricultural Indonesia declined dramatically. This is particularly visible when comparison is made with the Asian countries which entered the industrialization process later (Bangladesh, Vietnam, but also China), and the NIE countries. The process of structural

---

35 A. Amsden (2001): The Rise of "The Rest": Challenges to the West From Late-Industrializing Economies, Oxford: Oxford University Press; I. Chalmers, V. R. Hadiz (eds.) (1997): *The Politics of Economic Development in Indonesia: Contending Perspectives*, London: Routledge; K. S. Jomo (1993): *Industrialising Malaysia: Performance, Problems, Prospects*, London: Routledge; K. S. Jomo et al. (1998): Case of Malaysia: Industrial Policy and the Emergence of Internationally Competitive Manufacturing Firms in Malaysia, in: K. Takahashi [ed.] Asia's Development Experiences: *How Internationally Competitive National Manufacturing Firms Have Developed in Asia*, Tokyo: Foundation for Advanced Studies on International Development, pp. 178–261; K. S. Jomo (2001): *Southeast Asia's Industrialization. Industrial Policy, Capabilities and Sustainability*, Basingstoke: Palgrave; A. Ikeo (ed.) (1997): *Economic Development in Twentieth-Century East Asia: The International Context*, London: Routledge; Lee (2002).

transformation and modernization in the economies of ASEAN countries lost its dynamics, and within a decade after the Asian crisis there was also a significant slowdown in the rise of living standards and of the catching-up with the economies of well-developed countries. It has to be pointed out that the ASEAN countries only partly entered the developmental path typical of the Asian developmental state. The quality of political institutions in those countries under the conditions of political destabilization proved relatively poor, which stemmed from the scale of cronyism, clientelism and from the weakening legitimization of their regimes. The financing of industrialization came mainly from FDIs, rather than from internal accumulation or developmental aid as in the case of the first generation of developmental states in Asia.

Today, Malaysia – in the third decade of the trials – still aspires to the group of the most modern global economies, and in Thailand there are many manufacturing plants and plants assembling technologically advanced electronic products. However, and this needs to be stressed again, the relative positions of those two countries since the times of the crisis have undergone only slight changes at most. The process of civilizational advancement have slowed down significantly. It is worthwhile adding that since the times of the economic miracle, Malaysia has remained the most technologically advanced and most modern economy among Muslim countries worldwide (excluding those countries that finance economic development from profits generated by the sale of crude oil).

NIE countries (particularly the big ones) coped with the crisis much better. They maintained high economic growth dynamics and prevented the developmental levels of South Korea and Taiwan from departing significantly from the developmental level of Japan (measured against GDP per capita). However, even there the crisis entailed the cost of at least a partial departure from the developmental state model. As demonstrated by the example of Korea, liberalization and deregulation of the economy was not necessarily enforced by the expectations of the IMF, which granted stabilization aid in the crisis period. However, the effective adoption of a "neo-liberal" developmental model analogous to the one promoted by the IMF and supplemented with an extensive industrial policy, created the conditions for the continuation of developmental success. On the other hand, limited democratic traditions, a strong social position of the administration and universally felt economic success, effectively "translated" into the government's image-building success, have allowed for a change of the developmental model (i.e. in fact for a planned disassembly of the developmental state) without giving rise to a wave of social unrest.

As a result, in my opinion one can speak of a crisis or even the disappearance of the developmental state model in Asia, with the central role being played in this process by the economic crisis analysed here. The state limited its role in support of both economic and social development. Economic policy became reoriented; this was partly enforced by requirements of the aid packages granted by the IMF[36]. To a certain degree, Malaysia remained an exception; already after the crisis it intensively reached for instruments of protectionist policy, state interventionism and social policy, with a clearly ethnic profile: it aimed to improve the situation of the Malayan (not the Chinese) part of Malaysian society. But while in Japan, South Korea and Taiwan, the developmental state contributed to a visible reduction of any inequalities before the crisis (the crisis actually reversed this trend), then in the ASEAN states the high level of social inequalities proved lasting. Efforts aimed to reduce the said level were very moderately successful, also in Malaysia. In the richest countries with relatively effective public institutions, (partial) departure from the developmental state model in the name of maintaining growth proved to be a success, while in poorer countries with weak institutions the anti-crisis policies of the said type worked much less effectively, despite their diversification.

6 The Asian crisis and the European financial crisis. Parallels between crises of the models of the developmental state

The developmental models of European (capitalist) peripheries and South-East Asian countries were different[37]. They differed in terms of industrial policy, role of state and the trajectory of catching-up with the core. Also different has been the very concept of the developmental state, particularly since the time when European institutions started influencing developmental policy in Europe. However, even much earlier the point of reference in Europe was the capital-intensive industrialization of core countries, while the labor-intensive industrialization of Japan became the model in Asia. And last but not least, the long-term development paths were different. As a result, the industrialization process in European peripheries (both capitalist and communist) was capital- and resource-intensive. It contributed, particularly in Europe's southern part, to the development of highly productive but relatively small (particularly in terms of employment) manufacturing sectors.

In the case of Europe, developmental policy (particularly, industrial policy) in southern and eastern peripheries took place – in a gross oversimplification – in

36 L. Low (2004): *Developmental States: Relevancy, Redundancy or Reconfiguration?* New York: Nova Publishers.

37 Low (2004).

two stages. In the first stage, in the period on undemocratic (authoritarian) rule (until the 1970s), relatively effective attempts were made to build market economies through moderately weak links with the rest of Europe. In the case of the eastern peripheries, full economic dependence on the USSR took place instead and the development of so called state socialism. The development of free market economy in post-communist countries started after 1989. In the second stage, during the process of European integration, structural aid was intended to lead to a developmental convergence; at the same time it turned out that development was dependent in nature on the economies of European core states. Similar developmental stages can be observed in Asia too; although within the economic area which developed around Japan, the convergence policy played a much lesser (if at all) role there. In turn, a national industrial policy was of particular interest to the ruling elites in Asia, contrary to most European peripheries.

Despite the differences, one can still point out certain structural similarities between the regions: in either case, a dominant economic role is played by economies with large, modern and technologically advanced industrial sectors (Japan and Germany, respectively – although in Europe the core can be defined on a wider scale). In either, the economies of the periphery countries are strongly connected with the leading economy – via direct investments, position in the production chains, and business cycles. Their development has, therefore, – at least partly – the character of dependent development. It is also easy to point out significant differences: the greater diversification of developmental levels in Asia accompanied probably by greater diversification of the quality of public institutions and wider cultural gaps. Monetary policies between the two regions differed too: in Asia the currencies of periphery countries before the crisis were coupled to the US Dollar, and to the Japanese Yen; in Europe the Eurozone covered both core and periphery countries. Also different was the nature of the crisis itself: in Europe, the debt crisis was manifested as a result of the global crisis, leading to threats of insolvency (which did materialize in the case of some countries) in European periphery states. The Asian crisis described above had local origins, regional reach and started with the monetary crisis. In European conditions, the options to manage the economic crisis proved to be much greater, particularly at supranational level, than in the case of the Asian countries.

Taking into consideration both the similarities and differences, one may reflect on what follows from the comparison of the two crises[38]. Sources of the Asian

---

38 W. Pesek (2015): *What Europe Should Learn from the Asian Crisis*, Bloomberg View, 20.07, [Last accessed on-line on: 28.12.2015] http://www.bloombergview.com/articles/2015–07-20/lessons-for-greece-from-asia-s-1997-crisis.

crisis can be traced to the reorientation of Japan's policies in the late 1990s, and perhaps also to the Japanese crisis. On the other hand, apart from global factors, the reorientation of German economic policy at the beginning of the 21st century, including in particular the measures aimed at improving competitiveness, together were contributory factors that triggered the Eurozone crisis. Periphery countries in relation to Japan, but with relatively high developmental levels – South Korea and Taiwan – coped best during the Asian crisis. In Europe their 'peers' – southern peripheries, but also such countries as Ireland and Finland, coped relatively worse. This was particularly visible in the secular crisis in south European countries, and also – already after 2010 – by the weakening of the developmental dynamics of Finland. And last but not least, the group of less-developed periphery countries – i.e. in the case of Europe, the post-communist countries of the CEE region – handled the crisis and exited it in better condition than their Asian peers. However, it has to be stressed that compared to the regional core, their developmental level was higher at the moment of the crisis outbreak than that in the case of the ASEAN countries in Asia. Owing to high oil prices that were maintained until 2014, Russia – despite close economic ties with Europe – avoided the serious consequences of the European crisis paralleling those it experienced owing to "Asian flu".

Certainly such a comparison is a gross oversimplification, leaving aside many key differences between regions, but it enables us to ask an open question about the reasons underlying such different trajectories of the exit from the crisis. It seems that experiences from the Asian crisis, although at least partly taken into account in European policies, failed to prevent the emergence of another crisis. Perhaps such development is attributable to the fact that despite certain structural similarities, its origins were completely different.

Summary

The Asian crisis exerted a clear impact on the course of the developmental model and developmental state that took shape in South-East Asia after WW2, creating conducive conditions for the astonishing economic success of the region. Although owing to the success of China within 2 recent decades, it might seem that the crisis did not influence the region's development, in reality it undermined the foundations of the "Asian economic miracle" and the Asian developmental states, including in particular the political and economic consensus within societies of the region, which was necessary if growth was to be sustained. Therefore, successful anti-crisis policies were of central significance for further successful development of the states of the region and their convergence. The failure of such policies in many countries of the region being at medium and lower development levels became a barrier to catching-up with the highly developed countries.

At the level of empirical comparisons, it seems that the following factors can be considered as central factors to the success of anti-crisis policies: pre-crisis development level and (strongly correlated therewith) quality of public institutions. The countries that were better developed and simultaneously had better institutions, absorbed the incoming stabilization aid more effectively, introduced reform packages without destabilizing the socio-economic system and were capable of taking advantage of the global economic upswing. At the same time, some countries – like e.g. South Korea – swiftly liberated themselves from the "dictate" of the IMF and gained freedom in pursuance of sovereign economic policy – even though it bore resemblance to what the Fund required. Perhaps equally important was the structural misalignment of IMF policies with the developmental needs of underdeveloped countries. The issue of avoiding destabilization of the socio-economic system requires some comment to be made: it was avoided in NIE countries, but mainly because the societies accepted the change in the rules of the game, i.e. a departure from the developmental model founded on the focus on the reduction of inequalities.

It is worth mentioning that the failure of IMF aid programs in the region entailed serious political outcomes. It proved to be a driver of geopolitical changes, including in particular the rise in the significance of China, which besides its top economic position guaranteed by the dynamics and scale of its economy, also gained the status of the region's political leader.

References

Akamatsu K. (1962): A Historical Pattern of Economic Growth in Developing Countries, *Journal of Developing Economies*, 1(1):3–25, March–August.

Alavi R. (1996): *Industrialization in Malaysia. Import Substitution and Infant Industry Performance*, London: Routledge.

Amsden A. (2001): *The Rise of "The Rest": Challenges to the West from Late-Industrializing Economies*, Oxford: Oxford University Press.

Athukorala P. (2010): Malaysian Economy in Three Crises, *WP in Trade and Development*, No. 12/2010, Canberra: ANU.

Broedsgaard K.E., B. Heurlin (eds.) (2002). *China's Place in Global Geopolitics: Domestic, Regional and International Challenges*, London: Routledge.

Chalamwong Z. (1998): The Impact of the Crisis on Migration in Thailand, *Asian and Pacific Migration Journal*, Vol. 7, Nos. 2–3, 1998, pp. 297–312.

Chalmers I., V. R. Hadiz (eds.) (1997): *The Politics of Economic Development in Indonesia: Contending Perspectives*. London: Routledge.

Chancellor E. (2000): *Devil Take the Hindmost: A History of Financial Speculation*, New York: Plume Books.

Collins C., A. Senhadji (2002): Lending Booms, Real Estate Bubbles and the Asian Crisis, *IMF WP* 02/20, pp. 1–45.

Corsetti G., P. Pesenti, N. Roubini (1998): Paper Tigers? A Model of Asian Crisis, *NBER Working Paper* 6783, pp. 1–39.

De Vries, J. (2008): *The Industrious Revolution: Consumer Behavior and the Household Economy, 1650 to the Present*, New York: Cambridge University Press.

Goldstein M. (1998): *The Asian Financial Crisis. Causes, Cures and Systemic Implications*, Institute for International Economics, Washington D.C.

Hundt D. (2009): *Korea's Developmental Alliance: State, Capital and the Politics of Rapid Development*, London: Routledge.

Hundt D. (2014): Economic Crisis in Korea and the Degraded Developmental State, *Australian Journal of International Affairs*, vol. 68, pp. 499–514.

Huntington S. P. (1968): *Political Order in Changing Societies*. New Heaven: Yale Univ. Press.

IISD (2007): Regional Integration, Trade and Conflict in Southeast Asia. The Singapore Institute of International Affairs, *IISD*, [Last accessed on-line on: 28.12.2015] https://www.iisd.org/pdf/2007/tas_rta_se_asia.pdf.

Ikeo A. (ed.) (1997): *Economic Development in Twentieth-Century East Asia: The International Context*, London: Routledge.

IMF (2000): Recovery from the Asian Crisis and the Role of the IMF, IMF Report 00/05, [Last accessed on-line on: 28.12.2015] https://www.imf.org/external/np/exr/ib/2000/062300.htm.

Ishida K. (1998): Japan's Foreign Direct Investment in East Asia: Its Influence on Recipient Countries and Japan's Trade Structure, in: E. G. Adams, S. Ichimura (eds.), *East Asian Development. Will East Asian Miracle Survive?*, London: Praeger, pp. 156–169.

Jomo K. S. (1993): *Industrialising Malaysia: Performance, Problems, Prospects*, London: Routledge.

Jomo K. S. et al. (1998): The Case of Malaysia: Industrial Policy and the Emergence of Internationally Competitive Manufacturing Firms in Malaysia, in: Kazuo Takahashi [ed.], *Asia's Development Experiences: How Internationally Competitive National Manufacturing Firms Have Developed in Asia*, Tokyo: Foundation for Advanced Studies on International Development, pp. 178–261.

Jomo K. S. (2001): *Southeast Asia's Industrialization. Industrial Policy, Capabilities and Sustainability*, Basingstoke: Palgrave.

Jomo K. S. (2003): *Southeast Asian Paper Tigers. From Miracle to Debacle and Beyond*, London: Routledge.

Jomo K. S. (ed.) (2004): *After The Storm: Crisis, Recovery and Sustaining Development in East Asia*, Singapore: Singapore Univ. Press.

Kim S., J. H. Yoon, C. Viney (2001): Dynamic Interdependence and Volatility Transmission of Asian Stock Markets: Evidence from the Asian Crisis, *International Review of Financial Analysis*, vol. 10, No. 1, pp. 87–96.

Koo H. (2014): Inequality in South Korea. *East Asia Forum*. 1.07, [Last accessed on: 28.12.2015] http://www.eastasiaforum.org/2014/07/01/inequality-in-south-korea/.

Low L. (2004): *Developmental States: Relevancy, Redundancy or Reconfiguration?*, New York: Nova Publishers.

Lee Ch. H. (2002): *Financial Liberalization and Economic Crisis in Asia*, London: Routledge.

Myrdal G., (1968): *Asian Drama. An Inquiry into the Poverty of Nations*, 3 Vols., New York: Pantheon.

Ozawa T. (2005): *Institutions, Industrial Upgrading, and Economic Performance in Japan. The 'Flying Geese' Paradigm of Catch-up Growth*, Cheltenham: Edward Elgar.

Pesek W. (2015): What Europe Should Learn from the Asian Crisis, *Bloomberg View*, 20.07, [Last accessed on-line on: 28.12.2015] http://www.bloombergview.com/articles/2015-07-20/lessons-for-greece-from-asia-s-1997-crisis.

Raquiza A. (2012): *State Structure, Policy Formation, and Economic Development in Southeast Asia the political economy of Thailand and the Philippines*, London: Routledge.

Saxena S., K. Wong (2002): Economic Growth, Over-Investment and Financial Crisis, Mimeo, [Last accessed on-line on: 28.12.2015] https://faculty.washington.edu/karyiu/papers/invest-crisis.pdf.

Shin J.-S.; H.-J. Chang (2003): *Restructuring Korea Inc.*, London: Routledge.

Siriprachai S. (1997): Inconsistencies and Inequalities in Thai Industrialisation, in: J. D. Schmidt, J. Hersh, N. Fold (eds.) *Social Changes in Southeast Asia*, London: Longman, pp. 183–205.

Sugihara K. (2004): Labor-Intensive Industrialization in Global History, Background Paper for Osaka GEHN Conference [Last accessed on-line on: 28.12.2015] http://www.lse.ac.uk/economicHistory/Research/GEHN/GEHNPDF/SugiharaGEHN5.pdf.

Thorbecke W., N. Salike (2011): Understanding Foreign Direct Investment in East Asia, *ADBI Working Paper*, No. 290/2011.

Wong K. (2001): Housing Market Bubbles and Currency Crisis. The Case of Thailand, *Japanese Economic Review*, vol. 52, No. 4, pp. 382–404.

Łukasz Hardt[1]

Regulatory impact assessment and the creation of the economic policy in Poland

Abstract: The chapter focuses mainly on the quality and risks related to the regulatory decisions made by the governments, in general and subsequently in the case of Poland. The analysis demonstrates why the regulatory assessment mechanism has worked insufficiently during the creation of the economic policy process of the last two decades in Poland. The problem is often caused by the fact that the effects of the regulations are not consequently assessed in objective ways, because regulatory impact assessments are conducted by those who are responsible for creating regulations. Moreover, many policy drafts are not subjected to any impact assessment at all. If the government intends to avoid an insightful appraisal of a given regulation, it uses the way of submitting the draft as a legislator proposal of a group of PMs which does not require any regulatory impact assessment. Consequently, we can hardly speak of any evidence-based policy pursuit by the state. This occurs despite major actions of the government undertaken in order to improve the effectiveness of the legislation system.

Keywords: economic policy, Regulatory Impact Assessment, quality of governance, public policies, crisis management

Economists agree that regulatory quality is of prime importance for capital accumulation, technological progress, and knowledge creation, i.e. factors considered for decades to be major growth determinants. A state's regulatory activities have a significant impact on its economic development prospects[2]. If a state is largely responsible for the shape of the institutional environment within which economic entities operate, then the question arises emphatically of how those institutions should be designed to create optimal conditions for market exchange

---

1 The Faculty of Economic Sciences, Warsaw University (lhardt@wne.uw.edu.pl). The text presents exclusively the views of its author, and not of the institutions he is related to.

2 For more detailed discussions see: D. C. North (1990): *Institutions, Institutional Change and Economic Performance*. New York: Cambridge University Press; F. Fukuyama (2011): *The Origins of Political Order*. New York: Farrar, Straus and Giroux; D. Acemoglu, J. A. Robinson (2012): *Why Nations Fail, The Origins of Power, Prosperity, and Poverty*. London: Profile Books.

and consequently to allow for the maximization of social welfare[3]. In economic theories there is a consensus that Smith's invisible hand of the market cannot operate in an institutional vacuum[4]. This assumption underlies various concepts being part of the so-called positive economic theory of state, which recognises the government as an entity whose actions are aimed to counteract and eliminate market failures. This is the essence of papers written by e.g. B. Greenwald and J. Stiglitz, who proved that in a situation where economic entities do not have full access to information, market equilibrium will not be effective in Pareto sense[5]. Moreover, they demonstrated that in such circumstances a state's regulatory activity may bring the socio-economic system closer to optimal solutions, e.g. ones manifested through a lower unemployment rate. Such a perception of the function of the government is largely convergent with the thesis of Hobbes, according to which leaving the state of nature characterised by permanent conflict of everyone with everyone is possible through the renouncement by people of a part of the freedom they are eligible to for the benefit of the government.

Once economists recognised the key role of the state in the creation of economic development, their further research focused on going deeply into a state's structures and analysing not so much the regulations themselves, but the mechanisms underlying their creation. Therefore, similarly to neoclassical economics, which in the second half of the 20th century started to depart from the concept of a company as a production function and ventured to analyse its internal structure, also in the case of economic studies related to the state, researchers stopped just stating that institutions mattered and embarked on sophisticated studies on the dynamics of state's activities. This is the tradition under which one should locate the analyses by E. Maskin on mechanism design theory, including their compliance with incentive compatibility criterion, resulting, among other things, in the breakthrough research of J. Laffont and J. Tirole over regulations in the context of incentives they create, or of R. Guesnerie on taxation rules[6].

---

3 I understand institutions as rules of the game and adopt their conceptualization by D. C. North (1990), *op. cit.* I treat synonymously the terms 'institution' and 'regulation'.

4 See e.g.: J. Stiglitz (1991): The Invisible Hand and Modern Welfare Economics, w: D. Vines, A. Stevenson (eds.), *Information, Strategy, and Public Policy*, Oxford: Basil Blackwell.

5 E.g. B. C. Greenwald, J. Stiglitz (1986): Externalities in Economies with Imperfect Information and Incomplete Markets, *Quarterly Journal of Economics*, vol. 101, pp. 229–264.

6 J. J. Laffont, J. Tirole (1993): *A Theory of Incentives in Procurement and Regulation*. Cambridge MA: MIT Press; R. Guesnerie (1995): *A Contribution to the Pure Theory*

Through these papers economists increasingly analysed not just the existing institutions, but also pondered on what kind of regulations may contribute to the attainment of specific social targets.

At the same time governments themselves increasingly started to use such theories and to approach regulation drafting systematically, which usually entailed the institutionalisation of regulatory impact analysis (RIA) procedures[7]. Historically this process started in the United States when R. Reagan took over power and then a little later in the United Kingdom under the rule of M. Thatcher[8]. As the OECD points out in one of its reports, those are the countries where the RIA process is to a greater extent not only integrated with law-making mechanisms, but also with the political process as such[9].

In connection with the economic crisis of recent years in the European Union, following first and foremost from the dysfunction of the Eurozone and resulting – in the opinions of some – in economy governance panic, many researchers put forward the thesis that here in Europe we are experiencing a crisis of crisis management methods, or – on a wider scale – the crisis of pursuance of economic policy, including the mechanisms governing its creation[10]. I concur that this thesis and the permanent discussions around the methods of aiding Greece can only confirm this. However, in my paper I don't want to undertake a wide debate on the crisis in the European Union – it is discussed in the chapter authored by T.G. Grosse, but I will focus on the situation in Poland, although my starting thesis is similar – many of the mechanisms governing the formulation of economic policy in Poland are in crisis. This means that the drafted regulations are of an ad hoc nature, and those who designed them failed to take into account the long-term perspective or potential external effects. Moreover, an analysis of the

---

of Taxation, Econometric Society Monograph no 25, Cambridge UK: Cambridge University Press.

7 I treat synonymously the terms 'regulatory impact analysis' and 'regulatory impact assessment'.

8 C. Kirkpatrick, D. Parker (eds.) (2007): *Regulatory Impact Assessment. Towards Better Regulation?*, Cheltenham: Edward Elgar.

9 OECD (2012): *Sustainability in Impact Assessments. A Review of Impact Assessment Systems in Selected OECD Countries and the European Commission.*

10 D.M. Woodruff writes about governance by panic in the paper: *Governing by Panic: The Politics of the Eurozone Crisis*, LEQS Paper No 81/2014; see: M. A. Cichocki: (2015): *Unia w Unii? Strefa euro w przebudowie*, Nowa Europa. Przegląd natoliński, vol. 2(6), pp. 1–113.

impact of those regulations is frequently performed by those who drafted them. Therefore, a specific mental capture of regulations takes place – which are evaluated as beneficial, because they are authored by evaluators. Returning to the aforementioned papers by Greenwald and Stiglitz, one can state that although theoretically the government may cope better with managing transactions than the market when economic entities withhold information. At the same time the government may be characterised by such an objective function under which the value assigned to particular stakeholder groups, including regulators themselves, will be derivatives of their bargaining power and the results of so-called objective factors, and consequently social welfare will not be maximised. Market failure, therefore, can by accompanied by government failures. If, as I briefly indicated earlier, regulations are so highly relevant for economic development, then the crisis of their creation, including the mechanisms of regulatory impact analysis, gives rise to a dangerous situation in the context of building lasting growth foundations.

The said crisis takes place in a situation when Poland faces challenges of key significance for its future, i.e. the reduction of the risk of falling into the "medium-income trap" or a redefinition of its position in the European Union shaken by various types of crises. The world is changing dynamically and policy-makers need an effective system for the evaluation of their legislative proposals. In reality we are dealing with a paradoxical situation – the society and economy are under the influence of a growing number of external factors, while the public policy creation system becomes increasingly informationally closed, which is manifested, among other things, in the fact that legislators rarely analyse alternative methods for the attainment of adopted goals. This concerns in particular regulatory analysis mechanisms – civil servants saturated with information during the drafting of legal solutions are unable to assimilate additional and external information during the analysis of the said proposals. Consequently, the system is informationally ineffective and this underlies the thesis about its crisis.

As a consequence of the dysfunctionality of the RIA system, policy-makers are only to a limited extent able to tackle the challenges of growth, management and political legitimisation identified in this volume. So, if the economy's potential for sustainable growth depends on the law-making system's quality – and this is the thesis I put forward here, then the ability of policy-makers to tackle growth challenges becomes hampered. Similarly with reference to the issue of management: a system closed to information and not accepting – as supporters of a cybernetic approach would have it – energy from outside, is unable to attain a proper level of adaptive effectiveness, i.e. the ability of its structures to change in response to external stimuli[11]. The issue of legitimisation is more complex. On the one hand, a faulty RIA system may be used to legitimise political decisions by consenting to their implementation. In such cases the RIA mechanism is launched at the end of the legislative process, when changes to the proceeded upon legal solution are no longer possible. This situation is quite frequent in Poland. On the other hand, a correctly performed RIA may provide politicians with arguments to proceed with regulations even against circulating opinions about their outcomes and if the policy-makers attain the adopted goals then the legitimisation of the originators of specific legislative solutions will be reinforced. The RIA system should benefit legitimisation so understood. If the regulatory impact analysis is in a situation displaying symptoms of a crisis and prevents the government from responding properly to key challenges faced by the economy and society, it is worthwhile embarking on a wider analysis of the issues and propose remedial measures, something I am doing in this chapter of the volume.

In the first part of the paper I will present the issue of regulatory impact analysis from the perspective of economic theories. However, I do not analyse assessments of specific regulations, but I am concerned with the institutional system as part of which the analyses are performed. This is consistent with my general thesis that we are dealing with the dysfunctionality of the entire system governing the creation of economic policy, and one of its aspects – which I analyse in detail – are the faults of the regulatory impact assessment mechanisms. In the next section of the paper, starting from a general reflection on the quality of economic policy drafting, I proceed to a detailed review of the regulatory impact assessment system within the Polish government. Then – drawing extensively on international experience – I will try to propose several modifications of the present RIA system in Poland. The paper ends with a summary.

Regulatory impact assessment system – theoretical remarks

I have already pointed out that I will analyse the institutional framework underlying the process of the building of economic policy in Poland. However, I wish to specify that I confine myself exclusively to the regulatory impact analysis system and not the mechanisms underlying the creation of public policy goals. Referring to E. Maskin's mechanism design theory, I might state that I am interested solely in the implementation phase of the process leading to the attainment of a specific social goal. The above does not rule out, however, the fact that I will

11 See: A. Dudzińska (2015): *System zamknięty. Socjologiczna analiza procesu legislacyjnego*, Warsaw: WN Scholar.

be asking in multiple places in the text the question related to the extent to which deficits of RIA system follow from more general restrictions to good governance rules in Poland, and also to what extent the problems related to the operation of RIA mechanisms are characteristic also for other areas of government activities.

Before I proceed to a more theoretical view of the issues related to regulatory impact analysis, I will refer below to one of the more popular definitions of the system. The OECD suggests in the definition both an analysis of the potential impacts of specific actions and studies on alternative approaches.

"Regulatory Impact Analysis (RIA) aimed to be both a *tool* and a *decision process* for informing political decision makers on whether and how to regulate to achieve public policy goals. As a tool supporting decision making, RIA systematically examines the potential impacts of government actions by asking questions about the costs and benefits; how effective will the action be achieving its policy goals and; whether there are superior alternative approaches available to governments. As a *decision process* RIA is integrated with systems for consultation, policy development and rule making within governments in order to communicate information *ex ante* about the expected effects of regulatory proposals at a time and in a form that can be used by decision makers, and also *ex post* to assist governments to evaluate existing regulations. At the stage of regulatory implementation, RIA can be a tool to evaluate their impact"[12].

Under such an approach, RIA is not merely a tool, but also a decision process, strongly integrated with general legislative procedures and other elements of government activities. As a result of the transition from RIA as a *tool* to its treatment in terms of a *process*, in many OECD countries "RIA has evolved from narrow technical methods aimed at cutting costs toward more flexible and sophisticated techniques of problem-solving aimed at fostering a richer and more informed public debate about important public policy issues [...]"[13]. A detailed analysis of the popularisation of such an understanding of RIA is contained, among other things, in studies of OECD[14], as well as of I. Lianos and his associates[15].

As RIA mechanisms were disseminated, increasing attention was focused on their potential weaknesses. It turned out that there are significant differences

---

12 OECD (2009): *Regulatory Impact Analysis. A Tool for Policy Coherence*, p. 12.

13 S. H. Jacobs (2007): *Current Trends in the Process and Methods of Regulatory Impact Assessment: Mainstreaming RIA into Policy Process*, in: C. Kirkpatrick, D. Parker (eds.) (2007), *op. cit.*, p. 18.

14 OECD (2009), *op. cit.*

15 I. Lianos, M. Fazekas, M. Karliuk (2014): *The Diffusion of Impact Assessment Practices in Europe*, CLES Research Paper Series 2/2014.

between the RIA system ideal described in literature and its practical implementations in many countries. Here one can indicate, among other things, the universal absence of the application of RIA for the assessment of the most important regulatory actions focusing solely on those with much less political weight[16]. Moreover, analyses of alternatives to solutions proposed by the legislator are missing in RIAs performed in many countries. The practice of risk assessment related to the introduction of specific regulations is also far from being universal[17]. What is more, many RIA reports focus solely on financially measurable effects and completely forego an analysis of potential external effects[18].

Other researchers, e.g. C. Dunlop and her associates, stress that the cultural, historical and political context of a given country strongly influences how RIAs are used[19]. They indicate four possible functions of RIA systems. They name the first one as the political usage. Under such an approach, based on agency theory, the principal, e.g. the head of state and their chancellery, controls agents, e.g. sectoral ministries, through a centralized RIA system. Another option is the so-called instrumental usage. Under such situations RIAs serve the purpose of building an evidence-based policy. Attaching great importance to the idea of new public governance in state administration is conducive for the popularization of this approach[20]. The third option is to treat RIA as a mechanism building space for enhanced consultations with entities interested in the drafted regulation. Then the basic role of RIA is to provide stakeholders with possibly the most complete knowledge about the impact of a regulation – the so-called communicative usage of RIA. In many instances the consultation process based on the information matrix supplied by RIA serves the purpose of legitimizing the actions of regulatory agencies, which are frequently devoid of a clear democratic mandate. The last option is the perfunctory usage of RIA, where regulatory impact analysis is just a simple administrative exercise with no real influence over the legislative process. Those four usages of RIA are not mutually exclusive and in a given country RIA may be both a political control mechanism over law-making

16 According to OECD (2009), *op. cit.*

17 S. H. Jacobs (2007), *op. cit.*

18 C. Kirkpatrick, D. Parker. (red.) (2007), *op. cit.*

19 C. Dunlop, M. Maggetti, C. Radaelli, D. Russel (2012): *The Many Uses of Regulatory Impact Assessment: A Meta-analysis of EU and UK Cases*, Regulation & Governance, vol. 6(1), pp. 23–45.

20 Hood, Ch., Dixon, R. (2015), *A Government that Worked Better and Cost Less? Evaluating Three Decades of Reform and Change in UK Central Government*, Oxford: Oxford University Press.

mechanism and at the same time include elements of instrumental analysis of the impacts of specific legislative proposals. Many research studies indicate that the first and fourth RIA usages dominate in a majority of countries[21].

I will readdress these issues in greater detail when I make a diagnosis of the RIA system in Poland and refer to foreign experiences. But now I would like to make a few more general comments, so below I will raise the issue of independence and the democratic legitimization of agencies performing RIAs, including the risk of regulation capture, the issue of motivation and stimuli of entities performing regulatory analysis, as well as relations between the political level (determining targets for public policies) and the government's administrative level (performing assessment of various regulatory alternatives).

The problem of regulatory capture by entities affected by regulations has been widely analysed in literature for years[22]. In this context – among other things – detailed research is performed on the impact of imperfect information characteristic of regulatory agencies on the effectiveness of the institutional solutions they draft – those entities have a much lesser knowledge, e.g. on the industries they intend to regulate than the companies operating in those sectors. On the other hand, however, – and this has been stressed in recent years – the issue of informational asymmetry may take place between government agencies responsible for RIA and a government's political level. In this case, these are regulatory agencies that have more complete information about the subject of regulation than the politicians defining the targets for public policies. On the other hand, there is an observable and quite unambiguous trend to make units performing RIA largely independent from current government actions, particularly those involved in the creation of legislative solutions – the purpose is to avoid a situation where the evaluated is at the same time the evaluator[23]. So, this is where the problem of motivational agreement between regulators and politicians emerges.

21 E.g. C. Scott (2010): Reflexive Governance, Regulation, and Meta-Regulation: Control or Learning?, in: J. Lenoble, O. De Schutter (eds.): *Reflexive Governance: Redefining the Public Interest in a Pluralistic World*, Oxford: Hart, pp. 43–66.

22 Classic papers related to this issue include: M. D. McCubbins, R. G. Noll, B. R. Weingast (1987): Administrative Procedures as Instruments of Political Control, *Journal of Law, Economics, and Organization*, vol. 3(2), pp. 242–277; R. G. Noll (1989): Economic Perspectives on the Politics of Regulation, in: R. Schmalensee, R. Willing, *Handbook of Industrial Organization*, Amsterdam: North-Holland, pp. 1253–1287.

23 A. Dixit (1996): *The Making of Economic-Policy. A Transaction-Cost Politics Perspective*, Cambridge MA: MIT Press, p. 81.

An obvious benefit of the separation of a unit independent from the government to perform an assessment of draft legislative acts is the minimization of the risk of mental regulatory capture. The process aimed to make agencies of this kind independent is visible in many countries. It turns out, however, that even in the situation where an entity assessing regulations is autonomous, there is still a risk that the analysis will not be objective. Classic literature on the topic usually stresses that regulatory agencies may act for the benefit of regulated entities in exchange for defined material benefits[24]. But recently it is usually assumed that such capture is rare, at least in the case of highly developed countries, and a biased analysis of regulatory impact more often follows from information deficiencies on the part of the regulator, which are frequently related to manipulations performed by regulated entities – this is so-called information capture[25]. S. Davidoff also writes about social capture, where "These men and women may believe they are doing their best, but their worldview is affected by the people they interact with."[26]. A specific form of this social regulatory capture may be the fact that the regulators consider the interest of regulated entities to be identical with public interest. Still other researchers write about cognitive regulatory capture, i.e. a situation where "those in charge of the relevant state entity are internalizing, as if by osmosis, the objectives, interests and perception of reality of the vested interest they are meant to regulate"[27]. A detailed review of literature related to various types on immaterial regulatory capture is performed by D. Carpenter and D. Moss[28].

An interesting question is by how much the risks indicated above may be minimized when RIA is performed by an agency independent from the government. I define agency of this type broadly and understand by this term an entity not directly involved in the drafting of regulations, including the definition of their

24 M. E. Levine, J. L. Forrence (1990): Regulatory Capture, Public Interest, and the Public Agenda: Toward a Synthesis, *Journal of Law, Economics, & Organization*, Vol. 6, pp. 167–198.

25 This notion was introduced into literature by W. Wagner (2010): *Administrative Law, Filter Failure, and Information Capture*, Duke Law Journal 59 no 7 (April 2010).

26 S. M. Davidoff (2010): *The Government's Elite and Regulatory Capture*, DealBook, New York Times, June 11, 2010, http://dealbook.nytimes.com/2010/06/11/the-governments-elite-and-regulatory-capture [Access: 18.05.2016].

27 W. Buiter (2008): *Central Banks and Financial Crises*, in: *Maintaining Stability in a Changing Financial System* (proceedings of the Federal Reserve Bank of Kansas City Economic Policy Symposium, Jackson Hole, WY, 21–23.08.2008), p. 601.

28 D. Carpenter, D. A. Moss (2014): *Preventing Regulatory Capture. Special Interest Influence and How to Limit It*. New York: Cambridge University Press.

objectives, and not directly subordinated to those to whom the agencies drafting the regulations are subordinated. A possible example of this kind of institution is Dutch Actal (*Advisor Board on Regulatory Burden*). It is worthwhile pointing out that if in case of an independent regulatory entity any type of regulatory capture takes place, then the legislator – usually the government or parliament – will aim to subordinate (most frequently indirectly) the agency e.g. through the establishment of judicial control over its decisions[29]. As a result of actions of this kind, the RIA agency will issue rather negative opinions about a government's legislative proposals and will not suggest alternative change scenarios.

But on the other hand, even if the agency responsible for RIA functions correctly, it will still face the problem of its democratic legitimization. In the not too distant past some perceived entities of this type as constitutional anomalies, which cannot be described in terms of standard separation of powers[30]. However, recently, in line with a "non majority" democracy model, it is stated that achievement by those agencies of stronger democratic legitimization does not necessarily entail their politicization or even partisanship. G. Majone points out that the growth of the importance of independent regulatory agencies observed in recent years proves that contemporary societies are capable of legitimizing the functioning of these types of bodies of power not on the basis of political accountability, but more with reference to the level of their substantive competencies, transparency of operations, honesty, independence, as well as cohesion in action[31]. This independent "fourth regulatory power" gains in importance when we understand democracy in terms of rule of law, and not exclusively of the rule of majority, because then, independent regulatory agencies become an element of the democratic control system over those in power. Solidifying those reflections in the context of the topics addressed in this volume, it is beyond any doubt that the source of legitimization for an agency responsible for RIA must be its operation in accordance with the rules of professionalism, objectivism and other points as listed above. With regard to the regulations themselves, the perspective adopted here constitutes an incentive for a statement that a resolution to the problem of the lack of their legitimization does not necessarily involve further politicization of the process of their establishment, but rather their creation

29 See e.g.: J. Q. Wilson (1989): *Bureaucracy: What Government Agencies Do and Why They Do It*, New York: Basic Books.

30 See e.g.: C. Veljanovski (1991): *The Regulation Game*, w: C. Veljanovski (ed.): *Regulators and the Market*, London: Institute of Economic Affairs.

31 G. Majone (1996): *Regulatory Legitimacy*, in: G. Majone (ed.): *Regulating Europe*, London: Routledge.

on the basis of –among other things – a detailed RIA. I will address this issue once again further on in the paper.

Returning to the issue of the risk of regulatory capture by those responsible for the analysis of regulatory impact, these topics can be interestingly analysed with the use of papers studying multiprincipal agencies. It is particularly worthwhile here to reach for analyses by J. Tirole – the Nobel Prize winner in 2014, who successfully applies the economic analysis of business to studies on the internal dynamics of government functions. In a paper of 1994 he points out that many government agencies have a monopoly over the actions they pursue, which explains the difficulty with measuring their effectiveness. Moreover, it is frequently so that even the most sophisticated econometric analyses are not capable of estimating the impact of a given regulation on overall change of social welfare[32]. Tirole demonstrates that in a situation where a given decision of a government has multiple aspects and may impact on e.g. the condition of the natural environment, as well as on the manufacturing costs in a given economy sector, it is justifiable to create within the government a field of conflict between those who will assess the impact of the said regulation on the environment and those who will focus on its impact on business. Given such a situation, as Tirole demonstrates in his formal model, we will obtain more information about these two options than in the case when a single entity (a government agency) would have to analyse the two areas of regulatory impact on its own. A risk entailed by RIA decentralisation within a government is by growth in the likelihood of policy-makers receiving contradicting signals, e.g. arguments in favour of a regulation from people focusing on environment protection and those against the regulation coming from those who analyse its costs for business. On the other hand, “it is important to recognize, however, that RIA, even when operated well, is not a tool that substitutes for decision-making”[33]. It is RIA’s objective to provide comprehensive knowledge about regulatory impact, and consequently to improve the quality of debates within the government. I will return to these issues again when diagnosing the RIA system in Poland while formulating proposals for its modifications[34].

32 If it is so difficult to assess regulatory impact on welfare, then even more problematic will be the estimation of the power of impact of a given RIA system on a country’s wealth (see: Ch. Hood, R. Dixon (2015), *op. cit.*).

33 C. Kirkpatrick, D. Parker (ed.) (2007), *op. cit.*, p. 3.

34 Decentralization of RIA’s performance may influence the risk related to regulatory capture by interest groups external to the government, because their impact may in many

Another problem directly related to the aforementioned issue of regulatory capture is the fact that the political system does not create powerful stimuli for civil servants to make draft regulations that serve the common good. A. Dixit so describes the said issue: "[...] it is commonly observed that incentives for policymakers are quite low-powered; the marginal rewards for producing an outcome of greater value to society, or the marginal penalties for doing worse, are generally a very low percentage of the value added or lost"[35]. In this connection OECD countries made an attempt to introduce a pay per performance scheme for civil servants[36]. However, as it turned out attempts of this kind have usually failed, among other things due to difficulties in measuring the final benefits from civil servant's regulatory activities[37]. Moreover, overcoming such difficulties usually entails the necessity to bear prohibitive transactional costs.

A strategy that might contribute to the improvement of RIA quality is investing in competencies of agents[38]. In the majority of countries this process was coordinated by independent agencies performing RIA quality control. A good example of this would be the United Kingdom, Australia, and the Netherlands. In the latter country, Actal – an agency independent from the government and responsible for RIA, not only controls the quality of RIA coming from sectoral ministries, but also accompanies their officials at an early stage of RIA development. The example of the Netherlands is also interesting because in this country the first RIAs were relatively simple and consisted in estimation of the regulatory costs for business with the use of a standard cost model. Moreover, even today the Netherlands does not perform a detailed and in-depth regulatory assessment of all legislative proposals – only for the major ones. Actal is involved in a maximum of thirty assessments annually and they concern only the most important government legislative proposals. A similar approach is applied by Australia, New Zeeland, the United Kingdom, Ireland and the United States. This is a rational strategy, particularly taking into account the aforementioned problems with the pursuance of good quality RIAs. De Francesco and C. Radaelli indicate among other things that focusing on a small number of major RIAs usually reduces

---

cases enhance the contradicting signals reaching the government's decision-making centre.

35 A. Dixit, (1996), p. 94.

36 More on that topic in: OECD (2005): *Performance-related Pay Policies for Government Employees*.

37 Zob. np. E. Pilichowski (2009): Does Performance-Related Pay Work?, *Public Management Outlook*, vol. 30, pp. 1–17.

38 S. H. Jacobs (2007), *op. cit.*, pp. 25–16.

the risk that assessments will only be simple administrative exercises, with no influence over the political process[39]. Moreover, as indicated by the example of the Netherlands, a success of the RIA related only to a section of government activities may significantly contribute to the dissemination of this approach. In the Netherlands this concerned state policy towards certain undertakings; entrepreneurs themselves pressurised the government to use the approach to regulations affecting them as well as to other legislative proposals.

Describing the factors determining success in the introduction of the RIA system, it is worthwhile pointing out that in virtually all countries considered to be exemplary with regard to the operation of this mechanism, there is a visible strong involvement at the political levels of governments in the performance of assessments of legislative drafts. This minimises the risk of RIAs being simple administrative exercises, performed only to justify a previously made political decision. In countries where RIAs may lead to a conclusion like: "do not regulate and dispose of the legislative draft", RIA is always rooted in the political process. Wherever it is difficult to find examples of regulations abrogated as a result of their ex-ante assessment, the RIA process is usually of a strictly administrative nature. A good example of the evolution of the RIA system from a purely administrative tool to its association with real political process is provided by how regulations are assessed in the European Commission. The first change in the Commission's approach to RIA was already visible in actions undertaken by Günter Verheugen, the Vice President of the European Commission in the period between 2005–2010, who stressed many times that RIA must be of "political nature". The most recent actions of the European Commission in this area, described among other things in the *Better Regulation Package of* 19 May 2015, go in this direction and they strengthen even more the independence of bodies responsible for regulatory assessment, at the same time making it an important component of the legislative process. This purpose is served e.g. by the establishment of the Regulatory Scrutiny Board (RSB)[40]. One can expect – as Commission's officials point out in direct talks – that the RSB will be even more demanding in its assessments than that of the Impact Assessment Board it is supposed to replace. A negative opinion of the RSB will stop the legislative process within the European Commission. What is more, new regulations stipulate that

39 F. De Francesco, C. M. Radaelli (2007), in: C. Kirkpatrick, D. Parker (eds.): *Regulatory Impact Assessment. Towards Better Regulation?*, pp. 36–55.

40 See the detailed definition of its mandate in Art. 2.1. of the Decision of the President of the European Commission on the establishment of an independent Regulatory Scrutiny Board, Strasbourg, 19.5.2015, C(2015) 3263 final.

in the case of submitted legislative proposals it will be possible to appoint a tripartite panel for their assessment, composed of representatives of the European Commission, the European Parliament and of the Council. In summary, at the EU level the ex-ante regulatory assessment is heading towards strengthening the independence of the institutions responsible for this process accompanied by their stronger incorporation into the legislative process itself, already at its initial stage. If only regulatory impact assessment is performed at the early stage of regulation drafting, it is possible to strongly influence the shape of the regulations, including the abrogation of specific legislative drafts[41]. This is an important lesson for countries building their RIA system, including Poland.

In the context of the trend present in many countries to make agencies responsible for RIA as independent as possible from regulation drafters, it is worthwhile reaching for the British example, where on the one hand RIA quality is controlled at the stage of regulation drafting – with the Regulatory Policy Committee (RPC) being the responsible unit, but there is also ex-post control by The National Audit Office, being an equivalent of the Polish Supreme Chamber of Control. Although being outside the government and functioning as part of the Department for Business Innovation & Skills, RPC enjoys a significant independence, which follows among other things from the fact that its eight-person composition includes people being at the same time active in business, NGOs or in the academic world. They are aware that their activities manifested in the quality of regulatory reports, are subjected to a detailed analysis by the NAO, which strongly motivates them to work towards good regulation. However, even with reference to this system some criticism is voiced, and e.g. in its report of 2012 the OECD points out that it happens under the British system that RIA are sometimes of an illusory nature and serve the purpose of legitimising a purely political decision already made beforehand[42]. Accusations of this type are formulated not only against the British system, but also other systems, including that of the European Commission. My conversations with officials of various European agencies performing control over RIA systems suggest that –in their opinion – it is impossible to achieve a system capable of blocking a regulatory draft with high "political gravity". However, in such situations it is important to clearly communicate the information about assessment results, including the fact that a regulatory decision was made in spite of them.

41 See: OECD (2012).
42 *Ibidem.*

After the above presentation of the analysis of the operations of the RIA system from the perspective of conclusions made from the economy theory, and after invoking selected international experiences related to its functioning, in the next section of the paper I will focus on the central research question, i.e. to what extent is the RIA system in Poland an effective element of the process for formulating public policies.

A few remarks on the quality of governance in Poland

Before I start the evaluation of the operation of the RIA system in Poland, it is worthwhile making several comments on how public policies are formulated. Beyond any doubt, in recent years many tools have been implemented in our country that should improve the quality of the state's operations with regard to regulatory drafting – the practice of the performance of ex-ante and ex-post evaluations of various kinds of government programmes, including those financed from European funds have become widespread, while the number of government strategies has been reduced and solutions from the act on rules for pursuing developmental policy have been implemented. At government level, the RIA system has been strengthened, with regulatory reform programmes being regularly developed. The above has been largely forced directly or indirectly – through the so-called "soft" Europeanisation – by Poland's accession to the European Union. There would be no act on developmental policy, or such far-reaching popularisation of evaluation research, if it were not for the necessity to prepare the programmes governing the spending of funding transferred to Poland from the EU. In its recent report on an analysis of the effectiveness of the implementation of RIA mechanisms in various countries, the OECD writes about Poland: "Poland made significant progress in the implementation of RIA mechanisms"[43]. Nevertheless the system is still in need of a fundamental change, i.e. the transition from a tool with administrative and unfortunately perfunctory usage into that of being an important element, as well as at the political level of the entire legislative process[44].

If in this paper I am concerned with the issue of the quality of the public policy formulation process in Poland, with particular stress on the RIA system, I have to start with the statement that in the contemporary, interdependent world, it is the countries that pursue their economic policy under good governance and

43 OECD (2012), p. 19.

44 See: J. Górniak (ed.) (2015): *Ocena wpływu oparta na dowodach. Model dla Polski.* Warszawa: Akademia Leon Koźmińskiego, e.g. p. 173.

not a traditional governing framework that are more effective in the achievement of their objectives[45]. In other words, these are the countries that rely on the adaptive effectiveness of implemented regulatory solutions, which helps their economies to adjust well to swiftly changing external factors[46]. One may add that they are the countries, where those in power are aware of the challenges faced by the socio-economic system, and so apply strategic planning. The recent global financial crisis, combined with the still unresolved structural problems of the Eurozone, clearly show that the state and its policies do matter and we no longer ask only how much of the state should be in economy, but first and foremost what kind of state this should be, and how it should influence the socio-economic system[47]. This is the context in which we should view the transition in economic studies on regulations from simple assumptions of "deregulation" towards stressing the importance of "better regulation", which entails a general popularisation of proposals in favour of good governance and management of administrational operations[48]. When trying to apply these concepts to the assessment of the quality of economic policy formulation in Poland, it is worthwhile to more precisely define what the pursuance of such a policy is in the spirit of good governance. I propose the simple conceptualisation in the table below (See: Table 1).

In such a short paper as this it is difficult to analyse the economic policy of the Polish government in the context of the question of the features shortlisted in the table above. However, one should attempt to answer the question of whether this policy (and first and foremost the methods of its implementation) is closer to governing or good governance, or perhaps in some areas even the governing model is not pursued and the state only administers? If we look at the first feature of good governance, i.e. to what extent the government – through the making of relevant regulations – creates a structure of incentives for market game actors to attain objectives formulated beforehand, and to what degree it commands them to perform defined actions, it turns out that in recent years Poland has made some progress in the transition to the good governance model in this specific aspect thereof. First, as a result of the review of strategies and programmes, started back then by the government of J. Kaczyński, many of those outdated and undefined objectives have been eliminated. Then, as a result

45 World Bank (2001): *Building Institutions for Markets.*

46 See, e.g: D. C. North (1990), *op. cit.*

47 F. Fukuyama (2005), *op. cit.*

48 Those topics are discussed in detail in: J. Wilkin (2012): *Jakość rządzenia w Polsce: jak ją badać, monitorować i poprawiać,* Warsaw: WN Scholar.

Tab. 1: Comparison of the features of governing and good governance. Source: A modified Tab. 1 from: Wilkin, J. (2008). 'Badanie dotyczące stworzenia systemu wskaźników dla oceny realizacji zasady good governance w Polsce'. Warsaw: ECORYS Polska, p. 13.

Governing	Good governance
- stress on the effectiveness of enforcement of government's (state authorities') decisions; - domination of legal-administrative instruments in the enforcement of government's decisions; - small scale of the application of economic calculation in government decision-making and evaluation of such decisions; - high degree of the centralization of decision-making rights within the public sphere; - poor transparency of the methods of functioning of public authorities; - small scope of social participation in the performance of public functions; - performance of public functions mainly via state administration; - scarce potential for the society to vindicate the commitments assumed by the government; - monitoring, evaluation and assessment of regulations (if applied at all) remains in the government's domain; - domination of short-term perspective in the formulation of public policies.	- creation of conditions, mainly institutional ones, for the attainment of public objectives, both effectively and efficiently; - besides instruments of administrative nature, a wide application of economic instruments; - decentralization of decision-making rights in the public sector in accordance with subsidiarity principle; - use of public-private partnership and NGOs for the attainment of social objectives and delivery of public goods; - application of various methods to inform public opinion about activities of the public sector, particularly of the government; - social monitoring of the actions of the government (state) and creation of institutional conditions for vindication of commitments assumed by the government; - monitoring, evaluation and assessment of regulations applied widely and performed by entities largely independent from the government; - domination of long-term perspective in the formulation of the government's policies.

of the preparation of utilization of financing under the EU financial perspective 2007–2013, the act on pursuance of developmental policy was brought into force. Another major step was the building of the so-called new strategic order in connection with the next seven-year European budget. In this context one has to take note among other things of the preparation by the first government of D. Tusk of the Poland 2030 report on the most important long-term challenges faced by our country. In the intention of its authors it was in fact conceived as a supreme document defining the objectives and goals of all other strategies and operational programmes. Therefore, one can state that not only declaratively but also factually an attempt was made to build modern strategic governance at government level. Unfortunately this attempt was only partially successful – there is still no linkage between the objectives of the performance-based budget, programmes defining spending of European funds, or the regulatory actions of the government.

Moreover, inflation of programmes and strategies has taken place. It is true that there are fewer of such documents at government level than a few years ago – which is good, because this may improve the likelihood of their enforcement. On the other hand, however, there are more and more strategies emerging at the level of local government which are frequently poor quality documents, developed only owing to the formal requirements necessary to apply for European funds. And finally, although there are fewer of such government documents, they are often very broad and multifaceted papers, not infrequently of several hundred pages. But even bearing this in mind, "manual command" by the government of multiple aspects of the socio-economic system is presently performed to a lesser degree now than a few years ago. This also follows from the fact that as an EU member, Poland has quite limited possibilities to make interventions in many areas of economy, with the agricultural production sector being a prime example.

Another problem related to the quality of governance is the fact that the strategic system has largely assumed a life of its own and its influence over public debate and the political process is diminishing. One of the reasons underlying such a state of affairs is that government objectives are not hierarchical and the mechanisms of their implementation are deficient. Problems with the implementation of the performance-based budget, i.e. in fact with the dissemination of the methods of governance through objectives in the administration, demonstrate this quite well. In recent years there has been a regression concerning the interest of the political level in performance-based budgeting. Another unresolved problem is that the agenda of the government's actions is still dominated by that of a spending nature, which frequently leads to burying the structural problems of the Polish economy with EU funding. This in turn may indirectly contribute to the popularization of the opinion that the sole effective control over power is the mechanism of democratic elections at the cost of greater control over power by regulatory agencies[49]. Moreover, there is nothing to indicate

49 Here I am referring to the view of G. Majone, according to which decisions related to the redistribution of national income requires to a greater extent to be based on the will of the society as expressed in general elections than on measures of more regulatory

that sectoral thinking has been overcome in the Polish government administration[50]. In brief, one can state that although there has been some progress made in the transition into good governance with regard to the methods of attainment of the government's objectives, the current state of affairs is still not up to the challenges faced by Poland.

The RIS system in Poland and its role in the creation of public policies

After this, naturally, abridged reflection on the quality of the government's actions in the area of the formulation and pursuance of economic policies, the time has come for a more detailed analysis of the RIA system. In this analysis I will focus to a greater extent on the evaluation of the operation of the said system in de facto terms while devoting much less attention to how it is legally embedded de jure in the Polish system of governance[51]. To begin with, however, I need to make a few remarks in reference to formal rules of the RIA system. Its operations are defined in the rules of procedure of the Council of Ministers (Resolution No. 190 of the Council of Ministers of 29 October 2013), which in paragraph 3 of section 24 stipulates: "Before commencement of works on the development of a draft of a government document referred to in section 19 paragraph 1, hereinafter referred to as the "draft normative act", and of the draft assumptions of a draft bill, the applicant body evaluates the envisaged socio-economic effects". Then section 28 details this provision.

Additionally the body proposing a given legislative solution is obliged to make a regulatory test for assumptions underlying a normative act, "demonstrating the result of the assessment of envisaged socio-economic outcomes" (section 102, paragraph 1). Therefore both the draft bill itself, and its assumptions are assessed. Such an assessment is performed by the applicant body, most frequently by the sectoral ministry, and in particular cases RIA may be commissioned by the President of the Council of Ministers and done within the Chancellery of the President of the Council of Ministers (KPRM). What matters is that RIAs

---

nature, which could be to a greater degree entrusted to expert regulatory agencies (G. Majone (1996), *op. cit.*).

50 T. G. Grosse, Ł. Hardt (2010): *Sektorowa czy zintegrowana, czyli o optymalnej strategii rozwoju polskiej wsi*, Warszawa: Pro Oeconomia.

51 Here I am referring to well-known distinction between de jure and de facto institutions (see e.g.: D. Acemoglu (2009): *Introduction to Modern Economic Growth*, Princeton: Princeton University Press).

themselves are subject to evaluation by the head of KPRM (Section 32), who may turn to the applicant for correction, e.g. expansion, or ex-ante evaluation. This is an important mechanism, reinforcing the role of the central government in the RIA process. I will comment more extensively on this issue in a further part of the paper.

The rules of procedure of the Council of Ministers of 2013 also introduced the ex-post RIA mechanism. This issue is regulated by section 5 of the rules, according to provisions of which the performance of the assessment of a bill's functioning is not obligatory and may take place on the initiative of a member of the Council of Ministers or the Council may request such an assessment by itself. In each of such cases the assessment is developed by the sectoral ministry, within the area of competencies of which the given bill is. One of the main objectives of such assessments is the undertaking of potential corrective measures, e.g. taking the form of a bill's amendment. The quality of ex-post RIA is subject to control by the Council of Ministers. Similarly to the case of ex-ante RIA and regulatory tests, the central role in the process is played by the Department of Programming and Regulatory Impact Assessment. This unit performs not only control functions but also initiates important actions related to the entire RIA system, including training for civil servants, as well as taking part in the determination of the rules of operation of the said system.

Apart from the rules of procedure of the Council of Ministers, another major document organising the process of RIA development is: 'Guidelines for the performance of impact assessment and public consultation as part of the government legislative process' in the current version which was adopted by the government in May 2015. The guidelines are a kind of manual for those responsible for the development of ex-ante and ex-post RIA and regulatory tests. I evaluate this tool as being helpful for people preparing RIAs. On the other hand I am aware that its utility is dependent upon the competence of the people responsible for RIA, and this is an area where much is still to be done, something recognised even by KPRM officials themselves and in their report on the RIA system operation in 2013 they point out: "Analytical competences in ministries remain to be the bottleneck for RIA quality improvement". This is also confirmed by current representatives of KPRM.

Let us now have a look at some data illustrating the RIA system in action. In 2014 the Team for Government Work Programming in the KPRM refused to enter into the list of works of the Council of Ministers of two bill drafts/assumptions owing to the poor quality of the accompanying RIAs – this corresponded to 2 % of all submitted drafts (in 2013, 7 % were rejected). Entry into the list was delayed for 23 % of bills/assumptions, among other things owing to reservations that the KPRM had with relation to regulatory tests. In 2014 as part of inter-ministerial arrangements, the KPRM received approximately 150 draft/assumptions and bills and approximately 1250 draft regulations with a request to express opinions on them. It is difficult to unambiguously assess the fact of rejection by KPRM below 10 % of impact assessment studies. It seems that such decisions are made by the Team only in the situation of truly glaring shortcomings and in such a sense is quite surprising. On the other hand, such a low number of rejections may prove either that the quality of RIAs coming from sectoral ministries is improving, or that – and this is confirmed by representatives of the KPRM – the people responsible for performance of RIA are already in contact with the KPRM at the stage of their drafting. So looking from a de jure perspective at the RIA system it seems that significant progress has been made – RIA quality is improving and its authorisation by the legislative process is becoming more and more powerful (the new rules of procedure of the Council of Ministers).

Now the time has come for an evaluation of the actual effects of the operations of this system. And so to begin with one can raise a fundamental accusation that the RIA system encompasses only legal acts developed by the government while not covering the legislative proposals of MPs or the President. In other words, if the government is not interested in an insightful assessment of a given regulation, then it can submit the draft using a parliamentary path and evade the RIA requirements. What is more, a draft so proceeded upon does not have to undergo the strenuous procedure of social consultations. In the table below I present the number of draft bills submitted to the Parliament Speaker by the type of applicant.

The table below ignores drafts submitted by the President because first of all there were not many of them in the Polish Parliament of the 7th term, and secondly because Presidential bills as a rule are not "disguised" government proposals (See: Table 2). The high number of draft bills submitted via Parliament is notable – their number increased from 26 in 2012 to 68 in 2015. Even if we forego 2015, which was not a typical year due to Parliament's term ending then, still in 2014 there were as many as 58 drafts submitted by MPs. In the analysed period the total percentage of draft bills not requiring RIA performance fluctuated between 20 % (2011) to as much as 51 % in 2013. On average this corresponded to 42.9 % of all submitted drafts in the period under analyses. Therefore, in accordance with the methodology adopted in the rules of procedure of the Council of Ministers, RIAs concern only slightly over a half of the draft bills proceeded on in the Parliament. Private member's bills or those submitted by the Polish Parliament and Senate committees do not include RIAs.

Tab. 2: Number of draft bills submitted to the Parliament Speaker by applicant. Source: Own elaboration.

	2011	**2012**	**2013**	**2014**	**2015**	***Total***	
Group of MPs	1	26	66	58	68	*219*	
						Including*:	
						PO	105
						PSL	29
						SLD	20
						PiS	17
						Others	48
Parliamentary committee		3	9	7	13	*32*	
Senate		11	23	13	25	*72*	
Total	*1*	*40*	*98*	*78*	*106*	*323*	
Council of Ministers	4	93	94	122	117	*430*	
*non-CM**+CM*	*5*	*133*	*192*	*200*	*223*	*753*	
Non-CM(non-CM+CM)	*20 %*	*30.1 %*	*51 %*	*39 %*	*47.5 %*	*42.9 %*	

* I would deem a draft as submitted by a given political party if the rapporteur was a representative of such a party. PO stands here for The Civic Platform political party, PSL for the Polish Peasant Party, SLD refers to the Democratic Left Alliance, and PiS to the Law and Justice party.
** CM = Council of Ministers.

This obviously does not mean that their justification always lacks an analysis of impact upon the regulated matter, but they are usually superficial assessments and – naturally – hardly objective, because they are developed by the applicants themselves. There is, therefore, a huge gap in the RIA system at Parliament level. In many cases it is also highly likely –although this requires further research – that the Parliamentary path is chosen by the government intentionally to proceed on a draft bill faster, among other things by evading the requirement of social consultations and RIA performances. This thesis can be corroborated by the fact that a decisive majority of MP proposals were submitted by representatives of the PO-PSL coalition. Moreover, in many cases government materials were elements of the justification of private member's bills[52]. My interlocutors

52 G. Żmuda, P. Prokopowicz, W. Felcis, M. Król (2015): *Wykorzystanie oceny wpływu w procesie tworzenia polityk publicznych w Polsce*, in: J. Górniak (ed.) (2015), *op. cit.*, pp. 55–97.

also claimed that the very private member's legislative draft is frequently and wholly written within the government[53].

At the stage of parliamentary works on legal acts one more problem remains. In a decisive majority of cases, drafts submitted by the government are modified by amendments made in the Polish Parliament or in the Senate, and the latter - while frequently modifying the draft bill - are not subject to RIA procedure. In the context of ex-post RIAs there is another problem: an assessment of the impact of a bill as a rule is to be referred to estimates from ex-ante RIA, and the latter - in the context of amendments made to government drafts submitted in the parliament - may prove misaligned with the final tenor of the bill. The above does not mean that we should consider the initial ex-ante RIA as a document with no greater value, because even if the Polish Parliament significantly modifies government proposals, the information coming from the said RIA may still prove highly valuable for legislators. Moreover - and I will elaborate on this in recommendations - the value of RIA is not in the fact that it provides legislative drafts with estimates of their outcomes, but first and foremost in the establishment of a framework for the process under which a reflection can be made on the implications of a legal act - this is RIAs communicative usage. Such a system was successfully built within the government framework, although it still requires many modifications and improvements; but at Parliament level such a space for the analysis of the impact of legislative activities of Deputies and Senators has only just begun.

The problem indicated above is seen by experts but also by government representatives and employees of the Polish Parliament Analyses Office (BAS). Many claim that the analytical potential of BAS is not properly utilised and besides focusing on analyses of compliance of draft bills with the constitution and European law, the staff of BAS, similarly to people working on RIAs in sectoral ministries, should estimate the potential impact of legislative drafts. Moreover, my interlocutors point out that BAS officials should in such cases cooperate closely with the government administration responsible for the preparation of a given bill in the part related to RIA. This issue is seen by government representatives, who proposed I.B.6 action in the Better Regulation 2015 programme. The! "Development of recommendations underlying cooperation between the Government and Parliament of the Republic of Poland aimed to make

53 This is also confirmed by examples contained in the report: G. Kopińska, G. Makowski, P. Waglowski, M. M. Wiszowaty (2014): *Tworzenie i konsultowanie rządowych projektów ustaw*, Warsaw: Fundacja Batorego.

evidence-based law", whose description is as follows: "Recommendations will be developed for presentation to the Parliament of the Republic of Poland, and relating to cooperation between the Government and the Parliament as concerns the justification and creation of RIAs for private members' bills and amendments made at the stage of parliamentary works". And further on: "Development and implementation of the said recommendations will aim to bridge the existing regulatory gap, resulting in the absence of formal requirements to develop RIAs for the proposed parliamentary initiatives and for major amendments made during proceedings on draft legal acts in Polish Parliament and Senate committees". I agree with the change direction so proposed, but there still remains the problem of the absence of specific actions on the part of both government and Parliament in this area. I present proposals related to these issues in the recommendations.

Already in the theoretical part of this paper I have pointed out to the particular importance of the principles of independence and objectivism in the operations of the RIA system. The real issue here is that people assessing the legislative drafts must not be the same as those who are responsible for the drafting of the analysed regulations. At present the RIA system is almost fully located within the government framework and the accompanying analytical papers are rarely delegated outside. The said system is based on the one hand on the RIA units in sectoral ministries, and on the team of analysts in the KPRM, which is – among other things – a backup for the Team for the Programming of Government Works, on the other. A recurring problem in talks with people responsible for RIA in the ministries is that according to them their work frequently has no relevance for legislative process. This is true in some units to the extent that those officials do not know if their remarks eventually had any influence on the shape of the proceeded regulation. However, there are cases when RIA content does matter, e.g. at the stage of inter-ministerial consultations. Although RIA quality has improved in recent years, still making a specific sectoral ministry responsible for RIA development makes those RIA elements that are far-removed from the ministry's competence (e.g. an analysis of environment protection issues is hardly the domain of the Ministry of Labour and Social Policy) the weakest RIA link. Perhaps it is worthwhile considering a solution whereby, e.g. an analysis of regulatory impact on the natural environment is always located in the Ministry of the Environment. In other words, a given ministry would coordinate the development of RIA for a regulation drafted by that ministry, but they would be other ministries that would be responsible for the preparation of particular elements of the said RIA. This would also partially solve the problem of regulatory analysis by people drafting the regulation in question or being organisationally close to them. I elaborate on this issue in detail in the recommendations.

A positive change in the RIA system in recent years has been the strengthening of the role of the KPRM, which was indirectly contributed to by the introduction of the mechanism of regulatory test, which is attached by the applicant to the assumptions of the draft bill. The quality of that document is monitored by the Chancellery. On the other hand, people responsible for RIA in the KPRM at the same time play the role of those who promote the method itself, they organise training for officials, and attempt to influence the assessment system itself. I have already covered this issue before. In my opinion the technical and substantive level of the team for RIA is high. Nevertheless, considering various dysfunctions of the entire system, and lack of strong support from the government's political level, their real influence over the legislative process is limited.

As paradoxical as this may sound, the RIA system itself to some extent replicates the operations of the so-called silo structure of the Polish administration. The issue at hand is that the system is poorly integrated with other mechanisms placed within the government framework and is aimed to monitor the implementation of public policies. Here I have in mind first and foremost the evaluation system, which by the way suffers from the same dysfunctions as RIA, i.e. among other things the fact that the evaluators are not independent from those whose actions they evaluate. In the context of ex-post RIA it is central for those two systems – RIA and evaluation – to overlap to the greatest possible extent. Making RIA performers independent from regulatory drafters has to be accompanied by an identical process related to evaluators, who should become more independent from those designing and implementing the programmes whose effects are evaluated. Perhaps it would be pertinent to combine at least in part the two systems organizationally.

A significant dysfunction of the RIA system currently in operation is the absence therein of a precise mechanism for formulating the criteria that define regulations requiring a more detailed assessment at the ex-ante RIA stage. One can, therefore, speak of a certain absence of RIA hierarchization in terms of the weight of the matter they refer to. A forerunner of changes in this respect may be the introduction in the Better Regulation 2015 Programme of the notion of in-depth impact assessment and the ensuing formulation of the following programme performance indicator in this respect: 'the number of relevant projects for which a detailed Impact assessment will be performed'. Still the Programme lacks the definition of such a type of assessment. The KPRM has not developed such a definition either yet. It is also missing from the guidelines for RIA drafting. According to the Better Regulation Programme, thirty such impact analyses are to be performed in 2015. The KPRM was named as the entity responsible for its attainment. This is a good direction, particularly since the assessments of major regulations should not be left up to applicants themselves as an external assessment by the KPRM, in the form of RIA developed by the Chancellery itself, would be justified.

After the above analysis of the operations of the RIA system in Poland, I would like to turn to a more general theses of this volume. By doing so, I will verify to what extent this example confirms the presuppositions we formulated in the introduction to this volume on the one hand, while on the other hand on this basis I will try to draw more general conclusions related to the system of the formulation of public policies, and consequently I will refer to what I have already written before making a few remarks on governance quality in Poland.

Crisis of the system governing the formulation of economic policy in Poland?

One of the hypotheses of our research project is a thesis related to the crisis of economic policy creation in Poland. This may come as a surprise for many, particularly in the context of positive economic growth in recent years, or the convergence of the Polish economy in relation to the EU, the proof of which might be the approximation of Poland's GDP per capita to the EU average. However, it seems that this growth is attributable largely to the powerful foundations of the free market, established back in the beginning of the systemic transformation, or Poland's accession to the EU, and to a lesser degree from a well-thought-out and innovative state policy. In the coming years, however, one may expect that the state will have a much greater importance for economic operations than it has had throughout the last 25 years. So far there has been widespread conviction – also among elites and experts – that the less of the state there is, the better. Nevertheless, recently this problem has been formulated differently and it is rather stated that a well-governed state is necessary and the dispute over its size should no longer fire up the debates. This revaluation of the discussion is triggered on the one hand by the Eurozone crisis, which has demonstrated that nation-states do matter and that they are frequently the last stronghold protecting the market system from collapse. On the other hand, public opinion is increasingly interested in such issues as growing inequalities or climate change, i.e. the area where state activity is standard. The above is compounded by changes in economy theory itself, where there is a widening conviction that political and economic spheres influence each other and that, as D. Acemoglu and J. Robinson claim: "[...] distribution of political power in society is the key determinant of its development"[54]. Perhaps nothing better illustrates the change in the awareness of economists themselves with regard to the role of the state in economy than the words of M. Friedman, who said at a conference summarizing the first ten years of post-socialist transformation: "It turns out that the rule of law is probably more basic than privatisation."[55] In his best-selling book on the origins of nations' wealth, E. Beinhocker states that: "The question is not states versus markets – it is how to combine states *and* markets to create an effective evolutionary system"[56]. The central question in the context of my analysis and earlier example is to what extent the method governing the formulation of economic policy in Poland allows for the building of a policy that would stimulate development in a situation when external uncertainty is growing and the expectations of the society towards the state are different than those at the beginning of systemic transformation? In other words, this is a question of to what extent Poland may become an entrepreneurial state[57]? In other words, the question is to what extent the method governing the formulation of economic policy will lead to the government being able to minimize the risk of Poland falling into the middle-income trap?

My analysis of the RIA system in Poland leads to the conclusion that one can speak of elements of crisis situations in the context of methods governing the state's creation of economic policy. The issue at hand is that the RIA system deficit I have identified may give rise to such a situation in the socio-economic system that would have features of a crisis. On the other hand, however, in recent years some positive changes have been seen in the RIA system, starting simply from legal institutionalization of the system, and ending with the introduction of a regulatory test, i.e. ex-post RIA. However, these changes – similarly to evaluation systems or performance-based budgeting – are frequently quite deceptive and have no actual impact on reality (in this case: on economic policy). Can one really speak of the actual significance of the RIA system, if the gross majority of draft bills are not covered with the said system (private members' initiatives and amendments to drafts submitted by the government introduced in the Parliament)? This is related to an even more general problem in a state's

54 D. Acemoglu, J. A. Robinson (2012), *op. cit.*, p. 392.

55 M. Friedman (2002), interview in: J. Gwartney, R. Lawson (2002): *Economic Freedom of the World; 2002 Annual Report*, Washington DC: Cato Institute.

56 E. D. Beinhocker (2006): *The Origin of Wealth. Evolution Complexity, and the Radical Remaking of Economics*, Boston MA: Harvard Business School Press, p. 427.

57 See the description of the entrepreneurial state in: M. Mazzucato (2013): *The Entrepreneurial State: Debunking Public vs. Private Sector Myths*, London: Anthem Press.

functioning, i.e. total escape from responsibility both among political elites, and government administration. The RIA system is a good example of this as the responsibility for RIA quality falls "somewhere" between sectoral ministries and the KPRM. A parallel situation takes place in a performance-based budget, where it is difficult to name a single entity responsible for tasks in a given function[58]. And here I do not mean responsibility only in de facto terms but also in de jure.

The Polish government, therefore, still faces the challenge of management pointed out in the introduction to this volume. As many "technical" issues related to the institutionalisation of the RIA process have already been successfully resolved, although its further improvement will require a greater involvement of the political component, including the latter's consent for increasing the independence of RIA performers. Only in this way can the elements of a crisis situation in the system be overcome. The fact that issues related to the improvement of the efficiency of the legislative process are not usually a topic of politicians' attention demonstrates that there is still much to do in this area. This is also a manifestation of a wider trend to ignore the long-term perspective in thinking about the state and its activities. This is verified by the current absence within the government framework of an institution pursuing in-depth analytical works targeted at the building of lasting growth foundations in the time perspective of not a single term in office, but even of several decades[59]. Moreover, as a result of the absence of a RIA system which has a real influence over the legislative process, politicians frequently make decisions addressing crisis symptoms in specific areas instead of addressing their underlying causes, while the latter may simply result from the fact that instead of the market (or civil society) there is too much interference from the state, and of poor quality in given areas. The true measure of the quality and effectiveness of the operations of the RIA system might be if "don't regulate" became the order of the day as a RIA result as this would finally put paid to legislation initiatives. I will write below how this system can be changed.

---

58 M. de Jong, Ł. Hardt (2011): *Implementing Good Governance Approach in Polish Central Government Institutions through Performance Based Budgeting*, Warsaw: Ernst & Young.

59 Until March 2006 there was the Socio-Economic Strategy Board in operation in the Council of Ministers, and in the period of the first government of D. Tusk – the Prime Minister's Strategic Advisers Team headed by minister. M. Boni.

The RIA system in Poland – change proposals

I have pointed out above that the fundamental problem in the operations of the RIA system in Poland is not the quality of impact assessments themselves (although some work in this respect is necessary too), but by the fact that the units responsible for regulatory impact analysis are frequently the same as those that draft the said regulations. This results in the legislative proposals coming from sectoral ministries being evaluated by the staff of the same ministries. Naturally such evaluations can hardly be objective. The only problem to a lesser extent is resolved by the transfer of part of the know how related to the RIA and the KPRM, because they are still performed within the government framework. Even if both in the ministries and in the KPRM the regulatory assessors are not the same people as those who draft the assessed regulations, still the former may have internalized the targets and world views of the latter (see: Davidoff 2010). We need, therefore, an organizational separation of regulatory drafters from evaluators. Foreign practices are worthwhile taking advantage of here. In the Netherlands major regulations are assessed by Actal (*the Advisor Board on Regulatory Burden*), an institution largely independent from the government, which acts on the basis of a powerful statutory mandate and is managed by a three-person council. Its opinions have a large importance for the conduct of the process governing assessments of the most relevant regulations drafted by the Dutch government. Similar regulatory assessment councils, modelled on Dutch know-how, were also established in Sweden (*the Swedish Better Regulation Council*) and in Germany (*the National Regulatory Control Council*). They also operate in the United Kingdom (*the Regulatory Policy Committee*) and the Czech Republic (*the Board of Deputy Ministers for Regulatory Reform and Effective Public Administration*), although in those countries they are not as independent from governments as the Dutch board.

The next stage in the building of the RIA system, therefore, should be by the appointment of an independent unit for regulatory assessment, e.g. resembling the Dutch Actal, which would perform RIA for the most important legislative proposals proceeded upon by the government, and would also evaluate RIAs performed in the framework of the state's central administration. In the case of the latter, it should have the right to turn to a sectoral ministry, e.g. when their quality is unsatisfactory. The role of such a regulatory board should not only be to control but also to support government units responsible for RIA. In other words, the board would take over part of the responsibilities in the area of RIA, which are currently assigned to the KPRM. This should not be a large institution, but rather one composed of about a dozen people cooperating intensively with experts and the academic community. It would also be justified for regulatory assessments made by them to be performed largely by independent entities, i.e. research institutes and universities.

As I have already mentioned, the proposal to appoint such an independent agency may give rise to fears of its democratic legitimization and its ability to influence processes that should be left to the Parliament[60]. Such fears, however, would be unjustified for several reasons. First, the agency will not be just another vetoing point in the system of power, because even its negative opinion to a specific legal act will not be capable of stopping it being proceeded along if such is the political will of those in power. In none of the countries where such institutions operate do they have the *power of veto*. Second, and this is indicated by examples of the United States, the power of influence of such agencies follows from their procedural legitimization (observance of the operating rules defined by the lawmaker) and substantial legitimization, i.e. provision to the authorities and the society of top quality analyses performed by independent experts guided solely by the imperative of the maximization of social welfare[61]. Third, activities of the agency should focus on public policies of a regulatory rather than those of a distributive nature. In the case of the latter, decisions should be left to the Parliament[62]. In such cases, it should be left to an independent regulatory agency to assess legislative proposals from the viewpoint of the extent to which they eliminate market imperfections in a given area. It is obvious that the difference between regulatory and intervention policies is not clear, seeing that in particular the former may cause changes in GDP redistribution. However, as already pointed out by K. Wicksell in the 19th century, it is the signum specificum of regulatory policy that its primary objective is to reduce market imperfections, with the redistributive consequences being only an accompanying result. Fourth, such an independent regulatory council would only analyse major legislative proposals, which would facilitate the following of its actions by relevant stakeholders. Remaining issues to be discussed include the procedure governing the appointment of such councils and governing bodies of regulatory agencies.

During an earlier analysis I also pointed to the problem of a parliamentary gap in the RIA system. In this context it is worthwhile considering the introduction, e.g. pursuant to the rules of procedure of the Polish Parliament, of the obligation to attach private member's bills to the assessment of their potential impacts.

60 I use the terms "regulatory agency" and "regulatory council" interchangeably.

61 G. Majone (1996), *op. cit.*, p. 291.

62 *Ibidem.*

The Polish Parliament Analyses Office (BAS) now largely holds the competences which enable the performance of this task. With reference to amendments brought in at the stage of parliamentary works to government bills, I suggest that BAS should also present at least an estimate evaluation of their impact. Drawing on Dutch experience, we could also consider the introduction of an obligatory nature of support by sectoral ministries to the performance of RIA's for private members' bills. In the case of particularly important bills, consideration should be given to the introduction of the institution of RIA panels, i.e. the final shape of RIAs would be discussed by three entities taking part in the development of impact assessments, i.e. representatives of the new regulatory council, as well as the sectoral ministry and Parliament. A similar mechanism is to be introduced at the European level, where such a panel will be composed of representatives of the Council Commission and the European Parliament.

All actions indicated above should be accompanied by transparency of the entire process. On the other hand, I am aware – and this was confirmed in my talks with representatives of both the European Commission and of the Polish government – that it is impossible to create a system that would be capable of precluding – through a negative evaluation of RIA quality – further proceedings along with projects enjoying support of the highest political level. The cause underlying such a state of affairs is simple – it is in the very essence of the democratic mechanism to implement solutions that win the support of the majority, including those for which RIA unambiguously indicates that their implementation will bring about many negative outcomes. However, it should be the role of a good RIA system to inform policy-makers and public opinion that such solutions are proceeded upon despite their envisaged negative impact on the socio-economic system. Even in the Netherlands, legislative drafts happen that are proceeded upon along the fast "political track", virtually without taking into consideration results of impact assessments, but in their case such units as Actal aim meticulously to inform parliament and public opinion in such cases. In this context it is also particularly important to mobilize expert communities and monitor government activities in the RIA area. These communities frequently analyse the final regulations coming from the government, while to a much lesser degree formulating their expectations towards the legislative system, so as not to generate solutions that would later encounter their criticism.

With regard to ex-post RIA, I suggest that assessment of the impact of major bills should be carried out by an independent regulatory council. Here I have particularly in mind those acts whose ex-ante RIAs were performed earlier by the council. With regard to any issues related to the form of cooperation of the new institution, I will leave this with the Supreme Chamber of Commerce, or Parliament for further analysis. By the same token, similar studies will be required for the method of combination of performance of ex-post RIA with the simultaneous process of evaluation of several government programmes, including in particular those financed from European funds. Experience of other countries, as well as expert analyses indicate that success in one area of reforming state administration towards the pursuance of evidence-based policy swiftly spills over to other areas of state activities. Therefore, the new regulatory council should not at once develop many impact assessments, but rather focus on major regulations.

Owing to the special nature of this paper I am unable to refer to all RIA system deficits in Poland, or to propose a complete list of recommendations aimed to change this system. But I am still convinced that the change proposals indicated above are central. Their delivery will also in a sense become a touchstone of to what extent Polish political and administrative elites will be able to successfully face the challenges of state governance. I elaborate on this thought in the summary.

Summary

This chapter of the volume is aimed to demonstrate that there are elements of crisis situations present in the system of designing economic policy in Poland, and – on a wider scale – generally in regulatory assessment mechanisms. The issue at hand is that regulations are not necessarily assessed objectively, and a lot of them are subjected to no impact assessment (among other things bills that are drafted by MPs themselves). Consequently we can hardly speak of the pursuance by the state of evidence-based policy. The above takes place despite major actions undertaken by the government, which aimed to improve the effectiveness of the system. Those actions only to a very limited extent, however, addressed the fundamental problems in the operations of the system, i.e. the dependence of regulatory assessors on those responsible for regulation drafting, as well as the parliamentary gap in the RIA system. Nevertheless, I do not think that what was successfully done was irrelevant, because on the basis of achievements so far a modern RIA system could be built. I have put forward a few recommendations in this respect, and the central issue is related to making the entities assessing regulations independent from the administrative centres responsible for their drafting.

Like a magnifying glass, the RIA system in Poland shows all the general weaknesses of the Polish state, such as viewing the outcomes of government actions only in the short term, or escaping from responsibility, making it very difficult to define responsibility for given areas of state operations. One may also speak of the certain illusory nature of major de jure systems in operation in the area of central administration, but having very small actual impact on government functioning. Here I mean the system governing the evaluation of programmes financed from European funds, and performance-based budgeting. Hence, the proper way to improve governance quality must be via making those tools become mechanisms of genuine influence on the legislative process and – in more general terms – on state governance.

References

Acemoglu, D., Robinson, J.A. (2012): *Why Nations Fail: The Origins of Power, Prosperity, and Poverty*, London: Profile Books.

Beinhocker, E.D. (2006): *The Origin of Wealth. Evolution Complexity, and the Radical Remaking of Economics*, Boston MA: Harvard Business School Press.

Buiter, W. (2008): Central Banks and Financial Crises, in: Maintaining Stability in a Changing Financial System (proceedings of the Federal Reserve Bank of Kansas City Economic Policy Symposium, Jackson Hole, WY, August 21–23, 2008).

Carpenter, D., Moss, D.A. (2014): *Preventing Regulatory Capture. Special Interest Influence and How to Limit It*, New York: Cambridge University Press.

Cichocki, M.A. (2015): *Unia w Unii? Strefa euro w przebudowie*, Nowa Europa. Przegląd natoliński, vol. 2(6), pp. 1–113.

Davidoff, S.M. (2010): The Government's Elite and Regulatory Capture, *Deal Book, New York Times*, June 11, 2010 http://dealbook.nytimes.com/2010/06/11/the-governments-elite-and-regulatory-capture [access: 18.05.2016].

De Francesco, F., Radaelli, C.M. (2007), in: Kirkpatrick, C., Parker, D. (eds.): *Regulatory Impact Assessment. Towards Better Regulation?*, Cheltenham: Edward Elgar, pp. 36–55.

de Jong, M., Hardt, Ł. (2011): *Implementing Good Governance Approach in Polish Central Government Institutions through Performance Based Budgeting*, Warsaw: Ernst & Young.

Dixit, A. (1996): *The Making of Economic Policy. A Transaction-Cost Politics Perspective*, Cambridge MA: MIT Press.

Dudzińska, A. (2015): *System zamknięty. Socjologiczna analiza procesu legislacyjnego*, Warszawa: WN Scholar.

Dunlop, C., Maggetti, M., Radaelli, C., Russel, D. (2012): The Many Uses of Regulatory Impact Assessment: A Meta-Analysis of EU and UK Cases, *Regulation & Governance*, vol. 6(1), pp. 23–45.

European Commission (2015): Better Regulation Guidelines, *COM* 215 final.

Friedman, M. (2002), interview in: Gwartney J., Lawson R., (2002): *Economic Freedom of the World; 2002 Annual Report*, Washington DC: Cato Institute.

Fukuyama, F. (2005): *State-Building: Governance and World Order in the 21st Century*, London: Profile Books.

Fukuyama, F. (2011): *The Origins of Political Order*, New York: Farrar, Straus and Giroux.

Górniak, J. (ed.) (2015): *Ocena wpływu oparta na dowodach. Model dla Polski*, Warsaw: Akademia Leon Koźmińskiego.

Greenwald, B.C., Stiglitz J. (1986): Externalities in Economies with Imperfect Information and Incomplete Markets, *Quarterly Journal of Economics*, vol. 101, pp. 229–264.

Grosse, T.G., Hardt, Ł. (2010): *Sektorowa czy zintegrowana, czyli o optymalnej strategii rozwoju polskiej wsi*, Warszawa: Pro Oeconomia.

Guesnerie, R. (1995): *A Contribution to the Pure Theory of Taxation*. Econometric Society Monograph no 25, Cambridge UK: Cambridge University Press.

Hood, Ch., Dixon, R. (2015): *A Government that Worked Better and Cost Less? Evaluating Three Decades of Reform and Change in UK Central Government*, Oxford: Oxford University Press.

Jacobs, S.H. (2007): Current Trends in the Process and Methods of Regulatory Impact Assessement: Mainstreaming RIA into Policy Process, in: Kirkpatrick, C., Parker, D. (ed.), *Regulatory Impact Assessment. Towards Better Regulation?*, Cheltenham: Edward Elgar, pp. 17–35.

Kirkpatrick, C., Parker, D. (ed.) (2007): *Regulatory Impact Assessment. Towards Better Regulation?*, Cheltenham: Edward Elgar.

Kopińska, G., Makowski, G., Waglowski, P., Wiszowaty, M.M. (2014): *Tworzenie i konsultowanie rządowych projektów ustaw*, Warsaw: Fundacja Batorego.

Laffont, J.J., Tirole, J. (1993): *A Theory of Incentives in Procurement and Regulation*, Cambridge MA: MIT Press.

Levine, M.E., Forrence, J.L. (1990): Regulatory Capture, Public Interest, and the Public Agenda: Toward a Synthesis, *Journal of Law, Economics, & Organization*, Vol. 6, pp. 167–198.

Lianos, I., Fazekas, M., Karliuk, M. (2014): The Diffusion of Impact Assessment Practices in Europe, *CLES Research Paper Series* 2/2014.

Majone, G. (1996): Regulatory Legitimacy, in: G. Majone (ed.): *Regulating Europe*, London: Routledge.

Maskin, E. (2007): Mechanism Design: How to Implement Social Goals? http://www.nobelprize.org/nobel_prizes/economic-sciences/laureates/2007/maskin_lecture.pdf [access: 18.05.2016].

Mazzucato, M. (2013): *The Entrepreneurial State: Debunking Public vs. Private Sector Myths*, London: Anthem Press.

McCubbins, M.D., Noll, R.G., Weingast, B.R. (1987): Administrative Procedures as Instruments of Political Control, *Journal of Law, Economics, and Organization*, vol. 3(2), s. 242–277.

National Audit Office UK (2002): Better Regulation: Making Good Use of Regulatory Impact Assessments, London: Report by the Comptroller and Auditor General, HC 329 Session 2001-2002, November.

Noll, R.G. (1989): Economic Perspectives on the Politics of Regulation, in: R. Schmalensee, R. Willing, *Handbook of Industrial Organization*, Amsterdam: North-Holland, pp. 1253–1287.

North, D.C. (1990): *Institutions, Institutional Change and Economic Performance*, New York: Cambridge University Press.

OECD (2005): *Performance-related Pay Policies for Government Employees.*

OECD (2009): *Regulatory Impact Analysis. A Tool for Policy Coherence.*

OECD (2012): *Sustainability in Impact Assessments. A Review of Impact Assessment Systems in Selected OECD Countries and the European Commission.*

Pilichowski, E. (2009): Does Performance-Related Pay Work?, *Public Management Outlook*, vol. 30, p. 1–17.

Stiglitz, J. (1991): The Invisible Hand and Modern Welfare Economics, in: D. Vines, A. Stevenson (eds.): *Information, Strategy, and Public Policy*, Oxford: Basil Blackwell.

Veljanovski, C. (1991): The Regulation Game, in: C. Veljanovski (eds.): *Regulators and the Market*, London: Institute of Economic Affairs.

Wagner, W. (2010): Administrative Law, Filter Failure, and Information Capture, *Duke Law Journal*, vol. 59 (April 2010).

Wilkin, J. (2008): *Badanie dotyczące stworzenia systemu wskaźników dla oceny realizacji zasady good governance w Polsce*, Warszawa: ECORYS Polska.

Wilkin, J. (2012): *Jakość rządzenia w Polsce: jak ją badać, monitorować i poprawiać*, Warsaw: WN Scholar.

Wilson, J.Q. (1989): *Bureaucracy: What Government Agencies Do and Why They Do It*, New York: Basic Books.

Woodruff, D.M. (2014): Governing by Panic: The Politics of the Eurozone Crisis, *LEQS Paper* No 81/2014.

World Bank (2001): *Building Institutions for Markets.*

Jan Fałkowski

Public finance crisis and state fiscal competences

Abstract: The author of this chapter analyses the problem of the sovereign debt crisis. Hence, the recent crisis events in the EU member countries illustrate this problem which is reflected forward herein. The perspective adopted by the author allows to look at that issue from the angle of state's weakness and strength, defined in relation to its fiscal capacities. It is proved in the text that the low level of those capacities may result from deliberate decisions of political elites. There are arguments presented in the chapter according to which those who are in power are mostly guided by political rationality which may often result in poor capability of the state to secure fundings inquired for sustainable economic growth. The government may want chiefly to maximize its chances for the re-election by departing from solutions which are optimal from economic parameters. The author discusses in the chapter the linkage between the level of fiscal capacity of the state and social behaviours of citizens, which can be crucial for resolution of the excessive debt problem, particularly in a long-term perspective. The analysis ends in reflections on consequences of various types of adjustments which states might want to introduce into their fiscal policies in order to struggle against sovereign debt crisis.

Keywords: sovereign debt crisis, state fiscal competences, state power, public finance crisis

Introduction

Turbulence related to the last financial crisis, whose beginning is usually set at September 2008, when the Lehman Brothers bank announced bankruptcy, indisputably entailed a lot of diverse consequences. One of them is certainly a change in the way of looking at the issue of excessive sovereign debt. Something that for many years had been an indispensable element of the economic landscape of such states as Italy, Greece or Belgium – i.e. the level of sovereign debt in relation to GDP fluctuating around 100 % or even exceeding this threshold – started to be universally seen as a factor destabilizing the functioning of the economic and political order in place. What is important, in view of advancing globalization and integration processes, is that the related aftershocks began to be perceived not only in relation to particular countries, but perhaps – first and foremost – also on an international scale. This can be seen glaringly in the example of the European Union (EU).

In such a context it should come as no surprise that the problem of excessive sovereign debt (in relation to GDP) became one of the key points of reference in many discussions on the recent crisis[1]. Some opinions see the problem of excessive sovereign debt as the main driver of the Eurozone crisis[2]. Although one can certainly argue with such a statement[3], it is indisputable that excessive sovereign debt is a very significant problem, which both particular EU member states and the Community itself have to tackle. Moreover, bearing in mind the difficulties that some EU member states have with reducing their debts down to sustainable levels (periodically even with its servicing), it seems justified to put forward a thesis that besides crisis of trust in financial markets and crisis of trust in political elites, Europe is also currently struggling against a public financial crisis[4].

---

1 See inter alia: A. Alesina, F. Giavazzi, (eds.) (2013): Fiscal policy after the Financial Crisis, Chicago: The University of Chicago Press; G. Akerlof, O. Blanchard, D. Romer, J. Stiglitz, (eds.) (2014): What Have We Learned?: Marcroeconomic Policy after the Crisis. Cambridge: MIT Press; C. Cottarelli, P. Gerson, A. Senhadji (eds.) (2014): *Post-crisis fiscal policy*, Cambridge: MIT Press.

2 Addressed and accompanied by a discussion in: R. Baldwin, F. Giavazzi (eds.) (2015): *The Eurozone Crisis: A Consensus View of the Causes and a Few Possible Solutions*, London: CEPR, Vox.eu.org eBook, www.voxeu.org/sites/default/files/file/reboot_upload_0.pdf [access: 24.05.2016].

3 Identification of the present Eurozone crisis exclusively, or first and foremost, with the situation of public finance seems erroneous. Presentation of argumentation in favour of such position definitely goes beyond the framework of this paper. Nevertheless it is worthwhile stressing that even a casual analysis of statistics illustrating the state of public finance in the countries most affected by the crisis forces one to look more cautiously at such formulation of the issue. To illustrate those doubts one can e.g. contrast the situation of Belgium or Italy, which entered the crisis with sovereign debt to a GDP ratio at the level of 100 %, with the situation of Ireland and Spain, which recorded public debt to a GDP ratio at the level of 40 % at that time. While the former two countries did not have to take advantage e.g. of aid from the IMF, then the latter two had to resort to such aid (see inter alia: J. Fałkowski (2013): *Problem finansów publicznych w krajach UE z punktu widzenia nie tak odległej historii oraz kilku teorii nowej ekonomii politycznej*, in: T.G. Grosse (ed.) *Między polityką a ekonomią kryzysu strefy euro: Rozważania o teorii kryzysu w ekonomii politycznej*, Warsaw: Uczelnia Łazarskiego, pp. 41–59; see also: Baldwin and Giavazzi, 2015).

4 Addressed and accompanied by a discussion in: N. Roubini, S. Mihm (2011): *Crisis Economics: A Crash Course in the Future of Finance,* London: Penguin Books; R. Rajan (2012): *Linie uskoku. Ukryte rysy, które wciąż zagrażają światowej gospodarce.* Warsaw: Kurhaus Publishing.

In this chapter we also try to look closer at the said crisis. We will look at it from the angle of two basic aspects. First, our attention is focused on the so-called fiscal capacities of the states, which shape a states' ability to obtain funding for the performance of tasks set for their institutions[5]. In this way, such competencies can be viewed as key elements contributing to the risk of the emergence of a public financial crisis. They also define the potential actions a state can undertake with a view to reducing excessive debt problems. The other point of reference in the discussion presented herein, is the potential consequence entailed for economic growth prospects by various adjustments in fiscal policy brought about by pressure to bring public finance under control.

Focusing attention on the aforementioned threads may be justified by the fact that for a very long time both have been side-tracked in the discussion on the sovereign debt crisis in Europe. What is interesting is that, this situation continued despite some existing theories which assign high importance both to the problem of fiscal capacities and of the potential effects of various adjustments in fiscal policy as concerns the understanding of the problem of excessive sovereign debt. In this chapter we will try to indicate the potential reasons underlying such a state of affairs.

Owing to the constraints of space, in the discussion pursued herein we focus mainly on the challenges and adjustments defined at the level of a given country. Therefore, being aware of the related simplifications, we refer to a much lesser degree to the situation of the EU as a whole[6]. Nevertheless in some places we try to draw attention to basic dependencies governing relations between particular member states, as well as relations between national and EU institutions.

The optics we have adopted here is determined mainly by theories developed under a (new) political economy. This can be explained mainly by the fact that fiscal policy is greatly conditioned by political institutions in place. The latter will largely set out the potential leeway for policy-makers wishing to introduce certain reforms. In such a context, an approach looking for possible links between the areas of politics and of economy seems only natural.

---

5 See further on in the paper; addressed in: J. Migdal (2001): *State in Society: Studying How States and Societies Transform and Constitute One Another*, Cambridge: Cambridge University Press; T. Besley, T. Persson, (2011): *Pillars of Prosperity: The Political Economics of Development Clusters*, The Yrjö Jahnsson Lectures, Princeton: Princeton University Press.

6 Therefore, we are largely ignoring here a discussion on the consequences of the current crisis for further integration stages in the form of either a fiscal or political union.

Just as in the remaining parts of the book, as well as in this chapter we try to view the addressed issues from the angle of four basic challenges, which – in the face of the crisis – define both basic areas requiring activity on the part of political elites, and the instruments those elites might use to achieve the adopted goals. These challenges are: the developmental challenge, structural challenge, management challenge, and the challenge of inadequate political legitimization (addressed and accompanied by a discussion in chapter 1 of this volume). In a certain simplification, the linkage between these challenges and the case analysed in this chapter can be summarized in four points. First, any attempts aimed to resolve the problem of excessive sovereign debt in EU member states have to include deployment of structural reforms, because the crisis we are observing now has not been caused by the business cycle[7]. What remains unanswered is the question that to what extent will the introduction of those reforms entail in order to meet the structural challenges solely at the national level, and to what degree will it require adjustment measures at the EU level (expressed e.g. by a search for more effective instruments to support the process of convergence between member states). Second, if the reforms are to prove effective, they have to be introduced on the basis of efficient methods for coordination of efforts taken by both various social actors (citizens, banks, or entrepreneurs), and by the state. This obviously underlines the necessity to meet the management challenge, i.e. to find mechanisms that on the one hand will minimize the transaction costs of a search for consensus related to ways of exiting the crisis, while on the other hand, also creating sustainable foundations limiting the risk of similar situations repeating themselves in the future. Just as before, it is worthwhile asking about the extent to which the current situation requires a correction of coordination methods only at the national level, and to what extent a similar correction is needed at the EU level. Third, if they are to be effective, any structural reforms will require political legitimization. It can hardly be imagined that solutions forced against social expectations could be self-sustainable and enforceable in the long run regardless of how we assess them from the angle of dry economic criteria. Fourth, it can hardly be imagined that the meeting of a political legitimization challenge could be possible without prior stimulation of economic growth, because the costs and benefits of structural reforms would not be uniformly distributed. The creation of alternative sources for the accumulation of

7 See: G. Akerlof et al. (2014).

wealth and compensatory transfers must be financed from somewhere. Meeting the growth challenge will be necessary here, at least for these two reasons[8].

Below we attempt to present these dependencies in a more detailed way. We start with a brief discussion of three possible methods for the resolution of the excessive sovereign debt problem. In the case of one of them a key role will be played by the fiscal capacities of the states. We will devote some attention to them in the next part of the paper. Then we will look at the effects to which various adjustments in fiscal policy may lead to.

Three ways to resolve the excessive sovereign deficit problem

In the context of the discussion invoked above it should come as no surprise that a vast majority of efforts aimed at exiting the crisis afflicting the European Union focuses on the resolution of the problem of excessive sovereign debt. Such a perspective naturally directs attention onto necessary adjustments that should be implemented by states particularly stricken by the problem of excessive sovereign debt (in relation to GDP). Although the discussion draws attention to several issues, the bulk of proposals concerns corrections which EU member states should introduce as part of the fiscal policy they pursue.

In a certain simplification, the resolution of the excessive sovereign debt problem may take place on the basis of three paths (or possibly of a combination of steps from each of them). First, considering the fact that debt is calculated in relation to GDP, we can hope for an increase in economic growth rate. Therefore, the willingness to meet the challenge of growth can be viewed not only as an indispensable element of various anti-crisis strategies in a larger sense, but also as something permanently accompanying policy-makers (at least in rhetoric) in their endeavours to reduce excessive sovereign debt. The importance of economic growth for sovereign debt level is clearly visible in the example of Greece in the period 2008–2013. Throughout the entire period the Greek GDP went down on average by 5 % per year. At the same time sovereign debt rose from approximately 110 % GDP to almost 180 % GDP. It is worthwhile stressing that all of this took place despite significant reforms introduced in Greece from the onset of the crisis. In the years 2009–2014 their effects were manifested for example, in the form of a reduction of the budget deficit level from 15 % GDP to

---

8 It is worthwhile remembering that economic growth will help to limit the problem of excessive sovereign debt also mechanically. Sovereign debt is calculated in relation to GDP. Increasing the denominator in this fraction, will make the entire fraction smaller. We will refer to this thread also in a further part of the paper.

2.5 % GDP, a 28 % employment reduction in the public sector, or improvement of the position in Doing Business ranking by 48 places (from the 109th position in 2010 to the 61st in 2015)[9].

The second method to resolve the sovereign debt problem is based on corrections introduced into a state's spending policies. On the one hand, in Keynesian terms, one can look for sources to trigger economic growth in the stimulation of aggregated demand through government spending. On the other hand, more in neo-liberal terms, one can aim to reduce spending leading to the balancing out of the state budget. A good illustration for the application of the latter variant is covered by the example of austerity packages introduced in South European countries. Among many opinions in the discussion on the feasibility of the implementation of solutions of this type one can find both those claiming that this step was absolutely necessary and ones criticising not only the scale of introduced adjustments but also the speed at which they were made. From our perspective it is worthwhile drawing attention particularly to one thread emerging in this debate. It concerns the political legitimization for steps undertaken towards the introduction of austerity packages both at the level of the European Union itself and in particular member states. In this context the following aspect attracts particular attention. South European countries introduced reforms aimed at restoring fiscal discipline under pressure from other EU states. Under such an arrangement it is worthwhile reflecting on how much the shape of those reforms was designed in the gaining of political legitimization for actions of the political class with the southern countries in mind, and how much was aimed at gaining political legitimization by those in power in other EU states. Theoretically those two perspectives do not have to be mutually exclusive. Bearing in mind, however, the diversity of the goals and needs of particular EU states, which manifested themselves when the crisis started, the possibility to achieve political legitimization in either context seems quite doubtful. A good illustration of these divergences can be seen in the contrasting goals in the creation in South European countries of a proper institutional framework conducive for the maintenance of long-term fiscal discipline, with the need to satisfy in short-term (at least part of) the claims of creditors from other EU states holding Greek or Spanish debt securities. A potential conflict emerging against

---

9 Data about economic growth and sovereign debt come from Eurostat. Data on employment come from a European Commission's report "*The Second Economic Adjustment Programme for Greece, Fourth Review April 2014*". Data related to budget deficit level come from OECD. See: K. Whelan (2015): *The FT Lets Itself Down Again: Francesco Giavazzi on Greece*, http://karlwhelan.com/blog/?p=1550 [access: 24.05.2016].

such a background certainly challenges the effectiveness and sustainability of the solutions proposed under (successive) austerity packages. The results of elections in South European countries, which were held during the crisis and which largely undermined the legitimization for the anti-crisis policy pursued earlier, seem to confirm this quite well. As an example one can invoke here the election defeat of Mario Monti's camp in Italy (and the success of the Five Star Movement), the success of Greek Syriza or the recent election results in Spain, where the Podemos party received support of slightly over 20 %. The development of a new political consensus (both in the framework of the EU and of particular member states) regarding a further strategy for coping with the crisis, emerges as an urgent necessity for the near future. This will naturally be related to the problem of finding mechanisms that would help to coordinate the effective enforcement of agreements reached under such consensus.

And finally, the third method to resolve the excessive sovereign debt problem is the application of actions aimed to increase revenues into the public purse. This may take place through the introduction of new taxes, the optimization of current rates of existing taxation forms or through the improvement of tax collection efficiency under the existing system. Similarly, in the case of a path based on changes introduced into spending policy, the crisis resolution will largely boil down to the meeting of such challenges as: structural, management and political legitimization. Adjustments introduced as part of tax policies are frequently treated as quite obvious and relatively simple to implement (as requiring only a parliamentary majority to push through changes in the taxation system[10]). However, in reality they may entail unseen complications and consequences. While one may assume that in the face of a crisis (including sovereign crisis) those in power will aim at the maximization of budget takings, whose efforts can be implemented to various degrees[11]. The current Eurozone crisis has revealed this quite clearly. This might suggest that states in need of reform may greatly differ with regard to their fiscal capacities, which will determine their ability to acquire the funding to finance the required spending[12].

---

10 Formation of such majority does not have to be easy but once it is in place then the introduction of even very controversial bills is not particularly difficult. In such a sense, only a single boundary condition is required.

11 At this stage we leave aside specific motivations that may underlie such efforts.

12 Those capacities are an important component of the power of the state (see: J. Migdal (2001); T. Besley, T. Persson (2009): *The origins of state capacity: Property rights, taxation, and policy.* American Economic Review, 99, pp. 1218–1244). The other element distinguished here is the so-called legal capacity, defining state capacity to prevent the emergency to resolve social conflicts through good definition and safeguarding of

Fiscal capacities

Generally speaking, the fiscal capacity of a state refers to the capacity held or owned by a given state with regard to the effective acquisition of funding used to cover the expenditure planned by those in power. Also worth mentioning is that fiscal capacity is not limited exclusively to one-off maximizations of current budget takings or the application of possibly the highest tax rates[13]. It concerns the potential capacity to obtain required funding to finance specific plans made by those in power[14]. In an oversimplification, the fiscal capacity of a state can delineate the borders of the mobilization of financial resources by the state through the use of fiscal mechanisms. In this sense it is seen both from the angle of the capacity the state has to raise taxes, and from the angle of the capacity it has to counteract the behaviour of any citizens wishing to evade the payment of taxes. Viewed differently, the former of these perspectives will boil down to the level of legitimization of power and the leeway those in power will have when making decisions on increasing the fiscal burdens imposed on the society. The latter can be associated with the efficiency of how the system may take control over the way citizens make settlements with fiscal authorities.

In the context of the potential importance that the level of fiscal capacities of the states may have for the resolution of the problems of excessive sovereign debt, it may be slightly surprising that the discussion held so far on the crisis in Europe has largely neglected this thread. This certainly does not mean that it was ignored altogether. For example, problems with the collectability of taxes, which is an important component of the fiscal capacities of states, emerged in comments related to the situation in Greece, Italy and Spain. This may be supported by articles published on that topic e.g. by the BBC, Bloomberg, or the Wall Street Journal pointing out to losses suffered by the Greek, Spanish and Italian governments owing to universal tax evasion by local citizens. The only question is, to what degree did those issues become featured in the debate in order to convert into a subject of deeper reflection? Probably not to a high

---

property rights. Being aware of involved simplifications, particularly in view of the fact that fiscal and legal capacities interact with each other, in this paper we are focusing exclusively on the former.

13 Although in empirical works the level of tax rates or current budget takings from taxes are frequently used for measurement of fiscal capacity (see: e.g. T. Besley, T. Persson (2011)).

14 J. I. Herbst (2000): *States and Power in Africa: Comparative Lessons in Authority and Control.* Princeton, NJ: Princeton University Press.; J. Migdal (2001); T. Besley, T. Persson, (2009).

degree at all. Most discussions failed to go beyond a simple statement that "South European countries have tax collectability problems". Consequently, although noticed, this problem was treated as something to be faced in the future, while at the time, focusing only on other areas to lower the debt level[15].

In view of the available data, such a formulation of the issue seems quite short-sighted. For example, calculations for Greece estimate that the problem of unregistered income in the year 2008–2009 alone amounted to at least EUR 29 billion[16]. This in turn translated into a fiscal gap amounting to a record value of almost 32 % of high budget deficit in 2009, which amounted to as much as 15 % of the Greek GDP. Also quite revealing are the available estimates related to the size of the grey economy that place Greece or Italy, i.e. states where sovereign debt servicing issues are extremely painful, at the very top of the ratings among OECD countries[17].

Absence of a wider discussion referring to the significance of fiscal capacity in the context of a search for a resolution to the problem of excessive sovereign debt is also surprising against the background of existing theoretical papers. The latter afford a perception of fiscal capacity as one of the basic factors determining economic growth and development[18]. As argued before, the latter seem absolutely central for the reduction of the sovereign debt problem, particularly in the long term. A positive relationship between the level of fiscal capacity and economic growth can be justified in at least two ways. On the one hand, one can point to the importance of economic growth of investment spending financed by the state from tax-generated funding. On the other hand one can see that various forms of taxation are characterised by various degrees of inefficiency. Without going into greater detail, one can assume that a higher level of fiscal capacity should result in a transition from more to less inefficient taxation forms. This should in turn lead to a reduction of social loss with an enhancement of growth potential in a given society. Additionally it is worthwhile pointing out that by

---

15 Difficulties with introduction of the thread of fiscal capacity into a serious debate are also seen in the example of slim response to proposals of Van Rompuy and others, raising the issue of fiscal capacity that might be defined at the EU level (see:. H. Van Rompuy, J.M. Barroso, J.C. Juncker, M. Draghi (2012): *Towards a Genuine Economic and Monetary Union. Report of the Four Presidents*, 5 December).

16 N. Artavanis, A. Morese, M. Tsoutsoura, (2015): *Tax Evasion Across Industries: Soft Credit Evidence from Greece*, unpublished manuscript.

17 See inter alia: J. Slemrod, (2007): Cheating Ourselves: The Economics of Tax Evasion. *Journal of Economic Perspectives*, 21(1), pp. 25–48.

18 See inter alia: T. Besley, T. Persson, (2011).

defining the state's potential to generate budget takings, fiscal capacity will also determine the potential set and the effectiveness of the reforms that might be potentially introduced with a view to reducing the debt.

Bearing the above in mind, it is worthwhile asking why the fiscal capacities of some states are so low. Referring this fact to the public finance crisis and the necessity to find a swift solution, largely via political decisions, it becomes of particular interest as to what extent the poor level of fiscal capacities can be associated with deliberate actions of the political class. In this context one may ponder on any circumstances in which those in power may perceive investments in state fiscal capacity as contradictory to their particularistic interests.

Political rationality versus economic rationality

The first issue worthwhile raising here concerns the genuine willingness of the political class, if any, to increase the level of state fiscal capacities. From such a perspective, the central importance appears to be the motivation of those in power to reinforce state fiscal capacity, particularly in a period not marked by any kind of crisis[19].

Naturally, a lack of investments in fiscal capacity can be explained by the absence of awareness among political elites of the need for such actions. However, putting this explanation aside it is worthwhile asking if poor state fiscal capacity may directly follow from deliberate decisions of the people in power. Providing an answer to this question seems highly relevant insofar as it provokes one to ask more questions. In this context e.g. the question arises of how effective and sustainable the resolution of a crisis (in this case one related to excessive sovereign debt level) is possible under the rule of people who did not have the sufficient motivation to create in advance proper mechanisms to enable the undertaking of such actions *ex post*. If we assume that poor state capacities with regard to the acquisition of funds into the budget resulted from the deliberate decisions of those in power, then a resolution of the crisis may require either a radical change of preferences among those in power, or a radical change within the political elite. In other words, it is worthwhile asking to what extent the current excessive sovereign debt crisis has not become the beginning of a crisis of trust for the political elites of Europe.

19 Being in power may on its own enforce such actions during crisis under *ad hoc* principle.

Such a view is highly interesting insofar as it affords a different perception of the political successes of the Italian Five Star Movement, Spanish Podemos or Greek Syriza. By appealing to its potential constituencies for support in elections, each of these movements have pointed out that people/parties in power so far have not managed to cope effectively with the problem of the ever-widening income inequalities and uneven burden of citizens with the costs of anti-crisis policies. What matters from the perspective of the discussion pursued herein, is that both issues may be associated with the process of the creation and utilization of fiscal capacity in a given country.

With regard to arguments in support of a thesis associating the poor level of state fiscal capacity with the deliberate decisions of the political class, there are at least a few. In a decisive majority they are based on an observation that the rationality of politicians designed mainly to keep their power may not match the economic rationality determined by economic challenges. Three of these arguments are particularly worthwhile for deeper scrutiny.

The first of them refers to the classic problem of fierce rivalry between the ruling party and the opposition. Here we fall back on the assumption that those currently in power evaluate the consequences of their decisions not only from the short-term perspective, but also from the perspective of allowing for the coverage of a period beyond the coming elections. Consequently, we assume that by making specific political decisions, those in power try to assess how much their current actions will facilitate or hamper ruling for their political rivals if the latter assume power after the next elections. In other words, an important parameter in the utility function of those in power is not only the parameter measuring the direct effect of the decisions being made but also the parameter estimating how much such a decision will bring a potential benefit to those who will rule in the future.

In this context, what is worthy of attention is mainly the fact that incurring the costs of investments in a fiscal capacity by those in power – if they lose such power during the next elections – it may generate two kinds of benefits for the opposition. First, this will give them potentially greater spending leeway, which can be used for redistributive transfers towards those constituencies that have not had clearly defined political preferences so far. As a consequence, it may become more difficult to return to power during the next elections for those who made the decision on investments in a fiscal capacity. Second, the camp taking over power may use a high level of fiscal competence for the redistribution of incomes and reform costs in such a way that the main burdens are transferred chiefly onto the voters who traditionally support the previous government. Consequently, after taking over power the opposition will have the opportunity not only to pursue a political rent but also instruments for the abuse of power with a view to reducing the wealth of a selected group of citizens[20]. This may additionally hamper to those in power return to power in the first period, whenever possible depleting their political and economic resources.

The second argument supporting the thesis that political elites may deliberately abstain from investing in fiscal capacity may also be associated with models analysing the factors which improve the chances of the current ruling party to remain in the power, although here the mechanism is different than the one discussed earlier. The assumption we will use here is that investments in fiscal capacity constitute optimal policy from the viewpoint of society at large, particularly when this problem is viewed from a long-term perspective. In such a case, we may then perceive the absence of such investments as an ineffective situation, which will not enable the full use of the potential embedded in a given society. In this context valuable conclusions can be afforded by papers demonstrating that political elites wishing to remain in power may deliberately aim to create and maintain ineffective solutions. If we take into account recent papers analysing the motivations of politicians to make specific decisions during their term in the office, many of them indicate that by wishing to maximise their re-election chances, political elites do not necessarily have to seek choices that are optimal from the viewpoint of society at large[21]. What is important is that, political decisions being made may be disadvantageous not only for the constituencies supporting the opposition[22], but also for the electorate which supports

---

20 See; literature dedicated to the problems of a predatory state or the issue of the grabbing hand policy of a government favouring the interests of a narrow social group. See among others: D. C. North (1981): *Structure and Change in Economic History*, New York: Norton; M. Olson (1982): *The Rise and Decline of Nations: Economic Growth, Stagflation, and Social Rigidities*. New Haven: Yale University Press; J. B. DeLong, A. Schleifer (1993): Princes and Merchants: European City Growth Before the Industrial Revolution, *Journal of Law and Economics*, XXXVI, pp. 671–702; D. Acemoglu, S. Johnson, J. Robinson (2005): The Rise of Europe: Atlantic Trade, Institutional Change and Economic Growth, *American Economic Review*, 95(3), pp. 546–579; R. Myerson R. (2008): The Autocrat's Credibility Problem and Foundations of the Constitutional State, *American Political Science Review*, 102, pp. 125–139.

21 See e.g.: P. Krusell, J.V. Rios-Rull (1996): Vested Interests in a Positive Theory ofStagnation and Growth, *Review of Economic Studies*, 63 (2), pp. 301–329; D. Acemoglu, J. Robinson (2001): Inefficient Redistribution, *American Political Science Review*, 95 (3), pp. 649–661; T. Besley, T. Persson (2009).

22 See e.g.: E. Glaeser, A. Schleifer (2005): The Curley Effect: The Economics of Shaping the Electorate, *Journal of Law, Economics and Organization*, 21 (1), pp. 1–19.

those in power[23]. The latter thread, although at first glance may seem counter-intuitive, is based on the conviction that this type of politics may serve as a good tool for disciplining one's own electorate, which for many reasons (ideological, differently defined community of interests, etc.) will not be willing to vote for candidates of the opposition.

The third argument we wish to point out here, indicating that the poor level of fiscal capacities may result from the deliberate decisions of political elites, is supported by a model illustrating potential for the emergence of a certain coalition between those in power and the bureaucracy[24]. As mentioned earlier, an efficiently operating public administration will be an important factor contributing to the strengthening of fiscal capacities, as it is largely responsible for the quality of tax collection processes. Such a collation between those in power and the bureaucracy may take place when the people in power come from wealthy groups or from communities representing such groups. This is attributable to the fact that the strengthening of fiscal capacities may lead to the redistribution of incomes, which will obviously contradict the interests of those in power (or of their electorate). Consequently, those in power will have the motivation to weaken the potential of the fiscal control apparatus. To achieve such an outcome, the authorities may enable the public administration to take financial measures for services. From the viewpoint of society at large, such a situation generates two types of danger. Firstly, it suggests the poor level of a state's fiscal capacity. Secondly, it means that any change of such a state of affairs will encounter opposition not only from those in power (their constituency), but also from the bureaucracy. Consequently, to overcome such a *status quo* will require not only the replacement of those in power but also part of the existing bureaucratic apparatus. In such a sense, the aforementioned challenges (in this case, mainly the structural and management challenges) assume a new dimension. Although owing to the absence of relevant data, any predictions following from this model cannot be empirically verified, it is worthwhile asking the question of whether or not such a coalition between those in power and the bureaucracy did not emerge in the countries that are presently struggling against major fiscal problems.

---

23 See e.g.: T. Besley, S. Coate (1998): Sources of Inefficiency in a Representative Democracy: A Dynamic Analysis, *American Economic Review*, 88 (1), pp. 139–156; G. Saint-Paul, D. Ticchi, A. Vindigni (2016): A Theory of Political Entrenchment, *Economic Journal*, in print.

24 See among others: Acemoglu et al., (2011).

Circumstances conducive for the emergence of fiscal capacities

Regardless of the above mentioned discussion and the arguments indicating that those in power may have deliberately resigned from investments in fiscal capacities, it is worthwhile pointing out that certain circumstances may have made those investments more likely. One of the most frequently quoted factors increasing the likelihood of the improvement of those capacities is the external threat[25]. In the face of this threat the society becomes united under a single superior goal – that of security – and in the name of its achievement the society is inclined to increase state powers with regard to the acquisition of finance for defence. By analogy, one can ponder whether the society has similar, albeit on a slightly smaller scale, motivation to renounce part of its own resources for the benefit of the state during financial crises. Several important reforms that were introduced in Greece, Spain and Italy, which directly affected the pockets of local citizens, may support such interpretation[26]. It is worthwhile stressing here again, however, that in the case of South European countries the introduced reforms and the related costs largely resulted from the pressures of other EU states. The question arises, therefore, of how much the (re)building of state fiscal potential is effective when imposed from outside? The related legitimization problems we have mentioned above are hopefully a good illustration of what we may be dealing with here.

Second, it is pointed out that investments in fiscal capacity will be more likely in states characterised by smaller social diversity. This concerns both ethnic and religious diversity, as well as diversification in terms of resource ownership. This is based on the assumption that a community of purpose can be more easily achieved in more homogeneous societies, where it is easier to obtain approval for a decision transferring (as part of tax levies) private resources to be disposed of by those in power for the deployment of joint ventures[27]. The aggravating social

25 See inter alia: C. Tilly (1985): Warmaking and State Making as Organized Crime in: P. Evans, D. Rueschemeyer, T. Skocpol (eds.), *Bringing the State Back.* Cambridge: Cambridge University Press; C. Tilly (1990): *Coercion, Capital and European States, AD 990–1990*, Cambridge MA: Blackwell.

26 Here we leave aside the extent to which those reforms achieved their intended purposes or even to what extent they were really needed.

27 We obtain a more complex picture when we analyse the division of powers between particular social groups, where the differentiating elements of the latter is the level of owned wealth. In the case when wealthy people are in power, motivation to invest in state fiscal capacity is be weakened in fear of income redistribution (see: the discussion presented a little bit earlier in this chapter). A reverse situation may take place when those in power are representatives of poorer social groups. Income redistribution lies

conflicts which have been caused by the widening of income inequalities in South European countries, those that we have mentioned in the context of political choices being made there, may provide a good illustration that problems with the (re)building of fiscal capacities could have been caused by growing social diversification. Bearing this thread in mind, it seems interesting how many additional difficulties in the resolution of the sovereign debt crisis may be provided by the migration crisis Europe will face in the near future.

Third, it is assumed that society will find it easier to give consent for the delegation of potential powers to impose taxation for the benefit of those in power when there are stronger restrictions imposed on executive power in a given state. This is attributed to the fact that under such an arrangement it is less likely that the funds being at the disposal of those in power will be used against social interests. Restrictions imposed on the authorities constitute a kind of guarantee ensuring a relatively balanced distribution of political force between particular social actors. What is worthwhile stressing here is the fact that this argument is in-line with what we said before associating a resolution of the sovereign debt problem with the necessity to meet the management challenge, i.e. to find the proper tools to serve the purpose of coordinating actions submitted to anti-crisis policy.

As the fourth factor conducive for the creation of fiscal capacity one can list the issue of political stability. This follows directly from arguments presented above and explains why the poor level of fiscal capacity may have resulted from the deliberate decisions of those in power. Given the high likelihood of losing power, those currently in power will not be investing in the improvement of state fiscal capacity in fear that this might strengthen the situation of the opposition once it takes over power. Per analogy, greater chances of keeping power may reverse this situation. In this context it is worth pointing out that the fulfilment of this condition may be difficult in the circumstances of limited trust for the political elites we have mentioned above.

Social norms and values conducive for cooperation

As pointed out in the introduction, the power of a state in fiscal dimension will be largely determined by administrative resources and formal institutions. This does not change the fact that an important role can be played here by informal institutions. Here we mean social norms and values professed in a given

---

in their interest so motivations to invest in fiscal capacity (being a pre-condition for performance of pecuniary transfers) will be much stronger.

society, which determine the degree of specific social approval for tax evasion. Argumentation in favour of such a formulation of the issue is provided by several papers indicating that the motivations of individuals supporting cooperative behaviours (in this case we assume that such behaviour will come down to honest payment of taxes) largely depend on the norms and values present in the society[28]. As a consequence, cooperative behaviour is more likely in a society where professed norms and values are conducive for cooperation. If a given individual assumes that others will undertake actions in the spirit of cooperation, they will undertake such actions on their own. Otherwise their best response to the uncooperative behaviour of others will also result in a lack of cooperation. Such models of behaviour also originate in the fact that the problem of credibility of promises being made is embedded in each cooperative action: each person is obliged to make an *ex ante* promise related to their *ex post* behaviour[29]. What is important is that the credibility of such promises may be guaranteed either owing to formal rules, which are safeguarded by the state authorities, or through an informal mechanism forcing individuals to look after their reputations[30]. The latter will be based on universally binding norms.

If fiscal capacities, therefore, are to contain an important component based on informal institutions, it is worth asking to what extent their creation may be subjected to top-down activities, i.e. ones inspired and supervised by the state. Moreover, even if we assume that the state plays an important role in the shaping of civic attitudes anyway, the question arises as to what extent this process takes place on a day to day basis. It is worthy of note that although existing literature indicates that it is very difficult to change social norms (in this case norms conducive for uncooperative behaviour), it also provides arguments and examples illustrating the fact that this can be done[31]. The only question is whether this

---

28 See e.g.: E. Banfield (1958): *The Moral Basis of a Backward Society*, New York: Free Press; R. D. Putnam (1993): *Making Democracy Work: Civic Traditions in Modern Italy*, Princeton, NJ: Princeton University Press; G. Tabellini (2008): The Scope of Cooperation: Values and Incentives. *Quarterly Journal of Economics*, 123(3), pp. 905–950.

29 See inter alia: A. Greif, (2006): *Institutions and the Path to the Modern Economy: Lessons from Medieval Trade*. New York: Cambridge University Press.

30 See inter alia: M.O. Jackson (2008): *Social and Economic Networks*, Princeton, NJ: Princeton University Press.

31 See e.g.: A. Bisin, T. Verdier (2001): The Economics of Cultural Transmission and the Dynamics of Preferences, *Journal of Economic Theory*, 97, pp. 298–319; M. Doepke, F. Zilibotti, (2008): Occupational Choice and the Spirit of Capitalism. *Quarterly Journal of Economics*, 123(2), pp. 747–793. G. Tabellini (2008); D. Acemoglu, M.O. Jackson

is possible in the context of anti-crisis actions, when not only swift decisions but also – from the viewpoint of political legitimization – immediate action is needed. This may prove difficult in the South European countries presently in the spotlight, where expectations of both the political class, societies and international institutions are largely focused on swift and radical solutions.

Adjustments in fiscal policy

Bearing in mind the said pressure, it should come as no surprise that actions undertaken so far with the aim of improving public finance standing in the most crisis-stricken countries, were based on various adjustments introduced into fiscal policy. To another extent it is also understandable why for a long time the main stress was laid first and foremost on forcing the most crisis-stricken states to reduce (possibly too fast) their debt levels. On the other hand, it may be somehow surprising that for a relatively long time the fact that this goal can be attained through various means was definitely put into the shade in the discussions pursued[32]. Such diversity of opinion is particularly surprising in view of the increasing number of papers indicating that the choice of a path determining the necessary adjustments aimed to restore fiscal discipline will not be neutral for economic results neither in the short- nor long-term. We may, therefore, expect different effects if we opt for debt level reduction through spending cuts, than if we try to achieve the same goal by raising taxes[33]. It is worthwhile

---

(2015): Acemoglu, D., Jackson, M.O., 2015. History, Expectations, and Leadership in the Evolution of Social Norms, *Review of Economic Studies*, 82(1), pp. 1–34.

32 Compare with a discussion in an earlier part of the paper, see also inter alia: A. Alesina, F. Giavazzi (2013). Naturally some changes in this regard were forced by reality, and strictly speaking by extremely modest effects of austerity packages applied in South European countries. However one can still have doubts, particularly in the context of the discussion about the situation in Greece, whether the changes in the debate about necessary adjustments may be called a breakthrough.

33 See inter alia: A. Alesina, S. Ardagna (2010): Large Changes in Fiscal Policy: Taxes vs. Spending, *Tax Policy and the Economy*, 24, pp. 35–68; IMF (2010): Will It Hurt? Macroeconomic Effects of Fiscal Consolidation, in: *World Economic Outlook 2010*, International Monetary Fund, Washington, pp. 94–124; C. Favero, F. Giavazzi, J. Perego (2011): Country Heterogeneity and the International Evidence on the Effects of Fiscal Policy, *IMF Economic Review*, 59, pp. 652–682; R. Perotti (2013): The "Austerity Myth": Gain without Pain?, in: A. Alesina, F. Giavazzi, (eds.) *Fiscal Policy after the Financial Crisis*, Chicago: The University of Chicago Press, pp. 307–354; A. Alesina, C. Favero, F. Giavazzi (2015): The Output Effect of Fiscal Consolidations, *Journal of International Economics*, 96, supplement 1, pp.19–42.

bearing this in mind in particular in the context of the significance of the necessity to meet the growth challenge we mentioned in the beginning for the effectiveness of anti-crisis policy.

From this perspective it is worthwhile looking closely at the potential effects of various adjustments made under fiscal policy. Particularly if we once again invoke the aforementioned example of Greece where, despite the introduction of fiscal and spending reforms, the GDP shrank by almost 10 % annually, while the sovereign debt rose to previously unrecorded levels (reaching almost 180 % in 2013 in relation to GDP). Another point worth a mention is that the problem of recession and growing sovereign debt was experienced not only by Greece but also by other South European countries, which had been subjected to radical reforms[34].

Although existing papers dedicated to the consequences of various steps reforming fiscal policy differ in details, both concerning research methodology and the thematic scope of the performed analysis, the basic conclusion coming from either of them is quite accordant and can be summarized as follows: fiscal adjustments based on spending cuts are less costly from the viewpoint of GDP reduction than increased taxes. What is important is that this general conclusion is supported with results of papers which apply various methodologies for defining the periods in which fiscal consolidation took place. This, therefore, gives way to the assumption that the obtained results were not caused by a given methodology governing the assessment of the historical adjustment scale. It is also worthwhile stressing that some papers even indicate that spending cuts may have a positive impact on production output volume, the so-called phenomenon of expansionary fiscal contractions, although these results need to be treated with caution[35].

Having said that, it is worthwhile indicating here that a far less clear picture emerges from papers trying to estimate the size of fiscal multipliers, which indicate to what extent GDP reacts either to change in government spending or to a change in taxes. In spite of the clues coming from Keynes' model, the estimate we have at hand does not only assume values over one, but are most frequently within the range of 0.5–1.5. This obviously hinders assessments of the potential outcomes of our actions undertaken as part of fiscal policy. We would offer completely different indications to politicians if we decide that the

34 See inter alia: R. Baldwin, F. Giavazzi (2015).

35 See inter alia: C. Corsetti (2012): *Austerity: Too Much of a Good Thing*? London: CEPR. Vox.eu.org eBook, http://www.voxeu.org/sites/default/files/file/austerity_ecollection.pdf [access: 24.05.2016].

spending multiplier is closer to 1.5 than in a situation when we are more inclined to assume it is closer to 0.5. The fact that most estimations we have available are based on data for the United States, this additionally compounds the discussion because drawing conclusions for other countries on this basis may prove to be inaccurate.

Moreover, the size of those multipliers may largely depend on several economic determinants[36]. In this context the source literature lists e.g. various phases of the business cycle, the starting value of sovereign debt level in relation to GDP, unemployment levels, currently pursued monetary policies as well as the leeway the central bank's governing bodies have regarding e.g. a change in interest rates. As a consequence of this, the estimates available to us correspond to the average values of those multipliers from various periods, which may have been characterised by quite diverse economic conditions. Basing our conclusions on those averages, given the assumption that the actual value of the multipliers may vary a lot depending on the time and place and circumstances, may lead us to make inaccurate decisions with regard to the shape we should give to fiscal policy.

Within the framework of actions aimed at fiscal consolidation, it should also be taken into account the aforementioned fact that political calculations may have diverged from purely economic control. A worthwhile question here is of the political consequences those in power may suffer if they opt for a radical reduction of the sovereign debt level. If such consequences are too severe and translate into loss of social support, then the political class may avoid the necessary moves that would be advisable from an economic point of view. There are very few papers that would allow for the verification of such relationships. One of them is the study by Alesina et al.[37], which brings about very interesting results, and at a glance, may even seem counter-intuitive. By identifying cases of significant fiscal adjustments in OECD countries, the authors indicate that if we also control the economic results measured by GDP, then the reduction of the sovereign debt problem on average does not – for those in power – impose any additional costs in the form of being removed from the offices they hold. Consequently, such a paper would incline us to assume that politicians' fears related to the introduction of radical moves aimed at reducing excessive sovereign debt are unjustified.

---

36 C. Favero at al. (2011).

37 A. Alesina, D. Carloni, G. Lecce (2013): The Electoral Consequences of Large Fiscal Adjustments, in: Alesina, A., Giavazzi, F. (eds.) *Fiscal Policy after the Financial Crisis*, Chicago: The University of Chicago Press, pp. 531–570.

It is worth mentioning here that this paper only shows an average view of the situation without taking much into account of e.g. the differences that might arise in respect to the differences between right-wing and left-wing governments. This is important insofar as, for ideological reasons, it may be more difficult for right-wing governments to credibly justify to their constituency the necessity to make spending cuts. This is attributable to the fact that this assumption will be associated by the electorate as to whether there is crisis or not. On the other hand left-wing governments, which do not stray away from such slogans, may sound more credible once they articulate them.

Moreover, in their paper the authors measure the political consequences those in power may suffer owing to actions reducing the debt level, only by looking at personal changes within the government (a change of the prime minister or of the ruling party/coalition is not necessary). It remains an open question, therefore, to what extent general conclusions from the paper would be upheld if we adopted a wider approach and measured the political consequences of changes in fiscal policy by looking at the social support for a given formation (alternatively at the change in the division of seats in parliament).

Conclusion

Similarly, as in the case of previous economic upheavals, as well as in the case of the financial crisis that started in 2008, the attention of politicians and analysts have focused on reforms that would allow us to exit the crisis and minimize the latter's negative outcomes. In connection with the fact that the current crisis has sharpened the general perception of the sovereign debt problem, several reforms discussed in this context concern the fiscal policies of states which face the particular threat of insolvency. The stress that has been laid on the necessity to reduce spending in Greece may be a good illustration of this.

In connection to the above, in this paper we have attempted to look at this discussion from the angle of research carried out by economists on basic factors determining the possibility to make changes to fiscal policy, together with the effects of various adjustments made under such policy. Attention is focused mainly on three issues. First, centre stage is taken by the factors that facilitate or hamper an increase of the level of state fiscal capacity. Particular attention is attached to the motivation of those in power to make the necessary investments in this respect. Second, we look at how much the level of state fiscal capacity is determined by the efficient functioning of informal mechanisms, which are inherently not easily controlled from above. Third, we briefly discuss the differences, entailed on the one hand by spending cuts and by tax increases on the other, from the viewpoint of economic growth.

Two following threads in the performed discussion seem particularly interesting and worthy of further discussion. First, it is worthwhile looking closer at the factors determining the level of state fiscal capacity. The latter will define the action options for those in power with regard to any potential reforms aimed at reducing the sovereign debt level. In this context, familiarity with factors conducive for strengthening a state's fiscal capacity may prove crucial from the viewpoint of the choice of action on the basis of which one may create a strategy for the exit from a crisis as well as design mechanisms that reduce the risk of similar situations being repeated in the future. Second, it is worthwhile looking at what will prompt those in power to increase/use those capacities. Ignoring objective factors that may be conducive for the creation of state fiscal capacity, it remains unknown how much any actions along those lines would be undertaken by those in power. As a result, a succession of efforts aimed at increasing income into the state budget is in no way obvious. Moreover, as we have tried to demonstrate, even assuming that necessary and adequate conditions for emergence of state fiscal capacity are present, this process may take a long time.

References

Acemoglu D., Jackson M.O. (2015): History, Expectations, and Leadership in the Evolution of Social Norms, *Review of Economic Studies*, 82 (1), pp. 1–34.

Acemoglu D., Johnson S., Robinson J. (2005): The Rise of Europe: Atlantic Trade, Institutional Change and Economic Growth, *American Economic Review*, 95 (3), pp. 546–579.

Acemoglu D., Robinson J. (2001): Inefficient Redistribution, *American Political Science Review*, 95 (3), pp. 649–661.

Akerlof G., Blanchard O., Romer D., Stiglitz J. (eds.) (2014): *What Have We Learned?: Macroeconomic Policy after the Crisis*, Cambridge: MIT Press.

Alesina A., Ardagna S. (2010): Large Changes in Fiscal Policy: Taxes vs. Spending, *Tax Policy and the Economy*, 24, pp. 35–68.

Alesina A., Carloni D., Lecce G. (2013): The Electoral Consequences of Large Fiscal Adjustments, in: A. Alesina, F. Giavazzi (eds.), *Fiscal Policy after the Financial Crisis*, Chicago: The University of Chicago Press, pp. 531–570.

Alesina A., Favero C., Giavazzi F. (2015): The Output Effect of Fiscal Consolidations, *Journal of International Economics*, 96 (S1), pp. 19–42.

Artavanis N., Morese A., Tsoutsoura M. (2015): *Tax Evasion across Industries: Soft Credit Evidence from Greece*, unpublished manuscript.

Baldwin R., Giavazzi F. (eds.) (2015): *The Eurozone Crisis: A Consensus View of the Causes and a Few Possible Solutions*, London: CEPR, Vox.eu.org eBook, www.voxeu.org/sites/default/files/file/reboot_upload_0.pdf, [access: 24.05.2016].

Banfield E. (1958): *The Moral Basis of a Backward Society*, New York: Free Press.

Besley T., Coate S. (1998): Sources of Inefficiency in a Representative Democracy: A Dynamic Analysis, *American Economic Review*, 88 (1), pp. 139–156.

Besley T., Persson T. (2009): The Origins of State Capacity: Property Rights, Taxation, and Policy, *American Economic Review*, 99, pp. 1218–1244.

Besley T., Persson T. (2011): *Pillars of Prosperity: The Political Economics of Development Clusters*, The Yrjö Jahnsson Lectures, Princeton: Princeton University Press.

Bisin A., Verdier T. (2001): The Economics of Cultural Transmission and the Dynamics of Preferences, *Journal of Economic Theory*, 97, pp. 298–319.

Corsetti C. (2012): *Austerity: Too Much of a Good Thing?*, London: CEPR, Vox.eu.org eBook, http://www.voxeu.org/sites/default/files/file/austerity_ecollection.pdf, [access: 24.05.2016].

Cottarelli C., Gerson P., Senhadji A. (eds.) (2014): *Post-Crisis Fiscal Policy*, Cambridge: MIT Press.

DeLong J.B., Schleifer A. (1993): Princes and Merchants: European City Growth before the Industrial Revolution, *Journal of Law and Economics*, 36, pp. 671–702.

Doepke M., Zilibotti F. (2008): *Occupational Choice and the Spirit of Capitalism*, *Quarterly Journal of Economics*, 123 (2), pp. 747–793.

Fałkowski J. (2013): Problem finansów publicznych w krajach UE z punktu widzenia nie tak odległej historii oraz kilku teorii nowej ekonomii politycznej, in: T.G. Grosse (ed.), *Między polityką a ekonomią kryzysu strefy euro: Rozważania o teorii kryzysu w ekonomii politycznej*, Warszawa: Wyd. Uczelni Łazarskiego, pp. 41–59.

Favero C., Giavazzi F., Perego J. (2011): Country Heterogeneity and the International Evidence on the Effects of Fiscal Policy, *IMF Economic Review*, 59, pp. 652–682.

Glaeser E., Schleifer A. (2005): The Curley Effect: The Economics of Shaping the Electorate, *Journal of Law, Economics and Organization*, 21 (1), pp. 1–19.

Greif A. (2006): *Institutions and the Path to the Modern Economy: Lessons from Medieval Trade*, New York: Cambridge University Press.

Herbst J.I. (2000): *States and Power in Africa: Comparative Lessons in Authority and Control*, Princeton, NJ: Princeton University Press.

IMF (2010): Will It Hurt? Macroeconomic Effects of Fiscal Consolidation, in: *World Economic Outlook 2010*, Washington, pp. 94–124

Jackson M.O. (2008): *Social and Economic Networks*, Princeton, NJ: Princeton University Press.

Krusell P., Rios-Rull J.V. (1996): Vested Interests in a Positive Theory of Stagnation and Growth, *Review of Economic Studies*, 63 (2), pp. 301–329.

Migdal J. (2001): *State in Society: Studying How States and Societies Transform and Constitute One Another*, Cambridge: Cambridge University Press.

Myerson R. (2008): The Autocrat's Credibility Problem and Foundations of the Constitutional State, *American Political Science Review*, 102, pp. 125–139.

North D.C. (1981): *Structure and Change in Economic History*, New York: Norton.

Olson M. (1982): *The Rise and Decline of Nations: Economic Growth, Stagflation, and Social Rigidities*, New Haven: Yale University Press.

Perotti R. (2013): The "Austerity Myth": Gain without Pain?, in: A. Alesina, F. Giavazzi (eds.), *Fiscal Policy after the Financial Crisis*, Chicago: The University of Chicago Press, pp. 307–354.

Putnam R.D. (1993): *Making Democracy Work: Civic Traditions in Modern Italy*, Princeton, NJ: Princeton University Press.

Rajan R. (2012): *Linie uskoku. Ukryte rysy, które wciąż zagrażają światowej gospodarce*, Warsaw: Kurhaus Publishing.

Rompuy H. Van, Barroso J.M., Juncker J.C., Draghi M. (2012): *Towards a Genuine Economic and Monetary Union. Report of the Four Presidents*, 5th December.

Roubini N., Mihm S. (2011): *Crisis Economics: A Crash Course in the Future of Finance*, London: Penguin Books.

Saint-Paul G., Ticchi D., Vindigni A. (2016): A Theory of Political Entrenchment, *Economic Journal*, 126 (593), pp. 1238–1263.

Slemrod J. (2007): Cheating Ourselves: The Economics of Tax Evasion, *Journal of Economic Perspectives*, 21 (1), pp. 25–48.

Tabellini G. (2008): The Scope of Cooperation: Values and Incentives, *Quarterly Journal of Economics*, 123 (3), pp. 905–950.

Tilly C. (1985): War Making and State Making as Organized Crime, In: P. B. Evans, D. Rueschemeyer, T. Skocpol (eds.), *Bringing the state back*, Cambridge: Cambridge University Press.

Tilly C. (1990): *Coercion, Capital and European States, AD 990–1990*, Cambridge MA: Blackwell.

Whelan K. (2015): *The FT Lets Itself Down Again: Francesco Giavazzi on Greece*, https://medium.com/bull-market/the-ft-lets-itself-down-again-francesco-giavazzi-on-greece-92988bc675eb, [access: 24.05.2016].

Marek A. Cichocki

From crisis to strategy – against the backdrop of the EU

Abstract: The chapter explains a phenomenon of crises as well as the linkage between the crisis and a strategy set out for overcoming the troubles. Subsequently, the way how the crisis is perceived often results from the strategy chosen in the effect of political decisions. The problem of the strategy building as well as the ability for strategic planning remain the fundamental ways of governance, when it comes to states and supranational organizations. The author points out that the crucial aspect of each strategy is the mobilisation process requiring often political legitimisation. Thereupon, with regard to the Eurozone crisis, one can notice the problem of the input legitimacy which is a process understood as dispersed actions of various actors contributing to the mobilisation and to the resolution.

Keywords: crisis, strategy, state, mobilisation, input legitimacy, output legitimacy

The link between strategy and crisis may seem obvious but at the same time it is still inadequately subjected to in-depth analyses. This is an occurrence of a crisis that leads to the emergence of the need to search for forms of strategic action, which make us aware of the necessity to think and act in a long-term, strategic dimension. At the moment of a threat, growing uncertainty or the sudden collapse of existing rules, an expectation arises that disadvantageous phenomena will be countered with some planned, coordinated, long-term counter-action, enabling the recovery of control over the situation. Such interdependence between crisis and strategy seems to take place particularly frequently in the case of contemporary democratic societies, described also in terms of risk societies, which left the existing safe framework of modernity[1]. In their case, there is something like a particularly strong political dialectics linking the crisis and strategy. Expecting lasting growth and security, democratic societies react to any situation of threat or disturbance with the demand for a comprehensive and effective response from policy-makers, or the government[2]. Such expectations, whether

1 U. Beck (1986): *Risikogesellschaft. Auf dem Weg in eine andere Moderne*, Frankfurt a.M.: Suhrkamp, p. 25.

2 K. Borchardt (1990): *Przemiany w myśleniu o kryzysach gospodarczych*, in: *O kryzysie*, Warsaw: Res Publica, p. 120.

they are met or whether disappointment sets in, later translate into democratic choices made.

The link between crisis and strategy can also have an opposite meaning. The issue at hand is whether the concepts of what a strategic action is are what it should be, what its sense and nature is, whether it is at all possible or desirable, to what extent it e.g. allows us to achieve the assumed objectives, themselves based on specific assumptions, according to which we identify and understand the crisis as a phenomenon requiring the undertaking of proper, specific actions. In other words, how we imagine the make-up of a crisis, determines the way in which we formulate our strategies. On the other hand, and particularly in the context of the discussion on the issue of post-politics[3], the question emerges whether in the conditions of a post-modern world, an action – e.g. a political one – of a strategic nature is at all possible? The famous statement by Angela Merkel related to *Fahrt auf Sicht* (literally: drives by sight; usually translated into English as "assumes a reserved stance"), which she made at the climax of the financial crisis in Greece and of the entire Eurozone, may serve as an example of the resignation of post-political elites in Europe from strategic actions in the time of crisis[4]. The necessity for strategic actions in a crisis situation was negated slightly differently by Donald Tusk, after he become the President of the European Council[5]. Therefore, one can be under the impression that in contemporary Europe the political elites confronted with democratically articulated demand for systemic resolution of a crisis, negate the possibility and meaningfulness of a strategic action. This negation also demonstrates a specific cognitive attitude, a way of understanding the crisis as a phenomenon. So although it is a universal experience that a crisis leads to the realization of the need to develop a strategy (or negate it), in our paper we want to reflect not only on the nature of this relationship, but also on how the understanding of a strategy may determine the identification of crises.

---

3 See: J. Staniszkis (2008): *O władzy i bezsilności*, Warsaw: Wydawnictwo Literackie; J. Staniszkis (2003): *Władza globalizacji*, Warsaw: SCHOLAR; P. Sloterdijk (2008): *Krytyka cynicznego rozumu*, Wrocław: Wydawnictwo Naukowe Dolnośląskiej Szkoły Wyższej; S. Žižek (2008): *W obronie przegranych spraw*, Warsaw: Wydawnictwo Krytyki Politycznej.

4 U. Beck (2012): *Das deutsche Europa*, Berlin: Suhrkamp, pp. 47–55.

5 An interview with Donald Tusk, *Ja po prostu mam szczęście*, Polityka No. 49/2014.

Strategy

The Contemporary European Union has become a field of multiple crises, which implies a question on the capability of the Union to develop strategic responses. There is a certain paradox embedded in this if we realise that European integration, and its deepening, was intended to eliminate conflict and crises from European reality. Threats emerged rather in the external world and any potential strategic efforts were supposed to address those. In the case of the European Union, the problem of strategic planning and action emerges more or less in parallel to the process of development by Member States of the Common Foreign and Security Policy, and then of the Common Security and Defence Policy. A manifestation of those transformations is being created by the establishment of the European Security Strategy, gradual institutional changes within the Union and the political initiatives of Member States and EU institutions. The period concerned by those transformations covers the 1990s and 2000s; they relate mainly to the building of the EU capacity to provide a strategic response to external crises – and this is the direction along which the reflection on strategy and crisis develops[6]. However, since 2010 the problem has become greatly compounded. The European Union has become a field of several crises – financial, migration, geopolitical, structural, of political leadership and finally of identity, which emerge in certain sequences and in various areas. What is more, those crises interact with each other causing the effect of synergy of various crises, which may lead to a systemic crisis of the Union, being in fact an existential crisis. The new situation makes the issue of strategy much more complex. What should response strategies to particular crises be like, and can they be coordinated in the form of an imaginable European *grand strategy*? Anyway, it is becoming obvious that reflections made so far on the strategy in a narrowly adopted area of diplomacy, foreign policy and military capacity have ceased to be adequate. It is also worthwhile remembering that we are dealing the problem of the crisis of Member States themselves, remaining slightly in the shadow of grand crises of the European Union; this provokes a fundamental question as to whether a contemporary state is capable at all to make strategic planning and to act.

The problem is no way made easier by the very notion of strategy, which can be understood in many different ways. Depending on the subject-matter, we may speak of military, economic, state, political, business, as well as communication

6 See e.g.: Ch. O.Meyer (2006): *The Quest for a European Strategic Culture*, New York: Palgrave; B. Giegerich (2006): *European Security and Strategic Culture*, Baden-Baden: Nomos.

strategies etc. This diversity breeds a worrying arbitrariness and consequently for some researchers and analysts the notion of strategy becomes something like a bottomless pit into which we are throwing any kind of consciously undertaken initiative.[7] Can we freely transfer experiences collected in the scope of strategic action freely from one area to another? Can a talented general be an equally talented business manager or political leader? However, from our viewpoint the ambiguity of the notion of strategy can be an important advantage. Historical evolution of the notion of strategy covers three various areas: the art of war, the state's functioning, and finally business, or – more broadly – the economy. The latter two areas are of particular importance to us from the viewpoint of relations between behaviours in crisis situations in economy and in politics. However, generally speaking comparisons between theory and practice of strategic planning and action from those three basic areas can be deemed as promising from the viewpoint of the search for fundamental features of strategy as such.

Regardless of how diversified the use of the notion of strategy is, we can assume some general definition of the term. A strategy describes first of all a specific type of action, characterised by high cohesion, order and expected effectiveness in attainment of goals in uncertain situations, conflicts, disputes, fights, crises or rivalry. So naturally a strategy implies a high level of rationalization in the approach to decisions and actions taken to overcome the unknown. If we transfer strategies into the level of political relations, then the concept of a strategy turns out to be close to the realistic understanding of policy and conflicts. At least this is so on the face of it, although one has to remember that a high level of rationality of strategic planning or action was also subjected to heavy criticism[8].

Army

The history of the notion of strategy is related first and foremost to a specific area of military actions – to the battlefield and the art of war. It defines the ability to plan and carry out military campaigns together with the related know-how. *Strategos* – this term was used in ancient Greece to describe a commander of an army or fleet. According to this historical meaning of the term, strategy should be first of all referred to as the art of war, the military, therefore differentiating it from tactical or operational actions, and also understanding it as a separate

7 D. Hambrick, J. Frederickson (2001): Are You Sure You Have a Strategy?, *Academy of Management Executive* 15, No. 4/2001, p. 49, after: L. Freedman (2013): *Strategy. A History*, Oxford: Oxford University Press, p. 560.

8 I. Berlin(1993): *Jeż i lis*, Warsaw: Aletheia, pp. 45–66

area than e.g. politics, culture or management. The classic work by Thucydides, however, *The History of the Peloponnesian War*, which even today is an irreplaceable source and inspiration for reflections on military strategy in times of war, demonstrates that full separation of war from politics or culture is virtually impossible. With time the meaning of strategy, strategic actions and thinking, now expands into other areas, such as politics, state functioning, administration, business or the general management of a variety of resources. In such broad meaning, strategy refers to various types of human organisations and actions, and decisions made within its framework. This expansion of strategy into other fields, chiefly politics and operations of the state, has been enabled by modernity and the related process of rationalisation and centralisation of politics[9].

So it is impossible to separate military reflection on strategy from the state. This is why Colin S.Gray, an Anglo-American theoretician of military strategies and director of the Centre for Strategic Studies, defines strategy mainly with reference to a state's actions in a situation of conflict in international relations, defining it as "the use that is made of force and the threat of force for the achievement of policy"[10]. Colin derives such understanding of strategy directly from the classic writer on the topic, Clausewitz, and his work *On war*, although he is aware that Clausewitz sees strategy in a wider sense, as the use of engagements for the object of the war[11]. From such a perspective a strategy is any planned, orderly or though-out mobilization of available resources, and their engagement for the object of the war. Colin also quotes other definitions of strategy, which more or less confirm his own understanding thereof, although containing additional elements that slightly complicate the image. And so Basil H. Liddell Hardt, one of the most outstanding theoreticians of strategy and a military historian, considers strategy as "the art of distributing and applying military means to fulfil the aims of policy"[12] by which he understands the ability to coordinate and direct all the resources of a nation or band of nations, towards the attainment of the political object of the war. On the other hand, the definition of General Andre Beaufre insists that strategy "is therefore the art of the dialectic of force or, more precisely, the art of the dialectic of two opposing wills using force to resolve their dispute"[13]. The notion of art is notable in either definition. Strategy

---

9 S. Huntington (1996): *Political Order in Changing Societies*, New Haven: Yale University Press, pp. 99–109.

10 C. S. Gray (1999): *Modern Strategy*, Oxford: Oxford University Press, p. 17.

11 C. von Clausetwitz (2003): *O wojnie*, Warsaw: Mireki, p. 123.,

12 B. H. Liddell (1967): *Strategy. The Indirect Approach*, London: Faber and Faber, p. 335.

13 A. Beaufre (1963): *An Introduction to Strategy*, London: Faber and Faber, p. 22.

is a kind of art, which refers to the differentiation present in the reflections of Clausewitz between knowledge and art, knowledge and skill[14]. In such an aspect, strategy must not be considered to be a manifestation of strict knowledge on how one should behave in given circumstances. Still, it is not pure art either. There also appears an external factor for shaping up a strategy – the opponent's will, without which strategy as a certain form of behaviour would no longer make sense. So strategy created in conflict with others, just like war, in accordance with the classic view of Clausewitz, is an act of relations between people, is a phenomenon of social life, being a constant battlefield.[15] This means, however, that strategy must not be treated statically, simply as a plan of action targeted at the attainment of a defined goal, with the use of defined means, using defined resources, at a defined time. Strategy is something more, an attempt to respond to a reality much more complex, unknown and above all dynamic. This problem is best understood by the definition of strategy as a process (and not a plan) proposed by Murray and Grimsley. They claim that "strategy is a process, a constant adaptation to shifting conditions and circumstances in a world where chance, uncertainty, and ambiguity dominate".[16] From this viewpoint it is quite close to conclusions proposed in a popular book published by the Boston Consulting Group on inspiration that can be derived in business from strategic reflections of Clausewitz. The authors of the book come to a conclusion on the basis of the analysis of Clausewitz, that positive theory of strategy is unimaginable exactly owing to the dynamics of reality. Reality will evade any positive theory. Strategy, therefore, must not only be based on the concept of maximisation of the effectiveness of the use of means to attain intended objectives. Focusing on a target may completely reduce or limit any chances for further action if we attain the said target. Therefore, the possibility to continue an action (campaign) should be the supreme goal of any strategy.[17]

14 C. von Clausetwitz, *O wojnie*, p. 97.

15 *Ibidem*, p. 98.

16 W. Murray, M. Grimsley (1994): *Introduction: On Strategy* in: W. Murray, A. Bernstein, *The Making of Strategy: Rulers, States, and War*, Cambridge: Cambridge University Press; after: C. P. Gray, *Modern Strategy*, *op. cit*., p. 19.

17 B. von Oetinger, Ch. Bassford (2002): *Clausetwitz o strategii*, Warsaw: Polskie Wydawnictwo Ekonomiczne, p. 57.

Business

Reflections of Clausewitz over war strategy were born out of the breakthrough in the military area, with Napoleon playing a fundamental role. Wars were no longer fought by generals and their armies, but by nations, states, societies and economies. Therefore, on the one hand it was difficult to separate strategy in the military sense from policy in the situation of national armies. Those were the decisions of the political leaderships of states that defined strategies deployed through military actions[18]. On the other hand, strategic experiences in military areas could to a greater extent serve the dynamically developing economic organisations in industrial societies. Particularly in the case of the United States, when in the late 19th century large corporations started to emerge. The language of military strategy enabled an attractive description of the situation where economic competition became a battlefield, a company became something like an army and its owner or manager became a general. Strategy as an instrument of operation in business, and further on as knowledge related to how to best organise the operations of an enterprise, how to organise work most effectively, use the available resources, how to secure profits and further how to guarantee company development, appeared as a problem along with the shaping of the industrial society and emergence of the new role of a manager as the main organizer and planner of economic processes by a company. This was the moment when the first business schools were established (Wharton School at Pennsylvania 1881, followed by Harvard Business School 1908), and then followed in the 1960s by big consulting companies such as the Boston Consulting Group of Bruce Henderson of 1963 or McKinsey & Company.

Evolution in the approach to strategy in business, the road along which theories of strategic company management changed, provide many interesting examples for the understanding of the very problem of strategy; this is also possible owing to the relationship between the economic and political approach to the issue. The understanding of strategies in business is initially under the powerful influence of scientific and positivist rationalism. This is based on top-down management methods, clear internal hierarchy, the control and mobilisation and recognition of the unchangeable character of the basic rules of classic economy governing company environments. Those initial, highly rational management strategies in business, autocratic and scientific, with the most notable examples being Taylorism and Fordism of the turn of centuries, will, however, change

18 R. Aron (1995): *Pokój i wojna między narodami*, Warsaw: Centrum im. Adama Smitha, pp. 37–48.

with time towards a more flexible, non-dogmatic approach to organisation management. On the one hand, already in 1920s Alfred P.Sloan will propose in General Motors an innovative approach to the issue of the structure of the managed organisation, showing a direct relationship between effectiveness of a strategy and the complexity of the managed structure. In his opinion, a strategy must not lead to unilateral centralization of the managed structure; instead it has to be based on combining a centralised function of development and control planning with the diversification of independently performed tasks. On the other hand, the so-called Human Relations School, represented mainly by Elton May of the Harvard Business School, tried to expand the issue of organisation management to the issues of social, human relations in the workplace, in the company. According to Mayo, the problem of highly rational, autocratic and scientific management strategies does not follow from disregard for the democracy factor, which he considers to be rather an irrational element, introducing serious disturbances in business. Instead of democratization of a company, Mayo thinks that in organisation management and in designing its strategy one should also understand the social and biological facts that determine the functioning of an organisation and its control, influence e.g. its efficiency[19]. Such an approach paved the way for shifting the centre of gravity in theories of strategic management in business from economy into the domain of social sciences, psychology or anthropology, which takes place in the 1960s and 1970s. This change is related to cultural contestation of bureaucratic rigorism and hierarchism on the one hand, and to the emergence of post-modernism in the sciences[20]. If post-modernity questions the further existence of the basic assumptions of the industrial society, we need to change consistently the approach to basic forms of such a society's organisation. A new generation of management theoreticians, such Tom Peters of McKinsey or Gary Hamel, contested the traditional approach to strategy in business, based mainly on bureaucracy, control and calculations, attaching major attention to the human aspect, social relations, culture, capability to generate the feeling of the community, as well as the satisfaction from participation in processes. In their opinion the main power of strategy in business is comprised of inspiration, openness to continuous learning, and the readiness for a creative and critical change[21]. Therefore, the evolution of theories and practices of strategic governance in business will proceed from strictly rational, scientific

19 L. Freedman, *op. cit.*, pp. 468–471.
20 *Ibidem*, p. 542.
21 *Ibidem*, pp. 556–558.

and autocratic concepts to more complex, flexible models, where economic effectiveness in profit generation and the capacity to react to external challenges will be increasingly replaced with internal social, anthropological and psychological factors. Consequently, the aspect of a strategy's rationality falls into the concept of relativism, which is manifested among other things in the fact that the centre of gravity in the theory is set not on a strategy's purpose, intention and achievement of assumed effects, but on uncertainty and contingency, as Henry Mintzberg – among others – points out.[22] So one can assert that the development of social sciences and psychology in the 20th century had the most powerful influence over the change of understanding of strategic planning and action in business. Against this backdrop, the impact of democratization on methods of enterprise management is much less pronounced. This issue appears in management theories and in practice (mainly trade unions); however, in the perspective of the evolution of the approach to the problem of strategy in business, its significance is fundamentally much weaker.

State

Besides the military and private enterprise, it is the state that can be considered the type of organisation responsible first and foremost for strategic planning and action. Perhaps we should use the state as the starting point for any analysis of strategy as a concept and practice of goal-oriented action. Particularly so if we have in mind the *grand strategy*, i.e. one aspiring to use the entire spectrum of available means and resources that a state may have at its disposal. If we understand such a grand strategy after Wiliam C. Martel as the "science and art of using all forces of a nation to execute the approved plans as effectively as possible during peace or war"[23], in practice only a state organisation has the capacity for such comprehensive action. The state is the only structure able to mobilise all available means and forces, mainly owing to the centralization of political power and sovereignty, as analysed by Charles Tilly or Samuel Huntington[24]. Depending on the scale of resources and internal social and economic complexity of the state structure, when making attempts at centralised mobilisation of means for the attainment of the assumed goal, the government is forced to negotiate the interests

22 *Ibidem*, p. 555.

23 W. C. Martel (2015): *Grand Strategy in Theory and Practice*, Cambridge: Cambridge University Press, p. 4.

24 Ch. Tilly (2002): States and Nationalism in Europe, 1492–1992, in: *Stories, Identities, and Political Change*, Lanham: Rowman and Littlefield Publishers.

and needs of various internal groups. Historically the relationship between the state and strategy starts with the formation of the structures of a modern state in the 17th century, in the sense that strategic planning and action and functioning of the state as a centralised from of power become associated with each other[25]. When modernity emerges as an effect of industrialization in the late 19th century, this relationship becomes even more obvious, but also increasingly complex. The goal of the strategy is now "the effective organization of the state's policies and resources, in order to achieve the objectives of the strategy"[26]. Those changes transformed the traditional state's structure and function, which used to focus mainly around foreign and war-making policies. Anand Menon points out that for example, in the case of the United Kingdom the number of state officials was 27 thousand in 1821, increasing to 80 thousand in 1881, and finally reaching in 1985 the level of 1 million and 56 thousand officials in central government administration. Respectively spending on administration amounted in 1900 to 14 % GDP, rising in the 1950s to the level of 36 %[27]. According to such researchers as Robert Higgs, a follower of the Austrian school in economy, on the example of the evolution of government in the United States, we can observe certain regularity: the bigger the crises become, entailing more and more comprehensive strategic responses, the more expansive government function becomes[28]. Development of the grand strategy at state policy level, therefore, leads more to omnipotent political power of the state, rather than to actual problem-solving. The concept of grand strategy becomes fully conceptualised at the moment when a modern nation state achieves its greatest industrial potential and when economic and social power becomes fully located in the centre of the political power of the state.[29] Such ability to concentrate power in relation to resources will concern only the biggest countries – the world superpowers. In the context of WWII this leads to the emergence – mainly in the United States, but also on the European continent – of grand strategies and the establishment of a global, lasting order. In theory, a concept underlying such strategy is put forward in the 1940s by Henry Antony Sargeaunt and Geoffrey West in a book titled

---

25 This mode of thinking was encountered earlier, mainly in the concepts of Niccolo Machiavelli, in his Prince.

26 W. C. Martel, p. 4.

27 A. Menon (2013): *Europa stan Unii*, Warszawa: Natolin European Centre, p. 16 and following pages.

28 R. Higgs (1987): *Crisis and Leviathan*, Oxford: Oxford University Press, p. 57 and following pages.

29 W. C. Martel, p. 25

Grand Strategy (1941) and by Edward Mead Earle in Makers of Modern Strategy (1943). The latter states among other things that: "In the present-day world, then, strategy is the art of controlling and utilizing the resources of a nation--or a coalition of nations--including its armed forces, to the point that its vital interests shall be effectively promoted and secured against enemies, actual, potential, or merely presumed."[30]

Particularly following the changes brought about by the end of the so-called Cold War[31], the relevance of strategy in the understanding of the art of controlling and utilizing the resources of a nation in securing a nation's vital interests was greatly reduced in the military field and the area of foreign policy. The centre of gravity was shifted towards the issue of development and the related problem of strategic management of public policies by the state. In his book dedicated to strategic management in the public sector, Paul Joyce points out that particularly within the last ten or so years this problem has become central for the definition of good management and secure development. This may be evidenced by institutional changes at national level, such as e.g. the establishment in 2006 of a strategic analyses centre in the French government, or the functioning from 2002 to 2010 of the Prime Minister's Strategic Unit in the United Kingdom. Joyce sees powerful relations linking strategic planning and management in the public sector with experience in strategic management gained in business and its theories, e.g. the matrix of Igor Ansoff, often called the father of strategic management in business.[32] Simultaneously he perceives limits to this relationship and described differences in the approach to strategic management in various European Countries.[33]

Along with the development of European integration and also owing to the consolidation of the Eurozone and the discussion about economic governance in Europe, the issue of strategic management of policies has also become an important element of the issue of good governance at supranational level. In such circumstances, particularly when viewing European integration from the viewpoint of federalism or functionalism, the European Commission is perceived as an institutional nucleus of a future, supranational, strategic core of the European Union[34]. This opens up several questions of what conditions should be met for the

30 E. M. Earle (1943): *Makers of Modern Strategy*, Princeton: Princeton University Press.

31 J. L. Gaddis (1991): Toward the Post-Cold War World, *Foreign Affairs*, spring 1991 Issue.

32 P. Joyce (2015): *Strategic Management in the Public Sector*, London and New York: Routledge, pp. 5–20.

33 *Ibidem*, pp. 40–70.

34 M. Cichocki (2015): *Unia w Unii*, Warsaw: Natolin European Centre.

EU to become a strategic planning and action creation entity in the full meaning of the term. In the meaning of technocratic management we may encounter in scientific and authoritative concept of management in business and by state bureaucracy, the Union is already beyond any doubt a centre for the creation of strategic plans and actions. The problem remains unsolved whether it actually already has and whether it may have a political nature at all and whether it is underlain by something we may term a common, European strategic culture[35]

Crisis

In the context of various approaches to strategic planning and action we now want to refer to the phenomenon of a crisis as a source for all types of strategic concepts. We will be talking about a phenomenon, because it allows us to combine the problem of crisis and the incidence of crisis, i.e. a crisis event.

In the analyses of the problem of crisis, whether undertaken from the perspective of social science, history of economy or from a more abstract level of the history of idea or philosophy, frequently two similar statements appear. First, growing sensitivity of public opinion of Western societies to the issue of crisis is pointed out. In the public debate, newer and newer areas are indicated as ones affected by the crisis (global world order, international relations, European integration, financial markets, Western social model, democracy. culture). In this context some researchers will be talking about *crisis-talk*[36], others will point out the common nature of the term[37]. A crisis becomes an overused term, both in scientific theories and by the media, which is supposed to characterise the sensitivity of the modern, Western risk society[38] to all kinds of threats and dangers generated by post-modernity. In such cases the crisis becomes a kind of "bottomless pit". Second, it is pointed out that in spite 0 f such frequent use of the term, we still lack a satisfactory, complete meaning or theory of the phenomenon of a crisis. Crisis as a phenomenon remains poorly defined at the theoretical level.

---

35 J. Coelmont (2015): *An EU global strategy for foreign and security policy and even defence*, European Geostrategy, http://www.europeangeostrategy.org/2015/10/an-eu-global-strategy-for-foreign-and-security-policy-and-even-defence/, [Last accessed on-line on: 21.06.2016].

36 R. J.Holton (1987): *The Idea of Crisis in Modern Society, The British Journal of Sociology*, Vol. 38, No.4, p. 503.

37 K. Borchardt (1990): *Przemiany w myśleniu o kryzysach gospodarczych*, in: *O kryzysie*, Warsaw: Res Publica, p. 114.

38 R. Kosseleck (2013): *Crisis*, Nowa Europa. Przegląd Natoliński, 2(15)/2013, p. 33.

Some even say that the very term of a crisis has only a common meaning, being a fashionable expression which each time seeks some theoretical justification.[39]

Bearing in mind such a clear problem with the definition of a crisis, and troubles with a theoretical definition of the very crisis phenomenon (what it is and whether it is at all) we may initially identify first of all such aspects of a crisis as a phenomenon or event based on the identification of inherent, endogenous causes underlying the emergence of crisis situations. In such situations, a crisis becomes the manifestation of defined and unavoidable inherent contradictions of a process. Such understanding of a crisis as a disturbance or – at worst – destruction of a process, can be found mainly in various economic theories. A classic form of such a description of a crisis through the identification of inherent contradictions is represented by Marxist's criticism of capitalism. Marx recognises the unavoidable and cyclic nature of crises in capitalism, seeing its source in the conflict between the innovation of production means against the value of labour, which results in a declining rate of return in proportion to economic growth. Consequently, economic growth in capitalism becomes accompanied by growth in social inequalities and emergence of increasingly serious crises. With the outbreak of the financial crisis in the United States and in the European Union, this Marxist's approach to crisis is experiencing a clear renaissance. Chris Harman will assert that only Marxism provides a proper explanation of grand crises, which are not just straightforward setbacks, disturbances of a harmonious development process, but originate in the logic of inherent contradictions. In his opinion Marx rightly identified their source in the lasting decline of the rate of return, as a consequence of which the development of capitalism has to be a development towards self-destruction.[40] Other authors, however, like Marxists, Michel Husson, or Thomas Piketty[41] starting from the assumptions of the Marxist theory of crisis, will indicate that the rate of return is subjected to various factors, so its change and consequences manifesting e.g. as inequalities may not be presented as a simple downward spiral. Although they have clear causes, crises are not so predictable.

The dogmatic approach to the crisis phenomenon in Marxist theory from the viewpoint of the inherent contradiction of capitalism in place, is mitigated by a

39 N. Luhmann (1984): The Self-Description of Society: Crisis Fashion and Sociological Theory, *International Journal of Comparative Sociology*, vol. 25, p. 68.

40 Ch. Harman (2011): *Kapitalizm Zombi. Globalny kryzys i aktualność myśli Marksa*, Warsaw: Muza, p. 101.

41 M. Husson (2011): *Kapitalizm bez znieczulenia*, Warsaw: Książka I Prasa; T. Piketty (2013): *Capital in the Twenty-First Century*, Cambridge: Harvard University Press.

more evolutionary approach presented in the classic version by Schumpeter, in his concept of the creative destruction process. Inherent powers of capitalism consist here in a constant process of change and adjustment, based on innovation. "The basis stimulus that triggers and maintains the movement of capitalist machinery comes from new consumer goods, new markets, and new forms of forced organisation, created by a capitalist enterprise"[42]. Inherent economic forces still remain central for the definition of grand crises, while their character keeps changing. Consequences for other areas may remain dubious. Daniel Bell describes how the innovative development of American capitalism destroys traditional models of culture and values.[43] The Marxist theory of crises remains credible in a sense that it will delineate indirectly at least two main directions in search for answers to the crisis phenomenon so defined: the first one following from the Hayekian economic market self-regulation theory; the other one from the Keynesian concept of crisis cycles through state policies. Both standpoints may be deemed as two basic strategies underlying the answers to the hypothesis of endogenous sources of the crises of capitalism.[44] If the former one attaches the main stress to the issue of individual enterprise and competitiveness based on standards of exchange and mutuality, then the latter assigns primary importance to the projection role of the state as the creator of strategic responses and democracy as a factor of their legitimacy.

A different conclusion for the identification of the crisis as a phenomenon or an event follow from those concepts of capitalism that do not focus on economy as a separate, intrinsic, autonomous process of market equilibrium or growing inequalities, like it is in the case of neoclassical economic theory, such as Marxism or Neoliberalism. Such a different approach can be found e.g. in the concepts of Ordoliberalism, where management, market manufacturing are phenomena taking place within a defined, established legal, social and ethical framework. Proper or improper market behaviour, therefore, is determined by individual attitudes towards the observance of the binding rules. From such a perspective,

42 J. A. Schumpeter (1995): *Kapitalizm. Socjalizm. Demokracja*, Warsaw: PWN 1995, p. 101.

43 D. Bell (1994): *Kulturowe sprzeczności kapitalizmu*, Warsaw: PWN 1994, Part I, Chapter 1.

44 W. Streek (2013): *Gekaufte Zeit. Die vertagte Krise des demokratischen Kapitalismus*, Berlin: Suhrkamp, p. 157 and following pages.

these are not the rules of history or economy, but human choice made in relation to certain principles that determine the emergence of crises.[45]

The model of describing the crisis phenomenon from the viewpoint of inherent, permanent or repeatable contradictions of a process is not limited solely to criticism of capitalism. Since classical times, it has been applied in explanation and understanding of the nature of disturbances of political processes. Starting from Polybius and his cyclic theory of the development of the state system dating back to the 2nd century B.C., through Tocqueville and his theory of the outbreak of revolution, to the more contemporary theories of political crises of J.J.Linz or of the revolution of Crane Brinton, the sources of crises will be located first and foremost in political process, in the area of the power of social movements. This, however, naturally makes the purpose of permanent, intrinsic rules responsible for a proper or improper course of process in the case of policy, a much more difficult – if not simply impossible–task. Michel Dobry will make a precise analysis of various theories of political crisis, indicating their assumptions and describing their weaknesses[46]. He differentiates between three basic types of approach to a crisis. The etiological approach assumes the possibility to separate a crisis from its causes, which are studied as inherent and prior to. An approach from the viewpoint of natural history starts with the assumption that in the course of history there are regularities being objective rules underlying a change of reality with no alternatives, so consequently a crisis is studied through the identification of a certain chain of events as one departing from the rules. And finally the heroic approach, usually based on the charisma concept of Max Weber or decisionism, with the main stress attached to the role of the decisions of main actors. Dobry also proposes his own approach to a political crisis, perceiving it as a complex and dynamic phenomenon, which should be first described from the viewpoint of the theory of mobilisation and resource control change, which signifies a change in the "regular", routine flow or political exchange.[47] The proposal of Dobry attempts to depart more clearly from the processual understanding of a crisis in policy and the search for inherent or objective causes explaining its outbreak. The category of "moves" he introduced to describe political actions in its analyses also shifts the crisis phenomenon towards a situational phenomenon.

---

45 P. Pysz (2013): *Neoliberalizm/keynesizm versus ordoliberalizm a światowy ład gospodarczy*, in: *Polska i Rosja w procesie globalnej integracji i dywersyfikacji*, Warsaw: Instytut Nauk Ekonomicznych PAN, pp. 105–117.

46 M. Dobry (1995): *Socjologia kryzysów politycznych*, Warsaw: PWN, pp. 45–89.

47 *Ibidem*, p. 19 and following pages.

Fundamentally those divergent approaches to a crisis, both in economics and in political science, in my opinion can be divided into those that perceive a crisis as a processual phenomenon and those that stress its situational nature. The former are sometimes more fatalistic in purport; the latter are based on the fundamental role of choice. A processual approach to crisis in the example of the Eurozone crisis was described in chapter 1 of this volume as a situation of intensification of the dysfunctions of a system's limitations, whose sources are identified mainly in institutional gaps and inherent contradictions[48]. The very processual approach to crisis is sometimes likely to obscure a fundamental, general issue, without recognition of which perhaps no analysis of the crisis phenomenon makes any sense: crises are generated, caused, and defined by humans. Therefore, crises are a human matter, with deep cultural and existential roots[49]. So it is impossible to separate a crisis from human actions or views. We can go even further and associate the crisis phenomenon with human spiritual breakthrough. This would correspond to the famous formula of Thomas Paine: "These are the times that try men's souls" expressed in "The Crisis" magazine of 1776–1783. From such a perspective, the phenomenon of crisis as man's work would be tantamount to an event or events induced by human actions, which undermine the status quo leading to a shock, a change of the rooted image of the world, resulting in a spiritual transformation. This greatly compounds the perspective of a scientific – in the meaning of objective – aspect of the crisis phenomenon, identification of some rules. If the crisis phenomenon is first of all subject to human science, then a sectoral approach to crisis – e.g. in economics or exact science – is bound to lose its absolute character. Human actions and opinions, so central for the understanding of a crisis, can be studied under a constructivist approach. How can we study spiritual changes, however, without invoking such tools as the history of ideas and culture or philosophy? it seems that this is the precise starting point of criticism by Tomáš Sedláček, who asserts that economic crises are products of unpredictable human actions and opinions, and only through culture can they be explained through myths, ideas, beliefs and symbols[50].

48 T. Grosse (2019): *The Eurozone Crisis*, in this volume, pp. 11–52.

49 C. F. von Weizsäcker (1990): *O kryzysie*, in: *O kryzysie. Rozmowy w Castel Gandolfo*, Warsaw: Res Publica, p. 17.

50 T. Sedláček (2012): *Ekonomia dobra i zła*, Warsaw: Studio Emka.

The mobilising function of a strategy in times of crisis

So how shall we approach the relationship between a strategy and crisis? What direction shall we take in any potential further research on this obvious relationship? It seems that the fundamental problem in the approach to strategy lies in its too realistic and rational definition. A strategy is precisely targeted at the attainment of a specific goal or goals; otherwise it loses its basic value. So its nature is strictly teleological, goal-orientated. Its effectiveness is contained in a coherent method of operationalisation of the solution to a given problem owing to the effective calculation of owned means, resources, time schedule for their utilisation and efficient assessment of the potential actions made by the opponents or of adverse factors. However, such a dogmatically rational approach to planning and action is perhaps the main factor responsible for the fact that human history resembles an immense cemetery of strategies. Does a strategy really fail if the assumed goals are not attained using the assumed means and in the scheduled timeframe, as this is exactly what almost always happens? The reflections of Henry Mintzberg on the purposeful or accidental character of a strategy[51] may even suggest that no strategy provides optimal conditions for the attainment of assumed objectives. From the viewpoint of the opening assumptions of how we imagine a resolution to some crisis, there are no effective strategies because the planned and undertaken actions will also fall short of the mark – i.e. the imagined goal. This does not mean that strategies make no sense – this is because of their accidental, unplanned effects that also provide a solution. Michel Dobry embarks on a fundamental polemics against Raymond Aron and his analysis of Clausewitz[52] mainly on the fundamental issues by stating that each temptation to describe continuity in teleological or instrumental terms, particularly with the application the means-ends pattern, is bound to lead to a complete distortion of thinking about human action[53]. No straight line connects a planned action and its effects.

The problem, however, does not come down solely to a dogmatic, rational approach to strategic thinking and action. Another issue is how we understand critical states or contingencies, i.e. the exact elements supposed to comprise the subject of the solution. When identifying the crisis, we fall down on certain

51 L. Freedman, p. 554 and following pages.

52 R. Aron (1997): *Penser la guerre. Clausewitz*, t. 1: L'âge européen, Paris: Gallimard; R. Aron (1995), *Pokój i wojna między narodami*, Warsaw: Centrum im. Adama Smitha, p. 37 and following pages.

53 M. Dobry, p. 14.

hypotheses, of which at least three seem to have a particular power of influence on our perception. First, we are guided by the hypothesis of progress or development, in which we assume that in normal situations our interests move forward and do not stand still. We perceive any opposite situation as stagnation. Second, we assume the hypothesis of wholeness or equilibrium, which describes the situation – either existing or desired – demonstrating the capacity for self-stabilisation, perceived as its strength. And finally the hypothesis of continuity which assumes that things proceed along a normal course of events according to some permanent rules. Any situation fundamentally undermining any of those three hypotheses can be perceived as a crisis situation, a contingency, requiring intervention[54]. If this is the case, than it turns out that what we recognise as a crisis is determined by assumptions deeply embedded in a given culture. Whether things move forward or alternate or whether we deal with a stalemate, how we understand the state of equilibrium or what wholeness means for us and when we think it starts undergoing disintegration – all follow from specific cultural choices and normative beliefs. Certainly economics or statistics will use quantitative measures to describe a given state of affairs or changes taking place, e.g. by demonstrating the level of growth and its fluctuations. By selecting various factors comprised of our perception of economic, social or political reality, we can use such numeric values to describe any changes taking place and confront results against the three basic hypotheses related to progress, wholeness and continuity. However, conclusions may fundamentally diverge from dominant views and feelings, e.g. of public opinion. This explains a frequent political phenomenon: excellent performance parameters of the economy accompanied by a growing political dissatisfaction of citizens, leading to change in power. Whether a conviction appears of disturbance of continuity, disintegration of the wholeness or stagnation, accompanied by demand for a strategic counter-action, does not follow on only from material factors but is usually normatively and culturally motivated. Therefore, Gray rightly asserts in his book on strategy that strategies do not exist outside a cultural context, and he thinks that cultural differences are one of the major problems in describing the character of strategic planning and action in a crisis situation.[55]

Fundamentally one can divide strategies into two types depending on their approach to the issue of the future. Some are defensive, focusing their efforts mainly

---

54 C. F. von Weizsäcker (1990): *O kryzysie*, in: *O kryzysie. Rozmowy w Castel Gandolfo*, Warsaw: Res Publica, p. 15 and following pages.

55 C. S. Gray (1999): *Modern Strategy*, Oxford: Oxford University Press, see first of all the chapter *Strategic Culture as Context*, pp. 129–151.

on the prevention of changes perceived as negative phenomena. These are strategies based on defending the status quo and the conviction that the future has no good alternative solutions. Offensive strategies assume the ability for alternative, more advantageous, evolutionary shaping up of the future compared to current states of affairs.[56] Both types treat strategic planning and action instrumentally, as a rational tool to attain external objectives. And in such cases, as has already been pointed out, they are perhaps doomed to failure. But still one more understanding of a strategy is possible – the one put forward by Michel Dobry, which we have already invoked many times in the paper. This is about the understanding of a strategy as a mobilising process. So its effects are first and foremost inward-oriented, while the achievement of external objectives is rather accidental, albeit not negative. The mobilisation process leads to a reorganisation of the potential, of its internal flows as well as political, social and economic utilisation mechanisms. So, as a matter of fact we are dealing with the reconfiguration of the internal power arrangement through mobilisation. However in contrast to e.g. Charles Tilly, Dobry points out that the process of internal mobilisation is not centralised in nature and is frequently dispersed. To describe it better, he uses the term of "moves". In the situation of a conflict we deal with a response consisting in various moves of various actors, which comprises of the entirety of the mobilisation process. In such a case, a uniform external effect of the process, let us say its rational and strategic dimension, is less clear and uncertain.[57]

Dobry refers to the mobilisation process, because in his opinion it best serves the task of describing the changes taking place in policy under the influence of a crisis. The endemic effects of mobilisation have priority in such cases, which is quite understandable if we view the problem from the standpoint of the political legitimacy of an action. In this example it is also clear that the approach to the same problem in economics is different and would be guided by different, external grounds. The mobilizing character of the strategy and the problem of its internal consequences point out to what Fritz W. Scharpf in his analysis of the European crisis identifies as input legitimacy as opposed to output legitimacy[58]. When analysing problems related to the so-called *austerity* policy towards the

---

56 M. Reeves, K. Haanæs, J. Sinha (2015): *Your Strategy Needs a Strategy*, Cambridge: Harvard Business Review Press, pp.7–13.

57 M. Dobry, pp. 19–25.

58 F. W. Scharpf (2013): *Legitimierung, oder das demokratische Dilemma der Euro-Rettungspolitik*, Max-Planck-Gesellschaft zur Förderung der Wissenschaften, http://www.mpifg.de/people/fs/documents/pdf/Legitimierung_oder_das_demokratische_Dilemma_der_Euro-Rettungspolitik.pdf, [Last accessed on-line on: 21.06.2016].

Eurozone crisis and performance by EU institutions of deep reforms in some Member States as a strategy for exit from the crisis, Scharpf points out the fundamental significance of input legitimacy. In his opinion it is the fundamental weakness of anti-crisis strategies undertaken in the Eurozone. In the context of a democratic society and government, input legitimacy is one of the most important features of any strategy understood as a mobilisation process comprised of the dispersed moves of various actors. Instrumentally understood output legitimacy, which is expressed by beliefs related to effectiveness of attainment of assumed goals, is of secondary importance in this context.

The relationship existing between a crisis and strategic planning and action is, therefore, both obvious and ambiguous. A realistic and rational approach to this issue proves by far inadequate. At the same time the emergence of newer and newer forms of crises and undesirable situations in Europe and in its neighbourhood should become subjected to more in-depth analysis. This paper aims mainly to define the research problems. Simultaneously our analysis aims also to identify several key issues, which should be subjected to further research. First of all we should reflect on any limitations and potential benefits in the application of the strategy drawing on experience from other fields. Here we have mainly in mind experience in the field of military strategies, enterprise management strategies and state strategies in the shaping up of its public policies. We often take advantage of such experience from other fields, seeing it as a serious inspiration. At the same time we are aware that such experience can be used only to a certain, limited extent. For example we already know that political strategies, particularly in the context of a democracy, must not be based exclusively on the input legitimacy of undertaken actions. The second serious problem for further research is comprised of the description of relations between the operational aspect of the strategy as a tool for the achievement of an objective in an uncertain environment, and the understanding of the strategy as a process on inward mobilisation. We are under the impression that the issue at hand here is about the opposing ways of understanding how actions shall be organized in a crisis situation. And finally, the third research area demanding particular attention is the cultural context of the strategy, expressed in practice by the existence of different strategic cultures. This matter should lead to the description of a wider issue, namely of cultural sources underlying the definition of crisis situations.

References

Aron R. (1995), *Pokój i wojna między narodami*, Warsaw: Centrum im. Adama Smitha.

Aron R. (1997): *Penser la guerre. Clausewitz*, t. 1: *L'âge européen*, Paris: Gallimard.

Beaufre A. (1963): *An Introduction to Strategy*, London: Faber and Faber.

Beck U. (1986): *Risikogesellschaft. Auf dem Weg in eine andere Moderne*, Frankfurt a.M: Suhrkamp.

Beck U. (2012): *Das deutsche Europa*, Berlin: Suhrkamp.

Bell D. (1994): *Kulturowe sprzeczności kapitalizmu*, Warsaw: PWN.

Berlin I. (1993): *Jeż i lis*, Warsaw: Aletheia.

Borchardt K. (1990): *Przemiany w myśleniu o kryzysach gospodarczych*, in: K. Michalski (ed.), *O kryzysie. Rozmowy w Castel Gandolfo*, Warsaw: Res Publica.

Cichocki M. (2015): *Unia w Unii*, Warsaw: Natolin European Centre.

Clausetwitz C. von (2003): *O wojnie*, Warsaw: Mireki.

Coelmont J. (2015): *An EU Global Strategy for Foreign and Security Policy*, 10 October, http://www.europeangeostrategy.org/2015/10/an-eu-global-strategy-for-foreign-and-security-policy-and-even-defence [access: 20.03.2016].

Dobry M. (1995): *Socjologia kryzysów politycznych*, Warsaw: PWN.

Earle E.M. (1943): *Makers of Modern Strategy*, Princeton: Princeton University Press.

Freedman L. (2013), *Strategy. A History*, Oxford: Oxford University Press.

Gaddis J.L. (1991): Toward the Post-Cold War World, *Foreign Affairs*, 70 (2).

Giegerich B. (2006): *European Security and Strategic Culture*, Baden-Baden: Nomos.

Gray C.S. (1999): *Modern Strategy*, Oxford: Oxford University Press.

Grosse T.G. (2019), *The Eurozone Crisis*, in this volume, pp. 11–52.

Hambrick D., Frederickson J. (2001): Are You Sure You Have a Strategy?, *Academy of Management Executive*, 15 (4).

Harman Ch. (2011): *Kaptializm Zombi. Globalny kryzys i aktualność myśli Marksa*, Warsaw: Muza.

Higgs R. (1987): *Crisis and Leviathan*, Oxford: Oxford University Press.

Holton R.J. (1987): The Idea ofCrisis in Modern Society, *The British Journal of Sociology*, 38 (4).

Huntington S. (1996): *Political Order in Changing Societies*, New Haven: Yale University Press.

Husson M. (2011): *Kapitalizm bez znieczulenia*, Warsaw: Książka i Prasa.

Interview with Donald Tusk (2014), *Ja po prostu mam szczęście*, Polityka, 49.

Joyce P. (2015): *Strategic Management in the Public Sector*, London and New York: Routledge.

Kosseleck R. (2013): Crisis, *New Europe. Natolin Review*, 15 (2).

Liddell Hart B.H. (1967): *Strategy. The Indirect Approach*, London: Faber and Faber.

Luhmann N. (1984): The Self-Description of Society: Crisis Fashion and Sociological Theory, *International Journal of Comparative Sociology*, 25.

Martel W.C. (2015): *Grand Strategy in Theory and Practice*, Cambridge: Cambridge University Press.

Menon A. (2013): *Europa stan Unii*, Warsaw: Natolin European Centre.

Meyer Ch.O. (2006): *The Quest for a European Strategic Culture*, New York: Palgrave.

Murray W., Grimsley M. (1994): Introduction: On Strategy, w: W. Murray, A. Bernstein (eds.), *The Making of Strategy:Rulers, States, and War*, Cambridge: Cambridge University Press.

Oetinger B. von, Bassford Ch. (2002): *Clausetwitz o strategii*, Warsaw: Polskie Wydawnictwo Ekonomiczne.

Piketty T. (2014): *Capital in the Twenty-First Century*, Cambridge: Harvard University Press.

Pysz P. (2013): *Neoliberalizm/keynesizm versus ordoliberalizm a światowy ład gospodarczy*, w: J. Kotowicz-Jawor (ed.), *Polska i Rosja w procesie globalnej integracji i dywersyfikacji*, Warsaw: Instytut Nauk Ekonomicznych PAN.

Reeves M., Haanæs K., Sinha J. (2015): *Your Strategy Needs a Strategy*, Cambridge: Harvard Business Review Press.

Scharpf F.W. (2014): *Legitimierung, oder das demokratische Dilemma der Euro-Rettungspolitik*, Wirtschaftsdienst, 94 (special edition).

Schumpeter J.A. (1995): *Kapitalizm. Socjalizm. Demokracja*, Warsaw: PWN.

Sedláček T. (2012): *Ekonomia dobra i zła*, Warsaw: Studio Emka.

Sloterdijk P. (2008): *Krytyka cynicznego rozumu*, Wrocław: Dolnośląska Szkoła Wyższa.

Staniszkis J. (2003): *Władza globalizacji*, Warsaw: SCHOLAR.

Staniszkis J. (2008): *O władzy i bezsilności*, Warsaw: Wydawnictwo Literackie.

Streek W. (2013): *Die vertagte Krise des demokratischen Kapitalismus*, Suhrkamp: Frankfurt a.M.

Tilly Ch. (2002): States and Nationalism in Europe, 1492–1992, in: Ch. Tilly (ed.), *Stories, Identities, and Political Change*, Lanham: Rowman and Littlefield Publishers.

Weizsäcker C.F. von (1990): *O kryzysie*, in: K. Michalski (ed.), *O kryzysie. Rozmowy w Castel Gandolfo*, Warszawa: Res Publica.

Žižek S. (2008): *W obronie przegranych spraw*, Warsaw: Wydawnictwo Krytyki Politycznej.

Tomasz Grzegorz Grosse

Summary and conclusions

Abstract: This chapter concludes the whole publication and aims to compare two perspectives, namely that of political science and that of economy in an approach to crisis phenomenon. The analysis of the author focuses on the following four issues: (1) developmental challenge, (2) structural challenge, (3) crisis management, (4) and political legitimacy of anti-crisis measures. Finally, it aims at concluding similarities and differences between the Eurozone crisis along with the Asian crisis of 1997–1998.

Keywords: developmental challenge, structural challenge, crisis management, political legitimacy

In the approach to the crisis phenomenon our project aims to compare two perspectives, namely that of political science and the other, economic. We have focused on an analysis of four elements of the crisis, namely: (1) the development problem, (2) the structural problem, (3) the management problem, and (4) the problem of the weakening legitimacy of a specific crisis-stricken system[1]. This is our proposal for a methodological approach to the evaluation of crisis reality, and to research the ways of overcoming the crisis by state authorities. The four aspects of the analysis we have proposed are an attempt to view the crisis from various perspectives, which are interrelated but not always possible to be clearly separated. In this summary of the entire research I am attempting to draw a major conclusion in each of the four analysis' segments, and then to make a theoretical synthesis.

The starting point for further reflections will be by reiteration of the definition of the crisis embedded in our research. There are various types of crises and the same can be said about their scale, dynamics and duration; this follows from objective economic indicators and also – as Marek Cichocki argues – from social perceptions and dominant cultural values in a given community. This latter approach is close to the constructivist theory, because it makes the crisis phenomenon dependent on social perceptions and core values. Theoretical perspective of this kind is most completely visible in our study with regard to the issue of

1 For a broader discussion see: T.G. Grosse (2013) (red.): *Między polityką a rynkiem. Kryzys Unii Europejskiej w analizie ekonomistów i politologów*, Warsaw: Uczelnia Łazarskiego.

political legitimacy. Returning to the definition we recognise that in the case of major crises we deal with the highlighted dysfunctions and limitations of a given system. This may follow on from inherent institutional gaps or internal contradictions[2]. A crisis is manifested via several emerging economic problems, which lead to a loss of political stability. In our interpretation this signifies first of all a disturbance or even suspension of existing economic development processes, which then bring about political consequences. A crisis in the economic domain contributes to the weakening of the potential in the international arena of a given political entity and disturbs prior processes in its internal policies, which – by the way – hamper the possibility to manage the crisis. Another manifestation of the crisis in the political sphere is by the weakening of the legitimisation for the authority, which may impact on those in power or even challenge the entire political system.

(1) Development challenge

A Marxist approach is close to our understanding of the crisis and this is what Marek Cichocki points out in his chapter. In view of the said theory, a crisis disturbs the development of the capitalist system by revealing its internal contradictions. As representatives of the discussed school of thought argue, these first of all concern any discrepancies between the interests of capitalists and the proletariat, which gradually accumulate as the system develops, and eventually lead to a systemic crisis, i.e. a revolution. An interesting observation of Marxists is that the forces which guarantee the development of capitalism (i.e. to secure capital accumulation) also lead to its downfall, or at least a crisis. The growth of capital accumulation causes a widening of economic disparities which translate into increasing polarisation between social classes, and eventually leads to the outbreak of dissatisfaction and political rebellion[3]. Marxists also point out that maintenance of the capitalist system development follows from asymmetric access to political power between social classes for the benefit of capitalists.

It appears that some crisis phenomena identified by representatives of the Marxist school can be used for the analysis of contemporary crises and in view of other theories too, as in the case of our research. For example, the Eurozone crisis after 2010 followed on from the contradictions inherent in the said system, first

---

2 B. Badie, D. Berg-Schlosser, L. Morlino (eds.) (2011): *International Encyclopedia of Political Science*, vol. 2, London: Sage, pp. 489–493.

3 J.A. Caporaso, D.P. Levine (1992): *Theories of Political Economy*, Cambridge: Cambridge University Press, pp. 70–71.

of all between the states which based their economic development model on the export of capital, production and services and those that imported the products, while basing their own model largely on exogenous growth factors[4]. The axis of this division was brought about by the different levels of economic competitiveness between the two groups of states, but also resulted from different economic development models adopted in particular countries. Consequently the functioning of the Eurozone was based on the accumulation of macroeconomic imbalances between these two groups of states, which was manifested among other things by the differences between their respective current accounts, something that sooner or later was bound to lead to a serious crisis. The same reasons that drove the Eurozone development at the beginning of its existence – for example, the expansion of trade and financial investments from the richest and most competitive states to the remaining parts of the Eurozone – later became the cause of crisis phenomena, by increasing the sovereign debt in the states importing external goods, services and capital. Macroeconomic imbalances followed largely because of improperly designed Eurozone institutions and institutional gaps within the system.

It is worthwhile pointing out that the institutional approach was the theory most frequently used by the researchers. For example, Łukasz Hardt asserts that properly designed regulatory system assessment institutions can be an important development instrument. Moreover, overcoming multiple problems or even crisis phenomena in the Polish development policy system requires a fundamental institutional correction. According to the new institutional economy approach, properly designed public institutions can exert a positive impact on economic development processes, e.g. to better define strategic targets and then better design public policy instruments, including regulatory ones[5].

4 Exogeneity of economy in this paper signifies the dependence of developmental processes of a given economy on access to external investments, technologies or developmental aid, and consequently on strategic decisions made mainly by external political centres or investors. See: T.G. Grosse (2014): The Golden Straitjacket of Poland's Membership in the EU, *Yearbook of Polish European Studies*, vol. 17, pp. 117–138.

5 See: D. Acemoglu, J.A. Robinson (2012): *Why Nations Fail: The Origins of Power, Prosperity, and Poverty*, New York: Crown Publishing; T. Legiędź (2013): *Nowa ekonomia instytucjonalna a zmiany paradygmatu rozwoju gospodarczego*, Ekonomia – Economics, 4 (25), s. 77–91.

According to rational choice institutionalism, the shape of the designed institutions is a reflection of the interests of dominant political actors[6]. According to these assumptions, the design of the single currency regime resulted from political bargaining between member states; and in those negotiations the decisive voice belonged to the richest and most competitive states, which later also derived the greatest economic benefits from the European single currency system. The asymmetry of political power within the Eurozone led to an uneven distribution of benefits and costs related to its functioning. Exactly the same rule became manifest during the crisis and as part of the anti-crisis policy undertaken by Eurozone policy-makers. What is more, as I argue in my chapter – the aforementioned institutional dysfunctions were not fundamentally overcome during the crisis and the costs of the said crisis were largely transferred onto troubled states, which at the same time had a much weaker position in the political power system.

The chapter by Marek Cichocki associates crisis phenomenon with a strategy designed to overcome the crisis. The author demonstrates that the most important aspect of such a strategy is the dimension of social and political mobilization, which is much less about the possibility to implement all of the provisions outlined in such a strategy[7]. It seems that such an anti-crisis strategy may be referred to attempts at restoring development on the basis of prior mechanisms and sources or at finding new development opportunities, both in the economic and political domain. Cichocki points out two general anti-crisis strategies: defensive and offensive. The former tries to defend the *status quo*, i.e. to restore the arrangement of political and economic forces that would enable a return to a previously pursued development mode. In the case of the Eurozone this would translate into maintenance of the prior division of power and distribution of economic benefits within the system. On the other hand, the offensive strategy is tantamount to expansion towards new growth factors and such reconstruction of the political system that would secure improvement of its internal controllability and growth of its international power. In the case of the European Union this would mainly translate into an "institutional breakthrough" towards a political federation or at least into a deepening of political integration within

6 P.A. Hall, R. Taylor (1996): Political Science and the Three Institutionalisms, *Political Studies*, 44, s. 936–957; K. Shepsle (2005): *Rational Choice Instituionalism*, Cambridge: Harvard University Press.

7 See: M. Dobry (1995): *Socjologia kryzysów politycznych*, Warszawa: PWN, pp. 19–20 [original version: M. Dobry (1986): *Sociologie des crises politiques*, Paris: Presses de Sciences Po].

the Eurozone. It appears that the anti-crisis strategy in Europe was the defensive one, largely aimed at restoring the *status quo*[8]. However, as I assert in the chapter on that topic – it significantly modified the prior model governing the functioning of European integration, something I call the systemic tendency towards an *asymmetric confederation*. It is based on the expansion of intergovernmental governance and a growing power hierarchy between the biggest and richest states and those immersed in troubles – or located on the peripheries.

According to Jan Fałkowski, stimulation of economic development is an indispensable element of exit from a debt crisis. From such a viewpoint, the anti-crisis strategy pursued in the Eurozone was crucially opposite, as it was based on an austerity policy, which at least in the inception phase restricted economic growth opportunities, increased unemployment and led to serious tensions within the political system. It inadequately contributed to a change of the economic development model in the crisis-stricken countries, particularly as concerns enhancement of the competitiveness of local enterprises.

Regardless of the undertaken anti-crisis strategy, one can also imagine an (unintentional) outcome of the crisis that will have a disintegrating dimension for the economic regime or political system in place before. Thus it will reduce opportunities for further development, at least within the earlier institutional framework. With regard to economic theories this is the scenario of the so-called *creative destruction* of Schumpeter[9], for example, aiming to replace the old development model with a new one. In the case of the European Union or Eurozone this could translate into the replacement of one regional integration formula with a new one (or new ones). At least in its assumptions (and after a period of turbulence following from the said change) it could secure opportunities for a more stable internal and geopolitical development for the new arrangement.

Piotr Koryś refers to the economic development model in the context of the Asian crisis of 1997. He asserts that the majority of South-East Asian states based their development on the exogenous model, which was challenged by the crisis. The aforementioned model was based on the liberalisation of financial markets and the powerful inflow of foreign capital, and on the quite superficial economic competitiveness in the said countries. It was related to a cheap workforce and the relative weakness and stability of the local currency in the initial prosperity

---

8 T.G. Grosse (2015): Overcoming Crisis in the Process of European Integration, in: K.A. Wojtaszczyk (ed.), *Crises in the Process of European Integration and Approaches to their Management*, Warsaw: ASPRA-JR, pp. 61–80.

9 J.A. Schumpeter (1994) [1942]: *Capitalism, Socialism and Democracy*, London: Routledge, pp. 82–83.

period. What began as the development force of the model, i.e. the opening up to foreign capital inflows, in 1997 became the cause of the crisis resulting from the sudden outflow of capital from the said capital. The superficial competitiveness disappeared in the situation of the local currencies' appreciation on the wave of investment inflows before 1997, including speculative investments. The strong inflow of external capital in the said period caused the same side effects in the Asian states as those we observed just before outbreak of the crisis in the slowly developing states in the south of the Eurozone. The pressure on salary rises and inflation increased, the speculative bubble of certain assets, particularly of real estate, grew; moreover, there was a leapfrog of growth in lending volume and private debt, largely in foreign currencies. The disturbances in the financial area in both of the aforementioned crises (related among other things to the escape of foreign capital, a decline in the banking sector, and in addition, to the devaluation of local currency exchange rates in Asian countries) rapidly translated into real economy and then also into problems of the political system.

It is worthwhile pointing out that the approach to development policies in Asian states combined openness to globalisation and economic liberalism with state interventionism, as well as selective protectionism and industrial policy targeted at export promotion[10]. Some experts point out that the development model preferred in Eastern and South-Eastern Asia quite swiftly became differentiated into countries which based their competitiveness on cheap production costs (mainly wide availability of workforce), which was visible particularly in the south-eastern part of the continent, and into such states as Japan, South Korea, Taiwan, and later also China, which later, shifted their development model towards innovation and advanced technologies. So these were the different strategies governing the use of endogenous resources for the promotion of economic growth based on export[11]. The capital needs of dynamically developing economies and pressure from the International Monetary Fund (IMF) and the US government in the 1980s and 1990s led to the liberalisation of capital flows

10 M. Woo-Cumings (ed.) (1999): *The Developmental State*, Ithaca: Cornell University Press.

11 T.B. Pepinsky (2015): Political Business and External Vulnerability in Southeast Asia, in: T.J. Pempel, K. Tsunekawa (eds.): *Two Crises, Different Outcomes*, Ithaca – London: Cornell University Press, pp. 137–162 [140]; R. Doner (2015): Success as Trap? Crises and Challenges in Export Oriented Southeast Asia, in: T.J. Pempel, K. Tsunekawa (eds.): *Two Crises, Different Outcomes*, Ithaca – London: Cornell University Press, pp. 163–184.

in that part of the world as well as the opening up to external investors[12]. The main problem was because of the excessive inflow of short-term and speculative capital in mid 1990s. Economists point out that the shared feature of the above mentioned crises was the inflow of external capital, which excessively stimulated consumption, plus external debt and financial speculation, while it was inadequately targeted at investments in production or for the building of competitive advantages of local economies[13].

The Asian crisis particularly challenged the development strategy aspect that was based on the excessive liberalisation of capital flows and which enabled first the inflows and then a sudden outflow of funds focused on fast profits. The post-crisis reforms did not bring about, in each case, a fundamental change to the development model. The most successful in overcoming the crisis were such states as South Korea and Taiwan, which maintained the prior opening to globalisation and export promotion strategy combined with actions targeted at the building of an endogenous basis for economic development. This was done by strengthening the innovation of domestic companies and building the potential of the local scientific and research sector. It seems that in the case of the aforementioned states this was more of a correction of an earlier model than its thorough reconstruction. Both states already earlier had been building internal potential for development, largely based on exports to foreign markets. One outcome of the crisis in the case of the majority of the states of the region was the limitation of capital flows, an improvement of the quality of financial supervision and regulations, which resulted in a reduction of the scope of financial speculations. Moreover, capital reserves in central banks and the banking sector were increased in case of another contingent crisis[14]. Another consequence was the impulse for closer economic and political cooperation in the region, also in financial terms, which were manifested by bilateral contracts related to currency swaps[15] and the so

12 S. Greenville (2000): Capital Flows and Crises, in: G. W. Noble, J. Ravenhill (eds.): *The Asian Financial Crisis and the Architecture of Global Finance*, Cambridge: Cambridge University Press, pp. 36–56 [39–40].

13 A. Turner (2016): *Between Debt and the Devil. Money, Credit, and Fixing Global Finance*, Princeton – Oxford: Princeton University Press, p. 151; T.J. Pempel (2015): Two Crises, Two Outcomes, in: T.J. Pempel, K. Tsunekawa (eds.): *Two Crises, Different Outcomes*, Ithaca – London: Cornell University Press, pp. 17–40 [27].

14 W.W. Grimes (2009): *Currency and Contest in East Asia: The Great Power Politics of Financial Regionalism*, Ithaca: Cornell University Press.

15 A currency swap is a contract whereby the parties (in the case of contracts between states, the parties are their central banks) decide to exchange specific amounts with due interest in different currencies for a specified time.

called Chiang-Mai initiative[16]. There was one more major outcome: a stronger linkage between most states of the region and the Chinese economy. Therefore, the Asian crisis brought about significant changes of a structural nature in the region, both in economic and geopolitical terms.

(2) Structural dimension

The structural aspects of the crisis refer mainly to economy and concern a dysfunctional configuration of production factors, or – more widely – an improper development level and economic competitiveness. According to some economists[17] the recent global crises, and first of all the Great Recession which began in 2008, are manifestations of the structural problems of the neoliberal capitalism formula, which is characterised by growing social inequalities, excessive deregulation of financial markets, speculative financial institutions and underinvestment of the production sphere (or so-called real economy). A good example of structural problems was the development model preferred by some Asian states in 1990s. It was based on the liberalisation of capital flows, the stabilisation of the exchange rates of local currencies to the USD and additionally by quite shallow competitiveness following from cheap production costs accompanied by a growing current account balance deficit (particularly in the south-eastern part of the region). Such a development model was initially functional, but later proved to be a structural trap, which brought about excessive debt, appreciation of local currencies, inflation growth and declining competitiveness, and eventually resulted in a monetary, financial and real economy crisis.

In addition, in the research carried out, we were interested in the structural dimension in the geopolitical sphere. As Piotr Koryś asserts, the Asian crisis brought about serious changes in this respect, mainly related to the growing position of China in the region and the weakening influence of Japan and the USA. A fundamental role was played by economic processes, including the

16 The Chiang Mai initiative was initiated by a series of bilateral swap contracts at the meeting of ASEAN+3 group on 6 May 2000. Then it evolved towards a multilateral agreement within the group. The agreement takes advantage of a part of the currency reserves of central banks; in 2012 it concerned the total amount of 240 billion USD.

17 D.M. Kotz (2015): *The Rise and Fall of Neoliberal Capitalism*, Cambridge: Harvard University Press. Critical opinions about liberalisation of capital flows, and the austerity policy applied during crises instead of fostering economic growth were also put forward by leading IMF economists; see: J.D. Ostry, P. Loungani, D. Furceri (2016): *N eoliberalism: Oversold*?, Finance & Development, June 2016, 53 (2), pp. 38–41.

replacement of Japan by China as the country having the core role in the economic exchange in the region. This situation also brought serious implications for the geopolitical structure in this part of the world. Another consequence was the intensification of economic and political cooperation within ASEAN[18] in connection with China, Japan and South Korea (ASEAN+3)[19].

The Eurozone crisis can be also analysed in a structural dimension. In economic terms, strong macroeconomic differences became manifested within the Eurozone, including deepening disparities related to the competitiveness of particular economies. The structural reforms forced by the crisis encountered resistance, and the main burden of economic adjustments was transferred onto trouble-stricken countries. At the same time a deterioration of the economic situation strongly influenced geopolitics, both internally within the EU, and in external relations.

The leading theory for a structural analysis in international studies is so-called structural realism[20]. According to this approach, international relations create systemic relationships and power hierarchy between particular actors in the regional and global arena and the basic element of the said structure is the distribution of power or of geopolitical potentials between particular entities. Disturbance of the geopolitical is the cause and at the same time a manifestation of international crises. The crisis is also an opportunity to rebuild the international system, and establish new power relations, i.e. a new hierarchy between particular actors. In the case of the Eurozone, the structural disturbances took place in at least three dimensions even before 2008, and they intensified during the crisis. First, between the great powers and particularly between the weakening France and increasingly powerful Germany. Problems of the single currency even in the transitional period led to making Germany a state with an almost hegemonic status in Europe. Second, disproportions between core and periphery states within the said system deepened while some states previously recognised as core states experienced a significant decline in their international

18 The Association of Southeast Asian Nations (ASEAN) established on 8 August 1967 in Bangkok, whose seat is located in Jakarta. The members are (in the sequence of accession): the Philippines, Indonesia, Malaysia, Singapore, Thailand (the founding states), Brunei (since 8 January 1984), Vietnam (since 28 July 1995), Laos and Myanma (Burma) (since 23 July 1997), Cambodia (since 30 April 1999).

19 T.J. Pempel (2015): *Two Crises, Two Outcomes*, in T.J. Pempel, K. Tsunekawa (eds.): *Two Crises, Different Outcomes*, Ithaca – London: Cornell University Press, pp. 17–40 [36].

20 K. Waltz (1979): *Theory of International Politics*, Reading: Addison-Wesley Publishing Company.

positions and of their influence over EU and Eurozone policies. On the one hand an example of such a country is Italy, which was gradually losing its economic significance and became immersed in internal problems. On the other hand, the geopolitical role of the United Kingdom in European Union policies was declining, mainly because it remained outside the Eurozone, but also because it increasingly distanced itself from integration processes. Third, the relationship has deepened between the asymmetry of political power and distribution of the costs and benefits from European integration between particular member states. The aforementioned process was dramatically accelerated in the crisis for the benefit of the richest states – those having the biggest political influence in the EU. It created an opportunity to exert structural pressure by the biggest states on those stricken by crisis, mainly in the economic dimension, which also resulted in deepening of the hierarchy within the political system. This then, was the pressure of geo-economics, whereby economic instruments were undertaken on the basis of existing asymmetry of power and then additionally deepened.

The institutional theory, particularly its rational choice school and historical school, may also offer a good explanation for structural changes in the Eurozone. According to both of the aforementioned currents of thought, institutions are tools for the realisation of interests in the strategic dimension, and they also reflect the asymmetry of power between particular actors, e.g. states. Because their own potentials differ, these are mainly the countries with the biggest resources that contribute to the shaping of international institutions, and doing this in accordance with their own rationalities and interests[21]. In line with such an approach, the anti-crisis institutions in the Eurozone were designed by the most influential states, and first and foremost in conformity with their interests and preferences of their domestic constituencies, while much less accounting for the rationality of the functioning of the entire Eurozone or election preferences in the most crisis-stricken states. In my chapter, I called the described phenomenon as the "asymmetry of rationality" which in my opinion brought negative consequences for crisis management.

21 P.J. Katzenstein (ed.) (1978): *Between Power and Plenty: Foreign Economic Policies of Advanced Industrial States*, Madison: University of Wisconsin Press; S. Saurugger (2014): *Theoretical Approaches to European Integration*, Houndsmill: Palgrave Macmillan, p. 93.

(3) Management problems

The concept of maintaining controllability over the crisis situation seems to be of fundamental significance for crisis management. This can be understood as the ability to control the crisis and influence it in such a way as to solve the sources of problems and not only their symptoms, and consequently to aim at recovering from difficulties and restoring development processes. It seems that one of the elements of controllability so understood is "power over oneself", i.e. the fact that a given entity has adequate resources and political power to be able to perform anti-crisis measures effectively. I propose referring the analysis of controllability over the crisis to an external dimension with internal determinants. The attention of researchers under our project focused again first of all on the institutions that might restrict or facilitate crisis management, both those defined in the context of external influence on policy-makers and those treated as internal determinants.

Restrictions for crisis management can be brought about e.g. by external political pressures, which impose reforms or other internal adjustments aimed to overcome pressing problems. Other external restrictions on management may be by the impact of ideas, values or international regulations, which e.g. may enhance the exogenous development (or block the possibility to channel the economy towards endogenous development). Norms of that type may lead to a reduction of controllability over the crisis, particularly when sources of the crisis are to be found in the dysfunction of the existing development model.

The Asian crisis was an example of the aforementioned external determinants. The IMF influenced the applied anti-crisis policy through stabilisation loans granted in exchange for reforms expected by this institution. Those reforms were not only very difficult for the states receiving financial supports, as they transferred the burden of economic adjustments onto local authorities. They also upheld the exogeneity of the economic models in the said countries, putting stress on the openness of those economies to liberal financial markets, and also supporting privatisation and attracting foreign investors. As Piotr Koryś points out, the local elites in many states responded with efforts aimed at regaining autonomy towards the external pressures, which resulted either in the swiftest possible exit from IMF aid programmes or even in rejection of any external support and of conditions related to recovery measures. As an example, Malaysia tried to restore the internal autonomy through a strong turn towards protectionism: the protection of internal markets, as well as control over capital flows and import substitution. It is worthwhile pointing out that the aforementioned Chiang-Mai initiative was supposed to improve the region's independence from the IMF's conditionality and enhance the bargaining position of particular states in potential future negotiations with the IMF or other financial institutions[22].

Koryś thinks that the states of the region that had better economic and political institutions, including among other things more deeply and firmly established democracies, coped better with overcoming the crisis. It seems that the autonomy of those states was of great importance, and particularly the possibility to lever the features of the exogenous economic model towards the stimulation of endogenous development factors, while maintaining openness to regional and global economies. Success was particularly secured by such policy that built the competitiveness of the local economy on the basis of technological innovations accompanied by the building of safeguards against speculative investments.

During the Eurozone crisis we observed the same struggles of crisis-stricken states against external pressures from international institutions (the IMF, the European Central Bank [ECB] and the European Commission). Those institutions imposed a strategy for overcoming the crisis, which largely transferred the adjustment costs onto the aforementioned states while offering them very limited scope to negotiate recovery measures. Therefore, all states aimed at the swiftest possible exit from aid programmes, and more precisely from the necessity to implement restrictive political conditions accompanying the granted loans. This then was an effort on the part of those states which, to the greatest extent, aimed to regain internal autonomy and to relax the austerity policies imposed by international institutions and the states financing the aid programmes. An extreme example of an attempt to regain autonomy was Greece, which in the summer of 2015 openly revolted against the anti-crisis policy dictated in the Eurozone. This was manifested by the announcement of a referendum, whereby the society rejected such a policy. Nevertheless, the Greek government neither regained autonomy in crisis management nor did it reject the austerity policy imposed by external actors.

The question of the effectiveness of anti-crisis reforms undertaken under external pressure is also raised by Jan Fałkowski. On the one hand he argues that many states experiencing public finance (and excessive sovereign debt) problems are characterised by a very low level of fiscal competence, i.e. a given state's capacities with regard to the effective acquisition of public funding. This may entail the necessity to provide external support to improve those institutions and

22 T.J. Pempel (2010): Soft Balancing, Hedging, and Institutional Darwinism: The Economic-Security Nexus and East Asian Regionalism, *Journal of East Asian Studies*, 10, pp. 209–238; W.W. Grimes (2009): *Currency and Contest in East Asia: The Great Power Politics of Financial Regionalism*, Ithaca: Cornell University Press.

imitate the best foreign models with a view to strengthening the power of the state[23]. On the other hand, a negative perception of external pressures by the society and local elites may greatly hamper changes of this type. What is more, external pressure may lead to the introduction of desirable reforms, but may also serve external economic and political interests, e.g. ones related to the exogenous development model or the existing hierarchy of power in international relations.

The concept of isomorphism created as part of institutionalism, addresses the aforementioned issues. It investigates the possibility to transfer institutions from one economic and social context into another one. The same institutions are not always equally effective, for example, in states with strongly developed regulatory systems and a legal culture, against those with weak structures of the rule of law and widespread corruption[24]. The isomorphism concept, therefore, attaches stress to an institutional context, including in particular the local political and social culture in which a given solution is applied[25]. Equally important is the ability to adapt external institutions in accordance with local development interests, and with a view to maximising benefits for the local economy and society, and not e.g. to building competitive advantages for foreign entities, unilaterally benefitting from such transfer of norms. Such action may result in a lack of "institutional adequacy", which is evident in some integration processes in the EU, i.e. a match between European norms and local institutional determinants and economic interests in the member states[26].

Having internal autonomy, therefore, serves controllability over the crisis because it allows better matching of the anti-crisis strategy to local determinants, as well as social and local interests. This is of fundamental importance for the proper definition of the goals for such a strategy, as well as selection of the best instruments for its implementation. This also allows for better respect for the rules of democracy, and for adjustment of the costs of overcoming the crisis to the endurance of the local society, and for selection by such a society and its

---

23 See: T.G. Grosse (2007): *Koncepcja state capacity i jej odniesienie do współczesnej praktyki politycznej* [The concept of state capacity and its reference to the contemporary politics], Studia Polityczne, nr 20, pp. 35–62.

24 P.J. DiMaggio, W.W. Powell (2004): The Iron Cage Revisited: Institutional Isomorphism and Collective Rationality in Organizational Fields, in: F. Dobbin (ed.): *The New Economic Sociology. A Reader*, Princeton – Oxford: Princeton University Press,.

25 M. Granovetter (1992): *Economic Institutional as Social Constructions: A Framework for Analysis*, Acta Sociologica, 35 (1), pp. 3–11.

26 T.G. Grosse (2012): *W objęciach Europeizacji* [Embracing Europeanization], Warsaw: ISP PAN, pp. 69–70.

elites of such a strategy of exit from the crisis that creates the greatest chances of returning to a stable economic growth path.

The second aspect of the crisis management analysis is through internal determinants. Historical institutionalism draws attention to the role of history for the political decision-making process, including those referring to a crisis situation. They are path-dependent, which means that past institutional choices – including those related to norms, ideas or regulations, as well as procedural or organizational solutions – influence later decisions[27]. This fundamentally limits the possibilities to manage the crisis, which requires the disabling of prior systemic contradictions and dysfunctions, i.e. institutional creativity instead of imitation of past solutions. This particularly concerns a crisis of systemic nature, which disavows the fundamental functioning principles of a given arrangement, and consequently requires the introduction of new rules and institutions. Overcoming such a crisis is almost impossible under the old institutional arrangement or with reference to old recipes and action methods. European integration processes are examples of strong path dependency, making all changes incremental and distributed across time, rather than radical. Integration processes are the gradual layering of successive institutions[28] where rarely a punctuated equilibrium[29] or institutional breakthrough[30] takes place. Sometimes old institutions or configurations of interest related to them preclude any change or aim to uphold (rebuild) the political *status quo*. Therefore Schumpeter's creative destruction is not a method to overcome European integration problems. The described trends compound management in the EU of serious crises, because they lead to the undertaking of minimalist and partial actions, of a temporary or reactive nature, rarely responding to the real causes of the crisis, focusing to a greater extent on their manifestations or the postponing of problems in time.

Historical institutionalism argues that an institutional change does not always bring about the expected results, and at the same time is highly unpredictable. There are too many factors which can influence change and policy-makers

---

27 P. Pierson (2004): *Politics in Time: History, Institutions and Social Analysis*, Princeton: Princeton University Press.

28 C. de la Porte, E. Heins (2015) : A New Era of European Integration? Governance of Labour Market and Social Policy since the Sovereign Debt Crisis, Comparative European Politics, 13 (1), pp. 8–28.

29 V. Lowndes, M. Roberts (2013): *Why Institutions Matter. The New Institutionalism in Political Science*, New York: Palgrave Macmillan, pp. 112–120.

30 T.G. Grosse (2019): The *Eurozone Crisis*, in this volume, pp. 11–52.

designing new institutions do not fully control the consequences of their actions[31]. This, to a certain degree, recaps the conclusions drawn by Marek Cichocki, when he questions the possibility of attaining the goals of anti-crisis strategy owing to the complexity of the reality, as well as several variables and dynamics of social and political processes. In Consequence to this, crisis management is a great challenge, although in the case of the Eurozone there was an additional problem of the improper definition of goals, and also of the instruments of anti-crisis policies. Policy-makers decided this was the crisis of the excessive debt of some monetary union states and therefore applied austerity policy instruments. But the real source of the crisis was mainly systemic macroeconomic disparities in the zone, including in particular the difference of economic competitiveness levels and development models between the core and periphery states of the monetary regime. The proper goal should have been rather aimed at attempting to overcome those differences, with anti-crisis instruments being used to stimulate economic growth and structural changes towards the improvement of competitiveness in the south of the Eurozone. The erroneous crisis diagnosis therefore, led to the improper design of strategic goals and implementation measures.

It seems, however, that this was not an incidental situation but rather a function of the political arrangement in place in the monetary union. Such a definition of the goals for an exit from the crisis was related to a calculation of the implementation costs of various strategy variants, and in a broader dimension, also of the benefit distribution within the monetary union, and finally of the social approval for a given anti-crisis policy. The aforementioned calculations were made by entities which had the greatest influence over the decision-making process and first and foremost favoured their own interests, economies, fiscal situations in their states and domestic constituencies. The interests of politically weaker states, particularly the troubled ones, were much less reckoned with. Also much less cared about was a lack of consent on the part of the societies in those countries for such difficult reforms. What appears to be of equal importance is the particularistic interest of dominant states, mainly of Germany, and the rationality of anti-crisis actions of German politicians, which prevailed over the interests of the entire Eurozone, as well as over the rationality behind the functioning of the monetary union. I understand the latter first and foremost as being aimed at overcoming the fundamental problems and contradictions of the said system and the rebuilding of long-term and stable development under

---

31 J.P. Olsen (2009): Change and Continuity: An Institutional Approach to Institutions of Democratic Government, *European Political Science Review*, 1 (1), pp. 3–32.

the monetary regime. I termed the described phenomena as *asymmetry of rationality*. It was the fundamental feature characterising the method of monetary union crisis management, and it also fundamentally hampered a swift recovery of the said crisis, rather contributing to increased political costs and unexpected side effects. Jan Fałkowski also draws attention to this aspect of crisis management. He argues that the particularistic approach – instead of the general one – hampers reforms aimed at the improvement of fiscal competences and the inability to cope with excessive debt. This happens whenever policy-makers are guided e.g. by the interests of the political class and its clientele, instead of the needs of the state or strategic challenges related to economic development policies.

(4) Legitimacy challenge

According to Seymour and Lipset, legitimacy involves the capacity of a political system to engender and maintain the belief that existing political institutions are the most appropriate and proper ones for the society. The basic aspect leading to engendering such a belief is the effectiveness of the government or its actual achievements[32]. Therefore, the legitimacy of any political system is based on the effectiveness of the governance and utility of the given system, which covers both the qualifications of the political elites in power, and also – in a wider dimension – of the political institutions that elect a given governing party and enable the effective performance of governance thereto. Legitimacy authorises the political system, both the elites and political institutions, and also determines efficiency of governance because it may either facilitate or hamper the implementation of political decisions. A particular test for any political system is by going through an economic crisis, which because of the deterioration of social welfare and emerging economic and social problems exerts pressure on the reduction of political legitimacy. At the same time a declining legitimacy may contribute to difficulties when making and implementing anti-crisis decisions, particularly ones entailing costs, which for that reason are unpopular or even rejected by the society.

So a crisis is a difficult situation for politicians and the entire system, exactly in the context of growing legitimacy problems. Particularly dangerous are those crises that are profound or systemic, i.e. ones that cannot be swiftly overcome, bring about even more dysfunctions and new challenges. Another type of danger

32 S.M. Lipset (1960): *Political Man: The Social Bases of Politics*, New York: Anchor Books.

is because of weak foundations of a given system's legitimacy. Fragility of legitimacy in the times of prosperity is not a problem for political power, but when a protracting crisis takes place; such fragility becomes a systemic challenge.

We were dealing with the aforementioned challenges in the Eurozone. First, the crisis was a major one, it was not adequately or efficiently managed, which not only made it difficult to overcome the crisis, but also gave rise to serious side effects and new problems. More crises emerged, including immigrants, geopolitics and relations with Russia, which fuelled old problems and added new ones. Second, since its establishment the European Union has been struggling against the problem of legitimacy weakness, which is also sometimes defined as democracy deficit. Democracy was the basis for the legitimacy of political power in Western Europe after WW2. Democracy is the political system in all EU member states. Therefore, democratic values and procedures are the basis of political culture in Europe; this also means that the political power of the European Union should be authorised in reference to democratic criteria. And at the European level the latter are inadequately met[33].

If "permissive consensus" for integration progress prevailed among European societies before the crisis, then economic difficulties brought about the phenomenon of "constraining dissensus" towards further integration[34]. Dissatisfaction of the constituencies with protracting and accumulating crises was initially aimed against politicians currently in power at the national level, which led to a series of early elections and changes of governments in several EU states. Later this dissatisfaction gradually became anti-systemic. It was aimed at the EU and the existing political elites supporting European integration. This phenomenon was manifested in the popularity of new political groups, frequently euro-sceptical, challenging the existing integration processes, proposing among other things the

33 V.A. Schmidt (2004): The European Union: Democratic Legitimacy in a Regional State?, *Journal of Common Market Studies*, 42 (5), pp. 975–997; V. A. Schmidt (2006): *Democracy in Europe. The EU and National Polities*, Oxford – New York: Oxford University Press; T. Risse, M. Kleine (2007): Assessing the Legitimacy of the EU's Treaty Revision Methods, *Journal of Common Market Studies*, 45 (1), pp. 69–80; A. Follesdal, S. Hix (2006): Why There Is a Democratic Deficit in the EU: A Response to Majone and Moravcsik, *Journal of Common Market Studies*, 44 (3), pp. 533–562; T.G. Grosse (2012): *Changes in Western democracy: a systemic crisis, or a chance to overcome it?*, Politeja, 21 (3), pp. 133–154.

34 L. Hooghe, G. Marks (2009): A postfunctionalist theory of European integration: From permissive consensus to constraining dissensus, *British Journal of Political Science*, 39 (1), pp. 1–23.

restriction of EU regulations, as well as partial denationalisation of EU policies, withdrawal from certain integration areas and even from the EU itself.

The political system that took shape in the EU is two-tier, i.e. it functions simultaneously at national and European levels[35]. The exhaustion of ideas upholding this system in EU societies was an element of the legitimacy crisis. Criticism aimed at the Union largely concerned management ineffectiveness, but it was also aimed at the unfair distribution of power as well as at the costs and benefits following on from integration within the system. The double-dealing and hypocrisy of the European idea, therefore, was pointed out, as they increasingly masked the real political interests and processes, which did not serve the purpose of building a better political practice. Particularly stressed were the meagre democratic foundations for decisions made in the EU, as well as for any actions of European institutions that undermined or limited democratic power in the member states. This is how the foundations for political legitimacy of the entire system were disavowed. It was not by accident that opponents of integration used the institution of a democratic referendum as their main weapon. This is how the European anti-crisis policy was challenged – e.g. in Greece regarding the recovery actions in the Eurozone (in 2015), in the Netherlands with regard to the Association Agreement with Ukraine – being an attempt to stabilize the geopolitical conflict (2016) – and in Hungary in connection with methods for overcoming the migration crisis (announced in 2016). Referenda have also become methods to challenge staying in the EU, with the notable example of the United Kingdom (2016), but similar trends are increasingly visible in other states too, mainly in France and Italy[36]. Therefore, accumulation of the crises that started back in 2008 brought about a relaunch of the "revolt of the masses" in Europe[37] or revolutionary sentiments towards the two-tier political system in the EU and in defence of national democracy[38].

---

35 T.G. Grosse (2012): *Dwupoziomowy system polityczny w Europie* [Two-tier political system in Europe], Przegląd Europejski, 25 (2), pp. 7–26.

36 The Ipsos survey of April 2016 indicated that 58 per cent of Italians and 55 per cent of the French would like to have a referendum held on staying in the EU similar to the British one. See: *Brexit vote set to fuel more referendums*, Financial Times, 9 May 2016, p. 2.

37 J.O. Gasset (1994): *The Revolt of the Masses*, New York – London: W. W. Norton & Company.

38 T.G. Grosse (2015): *A Potential for Revolution in Europe?*, in: B.J. Góralczyk (ed.): *European Union on the Global Scene: United or Irrelevant?* Warsaw: Centre for Europe, University of Warsaw, pp. 203–223.

This led to profound divisions between the "old" and "new" elites within particular societies and between EU states. Instead of performing a fundamental correction of anti-crisis policies, the pro-European mainstream responded to legitimacy problems by trying to marginalise euro-sceptical groups or remaining silent about decisions of voters that collided with anti-crisis measures or integration ideas.

The institutional theory analyses the issue of political legitimacy quite well, particularly from the perspective of constructivism and discursive institutionalism[39]. In the latter case, legitimacy is based on normative discourse, and its dominant values and ideas are a source of authorisation (or challenging) of the existing political system. According to Michel Foucault discourse is a tool used to impose meanings, exert control over weaker or subordinated entities and to define the rules in a given political system[40]. The same happened also during the single currency crisis when narration coming from European institutions and major EU capitals stressed the necessity to respect prior commitments related to the observance of fiscal criteria and the need to introduce austerity measures in the states that lived above their fiscal and economic capacities. Consequently the aforementioned arguments were intended to mobilise implementation of the anti-crisis policy preferred by EU policy-makers, primarily German politicians[41].

It is also worthwhile pointing out that narration during each crisis is by nature delegitimising because it specifies the problems and dysfunctions that will sooner or later encumber the elites in power as well as inadequately efficient political institutions and hold them accountable for any emerging troubles. As I have already mentioned this mainly concerns the situation of a protracting crisis which particularly and painfully affects such systems that have fragile legitimacy foundations. As Piotr Koryś points out, democratic institutions were much stronger or more resilient to the economic crisis in Eastern and Southeastern Asia than those of an authoritarian nature. This provided a greater flexibility in responding to economic troubles in democracies, although at the same time resulted in a change of the ruling party or a rise in the popularity of extremist political groups. Nevertheless, this does not translate into anti-systemic movements, which are particularly dangerous for authoritarian regimes. It seems

39 V.A. Schmidt (2008): Discursive Institutionalism: The Explanatory Power of Ideas and Discourses, *Annual Review of Political Science*, 11, pp. 303–326.

40 M. Foucault (1990): *Politics, Philosophy, Culture: Interviews and Other Writings, 1977–1984*, London: Routledge; Revised ed. edition.

41 M. Matthijs (2016): Powerful Rules Governing the Euro: The Perverse Logic of German Ideas, *Journal of European Public Policy*, vol. 23, no. 3, pp. 375–391.

that authoritarian political systems also have more difficulty with the implementation of anti-crisis policies. Jan Fałkowski arrived at similar conclusions, asserting that democratic institutions ensure a better legitimacy, and consequently a more effective deployment of difficult fiscal reforms. In this context the pressure from international institutions, which may have a weak or no democratic mandate at all – can hamper political authorisation for such reforms.

Łukasz Hardt also pursues his reflections on legitimacy in an institutional context. On the one hand a fundamental role is played by democratic legitimacy, which assigns primacy in regulatory decision-making to elected politicians. On the other hand, their decisions can be enriched by reflections of experts in a given field, as part of properly designed regulatory impact assessment (RIA) procedure. The author defines this type of enrichment of a given public policy as procedural or substantive legitimacy. At the same time he asserts that such a function is not fulfilled by the superficial application of RIA, which "is just a simple administrative exercise" aimed at justifying decisions already made by politicians. This means that technocratic legitimacy must bring about a real substantive effect, and not only window dressing. This seems to be the fundamental pre-condition for any type of legitimacy. If any institution has no greater influence over reality and only feigns actions – it cannot effectively fulfil the legitimising function[42]. Moreover, there is a hierarchic dependency between various types of legitimisation. Technocratic (or procedural/substantive) legitimacy is clearly complementary to democratic legitimacy. This is how Hardt builds the institutional model for RIA, under which decisions are made exclusively by politicians holding a proper electoral mandate (and superior democratic legitimacy), while at the same time experts supply relevant information about regulatory impact, which enriches the knowledge of the politicians and makes the decision-making process more comprehensible and transparent for citizens (in accordance with the complementary technocratic legitimacy). The challenge is in building such technocratic institutions that provide maximally professional, transparent and objectivised (so not politicised) knowledge about the adopted regulations.

From such a viewpoint the institutional trends in the EU mentioned by Hardt seem alarming, because the boundaries between politicians and civil servants are becoming blurred under the designed system assessing EU regulations. On the

42 T.G. Grosse (2014): *Wyzwania legitymizacji demokratycznej w Unii Europejskiej. Przykład wzmocnienia roli parlamentów narodowych* [Challenges of democratic legitimacy in the European Union: strengthening the role of national parliaments], in: A. Pacześniak, R. Wiszniowski (red.), *Europejska scena partyjna i jej aktorzy*, Wrocław: Wyd. Adam Marszałek, pp. 30–57.

one hand, the Regulatory Scrutiny Board can gain the capacity to stop the legislative process, i.e. it will make decisions without a proper democratic mandate. On the other hand, the inclusion of politicians into regulatory assessment under the tripartite panel composed among others of representatives of Parliament and the Council, makes this panel rather a political forum than a group of independent experts responsible for supplying objectivised knowledge about regulatory impact.

(5) Summary

In conclusion, of the reflections so far I will refer to the institutional theory, particularly in the context of relations between power and institutions. Under the discussed theory, certain threads related to the notion of power are addressed, although they do not always have the leading role or are adequately explained[43]. The results of our project indicate that the power category is central particularly for the understanding of crisis management. A great deal of importance for such management is having "power over oneself"[44], i.e. the ability of a given entity to make decisions in order to overcome a crisis or to be autonomous towards external pressures, which may impose a strategy for exit from the crisis which may be disadvantageous to them. The fundamental challenge for policy-makers is not just to overcome any existing problems, dysfunctions or contradictions within a given system. The basic challenge is by the adoption of an optimal path out of a crisis, one that will be relatively swift, entail minimum social and political costs, and will lead to the initiation of long-term economic growth processes and to the most beneficial development model. So the anti-crisis strategy is at the same time an attempt to optimize the crisis costs, reinforce or reconfigure the system of political power, and finally to build the institutional foundations (including those related to management, main economic processes and competitiveness factors), which will define the economic development model emerging from the crisis.

It seems that both for the Asian and Eurozone crises, it has been of fundamental importance about which economic model will be in place once the biggest problems are overcome, what its long-term competitiveness and stability

43 See more: P. Pierson (2016): Power in Historical Institutionalism, in: O. Fioretos, T. G. Falleti, A. Sheingate (eds.), *The Oxford Handbook of Historical Institutionalism*, Oxford: Oxford University Press, pp. 124–141.

44 See: V. Lowndes, M. Roberts (2013): *Why Institutions Matter. The new Institutionalism in Political Science*, pp. 78–79.

will be, and last but not least, what the benefits and costs of its functioning will be. All those elements are determined by the power, and various categories of institutions (regulations, principles, procedures, ideas) and are subject to political games, instruments of anti-crisis actions and elements of post-crisis architecture of the political system and economic models. In the case on international relations, power is of a geopolitical and structural nature (in the understanding of hierarchical relations between particular entities). It is dependent on the potential of particular actors to perform strategic actions, to have control over crisis situations and influence other entities.

Institutionalism identifies two groups of actors: rule makers and rule takers. Both parties have their own interpretations of rules, norms, values and ideas[45]. However, it is the distribution of power between them that determines how institutions emerge and how they are implemented later. Powerful actors seek to institutionalise their advantages – that is, they use their power to change "the rules of the game" to create further advantages down the road[46]. These rules include both formal and informal institutions, as well as public policies. Winners get to impose their policy preferences on the losers. This often means imposing arrangements to which losers must adjust. The exercise of authority is not just an exercise of power; it is potentially a way of generating power[47]. A crisis is a unique opportunity to rearrange an institutional framework for the benefit of the most powerful players. New institutions or policy regimes are often the main prizes awarded to the victors during "critical junctures"[48], which are major events that disrupt the existing political and economic balance. In institutional terminology "critical junctures" refer often to crisis situations and anti-crisis institutional reforms. In an international context power over-rules, and their making or implementation, is most frequently of an asymmetric nature. This was the case among other things of the Eurozone crisis, which highlighted the prevalence of a small group of the most influential member states, which determined

45 W. Streek, K. Thelen (eds.) (2005): *Beyond Continuity: Institutional Change in Advanced Political Economies*, Oxford: Oxford University Press.

46 P. Pierson (2016): Power in Historical Institutionalism, in: O. Fioretos, T. G. Falleti, A. Sheingate (eds.), *The Oxford Handbook of Historical Institutionalism*, Oxford: Oxford University Press, pp. 130–131.

47 L. Gruber (2000): *Ruling the World: Power Politics and the Rise of Supranational Institutions*, Princeton: Princeton University Press.

48 J. Hacker, P. Pierson (2014): After the Master Theory: Downs, Schattschneider, and the Case for Policy-Focused Political Analysis, *Perspectives on Politics*, vol. 12, no. 3, pp. 643–662.

the anti-crisis strategy and the new institutions established to overcome the problems. Particular stress was attached to the execution of anti-crisis actions in the monetary union. Concentration of power refers to the actor-oriented institutionalism concept, according to which only entities with the biggest potential may initiate strategic actions, including anti-crisis ones[49]. These are the actors who on the one hand have the greatest resource of "power over oneself", and on the other hand, have the greatest capacities to influence other entities. In the case of the Eurozone crisis, the dominant actor was first of all Germany, with France lagging slightly behind. In critical situations a significant influence was exerted by an external actor, i.e. the United States of America, and also international institutions such as the IMF and ECB.

Another popular institutional concept is that of the principal – agent model[50]. It assumes a hierarchy of relations between particular entities, under which those having the greatest power (or political legitimacy) make decisions and then delegate their implementation to agency institutions. The aforementioned model was developed in the context of research over European integration and aimed at explaining relationships between member states and technocratic institutions in the EU[51]. With reference to the Eurozone crisis, the division into policy-makers and entities implementing political decisions, largely overlapped with the divisions into lending states and those who became their debtors, who had to subordinate themselves to the political will of their creditors. The role of technocratic (agency) institutions in the EU became largely that of instruments for the execution of that dependency. During the Asian crisis the role of the principal and main lender was fulfilled by the IMF, although the most influential western states with the USA in the lead remained in the shadow of the said organisation.

Another concept indicates concentration of power in political elites, as well as elites in administration, army and business[52]. However, in the case of a crisis,

---

49 See: F. W. Scharpf (1997): *Games Real Actors Play: Actor-Centred Institutionalism in Policy Research*, Boulder: Westview Press.

50 B. G. Peters (2005): *Institutional Theory in Political Science: The 'New Institutionalism'*, (2nd ed.) London: Continuum.

51 M.A. Pollack (1997): *Delegation, Agency and Agenda Setting in the European Community*, International Organization 51 (1), pp. 99–134; H. Kassim, A. Menon (2003): The Principal–Agent Approach and the Study of the European Union: Promise Unfulfilled?, *Journal of European Public Policy*, 10 (1), pp. 121–139; S. Billiet (2009): Principal–Agent Analysis and the Study of the EU: What About the EC's External Relations?, *Comparative European Politics*, 7 (4), pp. 435–454.

52 C. Wright Mills (1956): *The Power Elite*, Oxford: Oxford University Press.

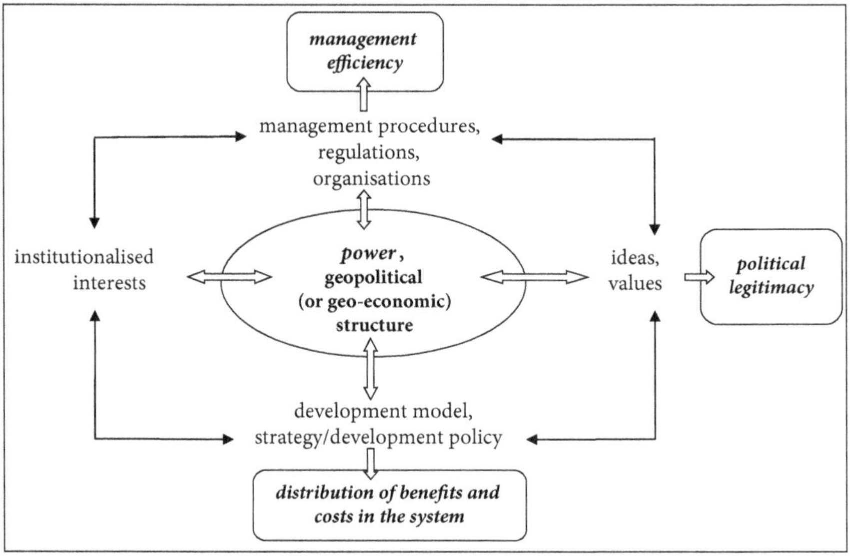

Chart 1: Power relation model with various institutional categories (author's own elaboration).

it is not only elites that matter, but societies too. This is most clearly visible with regard to the legitimacy aspect. Economic difficulties undermine legitimacy of power, and consequently contribute to bottom-up questioning of the elites in power or even of the existing institutional foundations of the political system. This might lead to rejection of both hitherto elites and political institutions, something we may call the "revolt of the masses" or "revolution" towards the existing system.

The above reflections lead me to an attempt to outline a theoretical model explaining relationships between power and institutions (see: Chart 1). In the very core there is political power, which is of a structural character, so it should be understood in a geopolitical (or geo-economic) perspective. Political power enters relations with various categories of institutions (they are located around the central power box). I identified four fundamental types of institutions. First, there are organisations, including international ones, but also regulations, procedures and all other mechanisms serving the purpose of management. The second institutional category is comprised of ideas, norms and values, which are of fundamental importance among other things for legitimacy of power, but also for the mobilization of societies in support for a specific policy, e.g. with a view to recovering from crisis[53]. The next institution is the economic development model, a preferred development policy, political vision or strategy. Among other things it is responsible for the distribution of costs and benefits within a given economic regime or political system, and consequently it is closely related to political economy. And finally the fourth category is that of interests, i.e. the perception of the benefits of particular actors or social groups, which is rooted in a specific political and economic arrangement, and consequently is of an institutionalised character.

The relationship between power category and institutions is bilateral. For example, power creates and uses institutions for the attainment of its own goals, including the reinforcement of an existing hierarchy of power or for the rebuilding (reconfiguration) of a specific political arrangement. A crisis becomes an excellent pretext for such actions. At the same time, however, institutions are a limitation on power. This concerns both the existing regulations and procedures, which may hamper an efficient decision-making process in a crisis. The situation is quite similar with norms and ideas, which narrow down the scope for political actions, sometimes to the detriment of the effectiveness of the attainment of goals, including the capacity to efficiently overcome a crisis situation. Similarly, the development model can be initially the source of benefits, to change later into a development trap, which not only contributes to problems and costs but also constitutes a serious challenge for a political system. It seems that particular categories of institutions can interact with each other (e.g. ideas shape regulations, and interests influence the preferred economic development model).

We can define a crisis itself with reference to the outlined model. A crisis could disturb the entire arrangement, also with regard to the power structure, the development trajectory (economic model), the distribution of benefits and costs within a system, management quality, the satisfaction of social interests and aspirations, as well as guiding ideas, values and political legitimacy.

References

Acemoglu D., Robinson J.A. (2012): *Why Nations Fail: The Origins of Power, Prosperity, and Poverty*, New York: Crown Publishing.

Badie B., Berg-Schlosser D., Morlino L. (eds.) (2011): *International Encyclopedia of Political Science*, vol. 2, London: Sage.

53 Cf. M. Blyth, O. Helgadóttir, W. Kring (2016): Ideas and Historical Institutionalism, in: O. Fioretos, T. G. Falleti, A. Sheingate (eds.), *The Oxford Handbook of Historical Institutionalism*, Oxford: Oxford University Press, pp. 142–162.

Billiet S. (2009): Principal–Agent Analysis and the Study of the EU: What about the EC's External Relations?, *Comparative European Politics*, 7 (4), pp. 435–454.

Blyth M., Helgadóttir O., Kring W. (2016): Ideas and Historical Institutionalism, in: O. Fioretos, T. G. Falleti, A. Sheingate (eds.), *The Oxford Handbook of Historical Institutionalism*, Oxford: Oxford University Press, pp. 142–162.

Brexit Vote Set to Fuel More Referendums, *Financial Times*, 9 May 2016, p. 2.

Caporaso J.A., Levine D.P. (1992): *Theories of Political Economy*, Cambridge: Cambridge University Press.

de la Porte C., Heins E. (2015) : A New Era of European Integration? Governance of Labour Market and Social Policy since the Sovereign Debt Crisis, *Comparative European Politics*, 13 (1), pp. 8–28.

DiMaggio P.J., Powell W.W. (2004): The Iron Cage Revisited: Institutional Isomorphism and Collective Rationality in Organizational Fields, in: F. Dobbin (ed.): *The New Economic Sociology. A Reader*, Princeton–Oxford: Princeton University Press, pp. 111–133.

Dobry M. (1986): *Sociologie des crises politiques*, Paris: Presses de Sciences Po.

Doner R. (2015): Success as Trap? Crises and Challenges in Export Oriented Southeast Asia, in: T.J. Pempel, K. Tsunekawa (eds.): *Two Crises, Different Outcomes*, Ithaca–London: Cornell University Press, pp. 163–184.

Follesdal A., Hix S. (2006): Why There Is a Democratic Deficit in the EU: A Response to Majone and Moravcsik, *Journal of Common Market Studies*, 44 (3), pp. 533–562.

Foucault M. (1990): *Politics, Philosophy, Culture: Interviews and Other Writings, 1977–1984*, London: Routledge; Revised ed. edition.

Gasset J.O. (1994): *The Revolt of the Masses*, New York–London: W. W. Norton & Company.

Granovetter M. (1992): Economic Institutional as Social Constructions: A Framework for Analysis, *Acta Sociologica*, 35 (1), pp. 3–11.

Greenville S. (2000): Capital Flows and Crises, in: G. W. Noble, J. Ravenhill (eds.): *The Asian Financial Crisis and the Architecture of Global Finance*, Cambridge: Cambridge University Press, pp. 36–56.

Grimes W.W. (2009): *Currency and Contest in East Asia: The Great Power Politics of Financial Regionalism*, Ithaca: Cornell University Press.

Grosse T.G. (2007): Koncepcja state capacity i jej odniesienie do współczesnej praktyki politycznej [The Concept of State Capacity and Its Reference to the Contemporary Politics], *Studia Polityczne*, nr 20, pp. 35–62.

Grosse T.G. (2012): Changes in Western Democracy: A Systemic Crisis, or a Chance to Overcome It?, *Politeja*, 21 (3), pp. 133–154.

Grosse T.G. (2012): Dwupoziomowy system polityczny w Europie [Two-Tier Political System in Europe], *Przegląd Europejski*, 25 (2), pp. 7–26.

Grosse T.G. (2012): *W objęciach Europeizacji* [Embracing Europeanization], Warsaw: ISP PAN, pp. 69–70.

Grosse T.G. (2013) (ed.): *Między polityką a rynkiem. Kryzys Unii Europejskiej w analizie ekonomistów i politologów* [Between Politics and the Market. The Crisis of the European Union in the Analysis of Economists and Political Scientists], Warsaw: Uczelnia Łazarskiego.

Grosse T.G. (2014): The Golden Straitjacket of Poland's Membership in the EU, *Yearbook of Polish European Studies*, 17, pp. 117–138.

Grosse T.G. (2014): Wyzwania legitymizacji demokratycznej w Unii Europejskiej. Przykład wzmocnienia roli parlamentów narodowych [Challenges of Democratic Legitimacy in the European Union: Strengthening the Role of National Parliaments], in: A. Pacześniak, R. Wiszniowski (red.), *Europejska scena partyjna i jej aktorzy*, Wrocław: Wyd. Adam Marszałek, pp. 30–57.

Grosse T.G. (2015): A Potential for Revolution in Europe?, in: B.J. Góralczyk (ed.): *European Union on the Global Scene: United or Irrelevant?* Warsaw: Centre for Europe, University of Warsaw, pp. 203–223.

Grosse T.G. (2015): Overcoming Crisis in the Process of European Integration, in: K.A. Wojtaszczyk (ed.), *Crises in the Process of European Integration and Approaches to Their Management*, Warsaw: ASPRA-JR, pp. 61–80.

Grosse T.G. (2019): The *Eurozone Crisis*, in this volume, pp. 11–52.

Gruber L. (2000): *Ruling the World: Power Politics and the Rise of Supranational Institutions*, Princeton: Princeton University Press.

Hacker J., Pierson P. (2014): After the Master Theory: Downs, Schattschneider, and the Case for Policy-Focused Political Analysis, *Perspectives on Politics*, 12, (3), pp. 643–662.

Hall P.A., Taylor R. (1996): Political Science and the Three Institutionalisms, *Political Studies*, 44, pp. 936–957;

Hooghe L., Marks G. (2009): A Postfunctionalist Theory of European Integration: From Permissive Consensus to Constraining Dissensus, *British Journal of Political Science*, 39 (1), pp. 1–23.

Kassim H., Menon A. (2003): The Principal–Agent Approach and the Study of the European Union: Promise Unfulfilled?, *Journal of European Public Policy*, 10 (1), pp. 121–139.

Katzenstein P.J. (ed.) (1978): *Between Power and Plenty: Foreign Economic Policies of Advanced Industrial States*, Madison: University of Wisconsin Press.

Kotz D.M. (2015): *The Rise and Fall of Neoliberal Capitalism*, Cambridge: Harvard University Press.

Legiędź T. (2013): *Nowa ekonomia instytucjonalna a zmiany paradygmatu rozwoju gospodarczego* [New Institutional Economics and the Paradigm Shift in Economic Development], Ekonomia–Economics, 4 (25), pp. 77–91.

Lipset S.M. (1960): *Political Man: The Social Bases of Politics*, New York: Anchor Books.

Lowndes V., Roberts M. (2013): *Why Institutions Matter. The New Institutionalism in Political Science*, New York: Palgrave Macmillan.

Matthijs M. (2016): Powerful Rules Governing the Euro: The Perverse Logic of German Ideas, *Journal of European Public Policy*, 23 (3), pp. 375–391.

Olsen J.P. (2009): Change and Continuity: An Institutional Approach to Institutions of Democratic Government, *European Political Science Review*, 1 (1), s. 3–32.

Ostry J.D., Loungani P., Furceri D. (2016): Neoliberalism: Oversold?, *Finance & Development*, June 2016, 53 (2), pp. 38–41.

Pempel T.J. (2010): Soft Balancing, Hedging, and Institutional Darwinism: The Economic-Security Nexus and East Asian Regionalism, *Journal of East Asian Studies*, 10, pp. 209–238.

Pempel T.J. (2015): Two Crises, Two Outcomes, in: T.J. Pempel, K. Tsunekawa (eds.): *Two Crises, Different Outcomes*, Ithaca–London: Cornell University Press, pp. 17–40.

Pepinsky T.B. (2015): Political Business and External Vulnerability in Southeast Asia, in: T.J. Pempel, K. Tsunekawa (eds.): *Two Crises, Different Outcomes*, Ithaca–London: Cornell University Press, pp. 137–162.

Peters B.G. (2005): *Institutional Theory in Political Science: The 'New Institutionalism'*, (2nd ed.) London: Continuum.

Pierson P. (2004): *Politics in Time: History, Institutions and Social Analysis*, Princeton: Princeton University Press.

Pierson P. (2016): Power in Historical Institutionalism, in: O. Fioretos, T. G. Falleti, A. Sheingate (eds.), *The Oxford Handbook of Historical Institutionalism*, Oxford: Oxford University Press, pp. 124–141.

Pollack M.A. (1997): Delegation, Agency and Agenda Setting in the European Community, *International Organization* 51 (1), pp. 99–134.

Risse T., Kleine M. (2007): Assessing the Legitimacy of the EU's Treaty Revision Methods, *Journal of Common Market Studies*, 45 (1), pp. 69–80.

Saurugger S. (2014): *Theoretical Approaches to European Integration*, Houndsmill: Palgrave Macmillan.

Scharpf F.W. (1997): *Games Real Actors Play: Actor-Centred Institutionalism in Policy Research*, Boulder: Westview Press.

Schmidt V.A. (2004): The European Union: Democratic Legitimacy in a Regional State?, *Journal of Common Market Studies*, 42 (5), pp. 975–997.

Schmidt V.A. (2006): *Democracy in Europe. The EU and National Polities*, Oxford–New York: Oxford University Press.

Schmidt V.A. (2008): Discursive Institutionalism: The Explanatory Power of Ideas and Discourses, *Annual Review of Political Science*, 11, pp. 303–326.

Schumpeter J.A. (1994) [1942]: *Capitalism, Socialism and Democracy*, London: Routledge.

Shepsle K. (2005): *Rational Choice Institutionalism*, Cambridge: Harvard University Press.

Streek W., Thelen K. (eds.) (2005): *Beyond Continuity: Institutional Change in Advanced Political Economies*, Oxford: Oxford University Press.

Turner A. (2016): *Between Debt and the Devil. Money, Credit, and Fixing Global Finance*, Princeton–Oxford: Princeton University Press.

Waltz K. (1979): *Theory of International Politics*, Reading: Addison-Wesley Publishing Company.

Woo-Cumings M. (ed.) (1999): *The Developmental State*, Ithaca: Cornell University Press.

Wright Mills C. (1956): *The Power Elite*, Oxford: Oxford University Press.

List of figures

List of tables

Biographical notes

Marek Aleksander Cichocki
Research director of the Natolin European Centre and editor-in-chief of the periodical "New Europe. Natolin Review". Professor at the Collegium Civitas. Former advisor to the President of the Republic of Poland in the field of the Constitutional Treaty and Sherpa for the negotiations of the Lisbon Treaty. He specializes in the subject of German affairs, European integration and history of political thought. Author of numerous publications on the abovementioned topics.

Tomasz Grzegorz Grosse
Sociologist, political scientist and historian. Professor at the University of Warsaw and head of the Department of European Union Policies. He specializes in the analysis of economic policies in the EU and the Member States, and also in public management. His recent publications include: "W poszukiwaniu geoekonomii w Europie", ISP PAN, 2014. He also edited the book: "Między polityką a rynkiem. Kryzys Unii Europejskiej w analizie ekonomistów i politologów", Uczelnia Łazarskiego, 2013.

Piotr Koryś
Expert in the field of economy in the Sobieski Institute. Assistant Professor in the Department of Economic History at the Faculty of Economic Sciences University of Warsaw. He specializes in the economic history, cliometrics, institutional economics and demography.

Łukasz Hardt
Economist, doctor habilitatus, member of the Monetary Policy Council in the 2016–2022 term. Assistant Professor and Manager in the Department of Political Economy at the Faculty of Economic Sciences University of Warsaw. Since 2015 – member of the National Development Council to the President of the Republic of Poland. He specializes in the institutional economics, methodology of economics and history of economic thought.

Jan Fałkowski
Economist, doctor habilitatus and Assistant Professor in the Department of Political Economy at the Faculty of Economic Sciences University of Warsaw. The winner of the scholarship of the Ministry of Science and Higher Education for young scientists. He specializes in the subject of political and economic institutions, political economy and agricultural economics.

Studies in European Integration, State and Society

Edited by Magdalena Góra, Zdzisław Mach and Katarzyna Zielińska

Vol. 1 Józef Niżnik: Democracy versus Solidarity in the EU Discourse. 2012.

Vol. 2 Grzegorz Żuk: Europe in Polish Public Discourse. 2013.

Vol. 3 Zdzisław Mach (ed.): Local Community, Power and European Integration. 2017.

Vol. 4 Janusz Węc: Germany's Position on the System Reform of the European Union in 2002–2016. 2018.

Vol. 5 Krzysztof Kowalski / Łucja Piekarska-Duraj / Barbara Törnquist-Plewa (eds.): Narrating Otherness in Poland and Sweden. European Heritage as a Discourse of Inclusion and Exclusion. 2019.

Vol. 6 Marek Aleksander Cichocki / Tomasz Grzegorz Grosse (eds.): The Many Faces of Crisis. An Analysis of Crisis Management from an Economic and Political Perspective. 2019.

www.peterlang.com

www.ingramcontent.com/pod-product-compliance
Ingram Content Group UK Ltd.
Pitfield, Milton Keynes, MK11 3LW, UK
UKHW060038151026
15625UKWH00086B/328

9 783631 791257